Literary Research: Strategies and Sources

Series Editors: Peggy Keeran & Jennifer Bowers

Every literary age presents scholars with both predictable and unique research challenges. This series fills a gap in the field of reference literature by featuring research strategies and by recommending the best tools for conducting specialized period and national literary research. Emphasizing research methodology, each series volume takes into account the unique challenges inherent in conducting research of that specific literary period and outlines the best practices for researching within it. Volumes place the research process within the period's historical context and use a narrative structure to analyze and compare print and electronic reference sources. Following an introduction to online searching, chapters will typically cover these types of resources: general literary reference materials; library catalogs; print and online bibliographies, indexes, and annual reviews; scholarly journals; contemporary reviews; period journals and newspapers; microform and digital collections; manuscripts and archives; and Web resources. Additional or alternative chapters might be included to highlight a particular research problem or to examine other pertinent period or national literary resources.

1. *Literary Research and the British Romantic Era* by Peggy Keeran and Jennifer Bowers, 2005.
2. *Literary Research and the Era of American Nationalism and Romanticism* by Angela Courtney, 2008.
3. *Literary Research and American Modernism Era* by Robert N. Matuozzi and Elizabeth B. Lindsay, 2008.
4. *Literary Research and the American Realism and Naturalism Period* by Linda L. Stein and Peter J. Lehu, 2009.
5. *Literary Research and Irish Literature* by J. Greg Matthews, 2009.
6. *Literary Research and the Literatures of Australia and New Zealand* by H. Faye Christenberry and Angela Courtney, 2010.
7. *Literary Research and British Modernism* by Alison M. Lewis, 2010.

Literary Research and British Modernism

Strategies and Sources

Literary Research:
Strategies and Sources, No. 7

Alison M. Lewis

THE SCARECROW PRESS, INC.
Lanham • Toronto • Plymouth, UK
2010

Published by Scarecrow Press, Inc.
A wholly owned subsidiary of The Rowman & Littlefield Publishing Group, Inc.
4501 Forbes Boulevard, Suite 200, Lanham, Maryland 20706
http://www.scarecrowpress.com

Estover Road, Plymouth PL6 7PY, United Kingdom

British Library Cataloguing in Publication Information Available

Library of Congress Cataloging-in-Publication Data

Lewis, Alison M., 1959-
Literary research and British modernism : strategies and sources / Alison M. Lewis.
p. cm. — (Literary research: strategies and sources ; no. 7)
Includes bibliographical references and indexes.
ISBN 978-0-8108-6901-1 (pbk. : alk. paper) — ISBN 978-0-8108-6902-8 (ebook)
1. Modernism (Literature)—Great Britain—Research—Methodology. 2. English literature—20th century—Research—Methodology. 3. English literature—19th century—Research—Methodology. 4. Modernism (Literature)—Great Britain—Information resources. 5. English literature—20th century—Information resources. 6. English literature—19th century—Information resources. I. Title. PR478.M6L45 2010
820.9'112—dc22 2009025825

Printed in the United States of America

Contents

Illustrations

Acknowledgments

First, I would like to sincerely thank the series editors, Peggy Keeran and Jennifer Bowers, for their support of my initial proposal for this volume, for their helpful guidance and feedback along the way, and most especially for their patience and forbearance in the face of my numerous missed deadlines.

It would be impossible to complete a work such as this without being able to look at and use the sources described herein. I'd like to thank the entire staff at Drexel University's Hagerty Library; the Interlibrary Loan Department was particularly instrumental in helping me to obtain the more elusive resources. I would also like to thank the University of Pennsylvania for access to the excellent collections held at both the Van Pelt Library and the Fine Arts Library.

On the home front, I send my love and thanks to my husband John Parrish, who did his best to keep my slow computer running as fast as possible. The household cats supplied much happy distraction, but Leila and Cleyre deserve particular recognition. Their constant desire to be in my lap helped keep me in my chair and, thus, working.

This book would probably not exist if it were not for the sounding board provided by the Quaker Ladies' Creativity Group. They listened to all my anxiety and excuses, gave sound advice, and inspired me by their own productivity. I'd particularly like to recognize our smaller "writer's group" members, Sara Palmer and Margo Tassi. They listened most attentively, helped hold me to deadlines, and even read some of the manuscript drafts. Karen Winner, a member of both of these groups and their permutations, deserves special acknowledgment. She was there through the entire process and was unfailingly generous in her encouragement, prodding, and sympathetic understanding of the challenges one faces in completing a task of this size.

I have every confidence that she will one day be the author of a best-selling mystery novel set in Philadelphia.

My appreciation extends to the British modernist writers whose works have inspired me and spoken to me across both time and the Atlantic Ocean. My own efforts at researching the lives and writings of D. H. Lawrence and Virginia Woolf remain some of the most satisfying experiences of my life. Finally, thanks go out to my "major professor," Sheldon Brivic of the English Department at Temple University. He infused in me the deepest appreciation for the quintessential modernist, and it is in his honor that a portrait of James Joyce graces the cover of this volume.

Introduction

Literary research, especially when it is conducted on an advanced level, is always challenging. Even if we confine our discussion to literature written in English, there is a bewildering array of potential resources for discovering information pertinent to a specific research topic. Many tools address literature in general, while others focus on a particular national literature, time period, or movement; a number will address a combination of these parameters. There are time-honored reference materials essential to the study of literature of any stripe, such as the Modern Language Association's bibliography, and new tools are being printed or made available electronically every year. More information is also becoming freely available on the World Wide Web, posted by individual scholars, scholarly societies, students, or "fans." Scholars who have worked in literary research for decades, along with those who are new to the field, may have a hard time seeing the "big picture" of not only what resources are available but where they can be found and how to use them. This volume is intended to pull out one thread of the literary research puzzle and expand upon both the library materials and the research processes related to advanced scholarship in a particular subfield, that of British modernism.

Before we proceed, it may be useful, if somewhat futile, to attempt to define the term *British modernism*. Any definitions of literary time periods by specific date ranges are false to some degree. Certainly the calendar did not turn to a new year and all writers suddenly began creating in a new manner with a new sense of aesthetics! Rather, scholars have noted that particular literary trends tend to come into fruition during certain time periods, and while the beginning and ending of each such era is somewhat vague, they serve as convenient categories for discussing dominant characteristics of that literature. Terms such as "romanticism," "Victorian," and "modernism" denote constellations of literary techniques and trends that have come to be seen as characteristic or representative of the best literature of a given era. They also serve as a means of categorizing information presented in the context of literature study in higher education and so are terms widely used by scholars and students alike, even if there is not necessarily agreement on precise definitions. For the sake of providing some structure and points of reference for the current volume, I am taking two historical events as bookends to roughly mark the "modern" era. On the one hand, the modern era may be said to begin with the death of Queen Victoria in January 1901, which marked the end of one of the longest reigns of any British monarch and from which society seemed to surge forth with a sense of new possibilities after decades of being constrained under a single, culturally conservative voice. On the other hand, I see the era of modernism ceasing in August 1945, with the United States' dropping of atomic bombs on Hiroshima and Nagasaki in Japan. This had the effect of not only heralding the end of World War II but also bringing about an irreversible psychological shift resulting from widespread awareness of the possible wholesale destruction of the human race. Certainly it could be, and has been, argued that modernism began decades earlier, in order to encompass the early works of figures such as Thomas Hardy and Henry James, or that it ended earlier with the start of World War II, or even that the modernist experiment is still ongoing. In any event, it is important to keep in mind that a certain amount of flexibility is called for when considering literary time periods and that many of the resources described in this volume will have varying definitions of the chronological scope of modernism.

The definition of the "British" part of the term *British modernism* is perhaps less fraught with controversy, although it is not entirely free from it. Most precisely, "British" may be said to refer to the people of Great Britain, comprising the countries of England, Scotland, and Wales. More broadly, it may be said to refer to the people of the United Kingdom, which includes Great Britain and Northern Ireland. Although Ireland as a whole has struggled with political and religious differences for centuries, there is still some common cultural heritage that crosses these boundaries and is reflected in its literature written in English. It is difficult to divorce figures as dominant and influential as W. B. Yeats and James Joyce, for example, from the mainstream of what is thought of as British modernism. Other figures might have their "Britishness" called into question as well, figures such as T. S. Eliot, who was born an American and later claimed British citizenship, W. H. Auden, who was born in England but later became an American citizen, and Joseph Conrad, a British citizen born in Poland whose major writings are all in English. Suffice it to say that flexibility remains called for and that while tools covered in this volume may have differing criteria for what constitutes "British," most of them define it broadly and inclusively.

As challenging as it can be to define the "when" and the "where" of modernism, there is also the important question of "what" constitutes modernism. Most critics agree that modernism is characterized by a high level of experimentation and innovation and that new forms of expression, such as stream of consciousness and imagism, were developed at this time. Modernism rejected the conventions of past literary forms and continually returned to the principle of "making it new." Sigmund Freud's psychological theories and James Frazer's anthropological writings were major influences upon modernist writers. The main innovators in the genre of fiction are generally agreed to be James Joyce, D. H. Lawrence, and Virginia Woolf. Other important novelists are Joseph Conrad, E. M. Forster, Ford Madox Ford, Graham Greene, and Evelyn Waugh. Among the poets, T. S. Eliot and W. B. Yeats are considered the major innovators, along with the highly influential American poet Ezra Pound. Mention of Pound draws into full relief the fact that modernism was an international movement, not confined to any one country or language. Ties and influences between British and American writers were particularly strong because of the shared language; many American writers came to Britain and Continental Europe during and after World War I. Influential European writers of this time period include Hermann Hesse, André Gide, Thomas Mann, and Marcel Proust, as well as Russian writers such as Leo Tolstoy and Anton Chekov. There was also a strain of exoticism in modernism, which exhibited interest in non-Western cultures in Asia and Africa. For all of these reasons, it is as difficult to impose geographical boundaries on modernism as it is to impose temporal ones. Modernism also was not confined to the realm of literature but affected other arts such as architecture, painting, music, dance, photography, and film. A great deal of cross-fertilization took place at this time between the various arts, particularly the visual arts and literature.

The intended audience for this volume is researchers in the field of British modernism, ranging from advanced undergraduate English majors, through graduate students, and on up to professional scholars. It should also be helpful to professional reference librarians, from generalists to subject specialists in literature, as well as graduate students in library and information science who wish to learn more about literature resources. A wide range of reference materials is considered, from the general and familiar (such as the *Modern Language Association International Bibliography*) to the more specialized (such as Sutton's *Location Register of Twentieth Century English Literary Manuscripts and Letters*). New researchers wanting guidance on where to find information beyond the library catalog and basic literature databases will find a variety of directions to follow and resources from which to choose. More advanced researchers seeking specialized primary resources will also have a range of options to pursue, from tools for finding contemporary reviews to those used for locating archival materials.

This guide covers resources and techniques for locating both primary and secondary research materials. While many of the reference materials are focused on the modern era, there are others that look at literature more broadly. These general tools are discussed specifically in terms of using them for research related to modernism. The chapters in this book focus on: general library reference resources; local and union library catalogs; print and electronic bibliographies and abstracting and indexing tools; scholarly journals relevant to modernism; contemporary review resources; journals, little magazines, and newspapers of the period; microfilm and digital collections; manuscripts and archives; and Web-based resources. Each chapter analyzes the strengths and weaknesses of the resources included as well as the best practices for using them. There is also discussion of the changing nature of literary research in British modernism due to the increased availability of reference materials in electronic formats and some of the challenges brought about by current copyright law.

In addition to best practices for using the print materials referenced here, detailed information is provided on search strategies for both local and union online library catalogs and for electronic bibliographies and indexing and abstracting tools. With the ubiquitous presence of such resources in libraries currently, most researchers feel confident in performing simple searches and obtaining "good enough" results. It is hoped that the tips and techniques recounted here will allow such researchers to upgrade their searching abilities and enable them to find better and more focused results with a shorter outlay of time. Obtaining an understanding of the most important searching techniques and strategies will serve as a core research skill transferable to any number of electronic resources.

This volume can be read from start to finish as a narrative of the research process. This may very well be the best strategy for newer and less-experienced scholars as they first approach their topics of interest. More experienced researchers or those with specific goals in mind may prefer to dip into particular chapters that focus on their current needs. No matter how a reader chooses to use this volume, it is hoped that it will open up new understanding of the research process, new options for materials to explore, and new possibilities for further extending our appreciation of the "ongoing tradition of experimentation" that is modernism.[1]

NOTE

1. See Daniel R. Schwarz, *Reading the Modern British and Irish Novel, 1890–1930* (Hoboken, NJ: Wiley-Blackwell, 2005), 1.

Chapter One

Basics of Online Searching

Researchers in today's electronic environment have many advantages over earlier generations of scholars. Personal computers and electronic databases have revolutionized how literature scholars conduct their work. They can quickly and efficiently find information through electronic database searching that would take hours or days longer to find with print indexes and abstracting tools, and they can do this without ever leaving their home or office. Trips to libraries and archives are still being made, but they are quicker and more focused on obtaining hands-on access to materials already identified online. Availability of full-text articles, electronic books, and digitized archival materials sometimes make the trip to the library or archive completely unnecessary.

In spite of the many advantages of the electronic research environment, there are pitfalls as well. Undergraduate students are sometimes surprised and disappointed to learn that we are not yet living in a science fiction universe where the whole of human knowledge is instantly available through the computer or are misled by super search engines like *Google* into believing that this is indeed the case. Even experienced electronic resource users can be overwhelmed by the range and complexity of information sources available. As good as many of the electronic databases are, their search interfaces can be confusing to the uninitiated. Each may have unique features or special search requirements that are not immediately obvious. And although certain search conventions do exist, there is no true standardization among electronic databases, and even the same resource may look very different, depending on which vendor is providing access to it.

This chapter is intended to help the researcher, of whatever experience level, to navigate some of these pitfalls and approach the research process in a more efficient manner. Portions of the material included here may already be well known to some researchers, depending on their experience level. It is hoped that everyone can learn something new and will indulge the presentation of known material as reminders of good habits.

STEP ONE: WRITING THE RESEARCH QUESTION AS A TOPIC SENTENCE

Whether you are an undergraduate who has been assigned a research topic, an upper-level student working on a topic of choice, or a seasoned scholar looking for a new area of research, you will need to reach a point where your topic can be simply stated in one sentence or as a single question. Prior to this, you may spend time thinking about your interests, sifting through what is already known, or taking some preliminary stabs at research just to see what's out there. But to proceed efficiently, you will sooner or later need to boil all your disparate thoughts down to one coherent topic sentence. "How did George Orwell use the concept of journalism in his work?" you might ask. In this case the key concepts to pull out are *George Orwell* and *journalism.* Or perhaps you are interested in exploring the critical response to women's poetry in the twentieth century: "I want to know how women's poetry in the twentieth century was received by critics." Your key concepts here would be *women, poetry, twentieth century*, and *critics*.

STEP TWO: BRAINSTORMING KEYWORD CONCEPTS

Once you have a single, focused topic sentence and have pulled out the major concepts, you need to start brainstorming for related terms. The reason this is particularly important with electronic searching is that computers are very literal-minded. If you put in the term *women,* they will find records containing the word *women.* But if the perfect resource you're looking for uses the term *female* or *woman*, computers will not find it! For this reason, you'll need to think about all the ways the English language has of expressing the same or similar concepts. Thus, for the second example above, you might come up with a list of potential search terms that looks something like this: *women, woman, female* and *poetry, verse* and *twentieth century, modern, modernism* and *critics, criticism, critical, appraisal, analysis.*

STEP THREE: THE STRUCTURE OF ELECTRONIC RECORDS: MARC AS AN EXAMPLE

Before we go on to the next step, it can be helpful to have a better understanding of the structure of electronic records. Knowing how these records are set up and "work" will aid you in developing the best search strategy for finding the materials you need. Most people are familiar with electronic library catalogs, so we'll use that as our example. The records found in almost all electronic catalogs use the same standardized set of rules based on the conventions of Machine-Readable Cataloging (MARC), established by the Library of Congress. MARC allows for the information included in library records to be categorized into various searchable indexes that enable the user to find specific works.

Figure 1.1 shows a typical public catalog record for a book related to twentieth-century literature. You'll note all the familiar categories one might use for searching for such a book in the catalog: author, title, subject. Figure 1.2 shows the MARC record for the same book. Many electronic library catalogs allow users to see this version of the record by clicking on a link for "MARC View," "MARC Record," or "Librarian View." Note how numbers are associated with various parts of the record: the author's name is found in the 100 field, the book's title is found in the 245 field, and subject headings each have a separate 600-level field. This will give you some insight into how a catalog search works. If you perform a search for an author, for example, the computer will search within the index of the 100 field for the information you input in the search interface. If you perform a title search, the computer looks in the index of the 245 field.

STEP FOUR: BUILDING A SEARCH STRATEGY

Field Searching

The next step in finding the information you need is to build an effective search strategy. Luckily, a few basic rules tend to apply to all electronic resources concerning how search strategies are constructed. In the previous step, we discussed MARC records and how they consist of various fields that

Author: Menand, Louis.
Title: Discovering modernism : T.S. Eliot and his context / Louis Menand.
Publisher: Oxford [Oxfordshire] ; New York : Oxford University Press, 1986.
Description: Book
211 p. ; 22 cm.
LC Subject(s): Eliot, T. S. (Thomas Stearns), 1888-1965 --Criticism and interpretation.
Modernism (Literature)

Figure 1.1. Library catalog record for a scholarly work related to modern British literature.

000 00943cam a22002898a 450
001 88394
003 PU
008 861208s1986 enk b 00110 eng
010 __ |a 86008646
035 __ |a (CStRLIN)PAUG86-B50442
035 __ |a (CaOTULAS)185131829
035 __ |9 AAK9992
040 __ |d CStRLIN |d PU
050 0_ |a PS3509.L43 |b Z7854 1986
082 0_ |a 821/.912 |2 19
090 __ |a PS3509.L43 |b Z7854 1986 |i 12/08/86 CTZ
100 10 |a Menand, Louis.
245 10 |a Discovering modernism : |b T.S. Eliot and his context / |c Louis Menand.
260 0_ |a Oxford [Oxfordshire] ; |a New York : |b Oxford University Press, |c 1986.
263 __ |a 8610
300 __ |a 211 p. ; |c 22 cm.
500 __ |a Includes index.
504 __ |a Includes bibliographical references.
600 10 |a Eliot, T. S. |q (Thomas Stearns), |d 1888-1965 |x Criticism and interpretation.
650 _0 |a Modernism (Literature)
950 __ |l VPL |i 12/08/86 C
955 __ |l VPL |c 1 |q YAP |r [00855 7063] |i 12/08/86 C

Figure 1.2. Modified MARC record for same title as previous figure.

are broken down into separate indexes and are searchable through a front-end search interface (the library catalog, as seen by the user). The same principle holds true for other electronic databases you may have access to through your library. Most of these provide information regarding scholarly journal articles, while some may also include information about books, reviews, dissertations, conference papers, and other materials of scholarly interest. As with your library catalog's MARC records, these databases' records are organized into fields whose contents make up individual indexes that are searchable. So likewise, you can perform an author search in these databases to find articles or other items authored by a particular person. Most databases allow for searching in a number of the available fields, most often through the selection of a particular field from a drop-down menu in the search interface. Usually the default search is a "keyword" or other broad, multifield search option, which will return the widest array of results.

Although searching by fields is fairly straightforward, there is still some potential for confusion. Sometimes students are frustrated when looking for critical works about an author and they are finding only the author's own works in the library catalog. They logically assume that because they are looking for works about an author, they should be performing an author search. However, librarians and databases work on a slightly different logic. An "author" search for *Joyce, James* is used to find books written *by* him; a "subject" search for *Joyce, James* is used to find books written *about* him and his work.

Subject versus Keyword Searching

Electronic databases normally allow for some type of subject searching, although this field may go by a different name, such as "descriptor." A frequent point of confusion in database field searching is the difference between "subject" searches and "keyword" searches. Subject searches in MARC catalog records look for information in the 650 and related 600-level fields. These areas contain the official Library of Congress subject headings assigned to that book. These are standardized headings developed by the Library of Congress and used consistently by libraries. The 2007 version of the *Library of Congress Subject Headings* (otherwise known as *LCSH*) is the thirtieth edition. It has five volumes and provides over 280,000 headings and references. Many libraries make a copy of the *LCSH* available to their patrons to aid in their use of the library's catalog. Figure 1.3 shows a library catalog record with a wide range of Library of Congress subject headings.

Library of Congress subject headings are a bit more complicated than simple subject labels. For instance, the system recognizes that a term like *modernism* is very complex and has applications for a variety of fields. While

Author: Miller, Andrew John.
Title: Modernism and the crisis of sovereignty / Andrew John Miller.
Publisher: New York : Routledge, c2008.
Description: Book
xxix, 222 p. ; 24 cm.
LC Subject(s): Yeats, W. B. (William Butler), 1865-1939 --Criticism and interpretation.
Eliot, T. S. (Thomas Stearns), 1888-1965 --Criticism and interpretation.
Woolf, Virginia, 1882-1941 --Criticism and interpretation.
English literature --20th century --History and criticism.
National characteristics in literature.
Sovereignty in literature.
Geopolitics in literature.
Authors, English --20th century --Political and social views.
Modernism (Literature) --Great Britain.
Series: Routledge studies in twentieth-century literature ; 4
Web Link: Table of contents only

Figure 1.3. Library catalog record with numerous Library of Congress subject headings.

Author: Gan, Wendy.
Title: Women, privacy and modernity in early twentieth-century British writing / Wendy Gan.
Publisher: Basingstoke [England] ; New York : Palgrave Macmillan, 2009.
Description: Book
ix, 182 p. ; 23 cm.
LC Subject(s): English literature --20th century --History and criticism.
English literature --Women authors --History and criticism.
Women in literature.
Privacy in literature.
Home in literature.
Space in literature.
Women --Identity.
Modernism (Literature) --Great Britain.
Web Link: Contributor biographical information
Publisher description
Table of contents only

Figure 1.4. Library catalog record found as a result of a keyword search for variations on the term *modern*.*

you can do an LC subject heading search for *modernism*, it's helpful to know that the term is further broken down as "Modernism (Art)," "Modernism (Architecture)," "Modernism (Literature)," and so on. Library of Congress subject headings can often be further narrowed by geographical region or time period: for example, "Modernism (Literature)—Great Britain" and "English literature—20th century." Knowing that these conventions exist can help you focus your research more easily. More information on relevant Library of Congress subject headings can be found in chapter 3.

In contrast to a subject search, a keyword search tends to be much broader. It will look not only in the 650 and related subject fields, but also in the 245 title field, the 100 author field, the 500-level note fields, and other specialized fields. Figure 1.4 shows a library catalog record that was found as a result of a keyword search for variations on the term *modern**. Note how the search term is highlighted not only in the subject area but also in the title field. Generally speaking, a subject search tends to be more concise, while a keyword search is broader. It is likely that you'll get a larger number of "false hits" (incorrect or inappropriate search results) using a keyword search, but this approach is often useful for finding obscure or elusive materials.

Boolean Searching

The basic building blocks of a database search consist of the Boolean operators *and*, *or*, and *not*. These familiar terms are used in specialized ways to help focus, expand, or limit the search results you obtain. Use of the operator

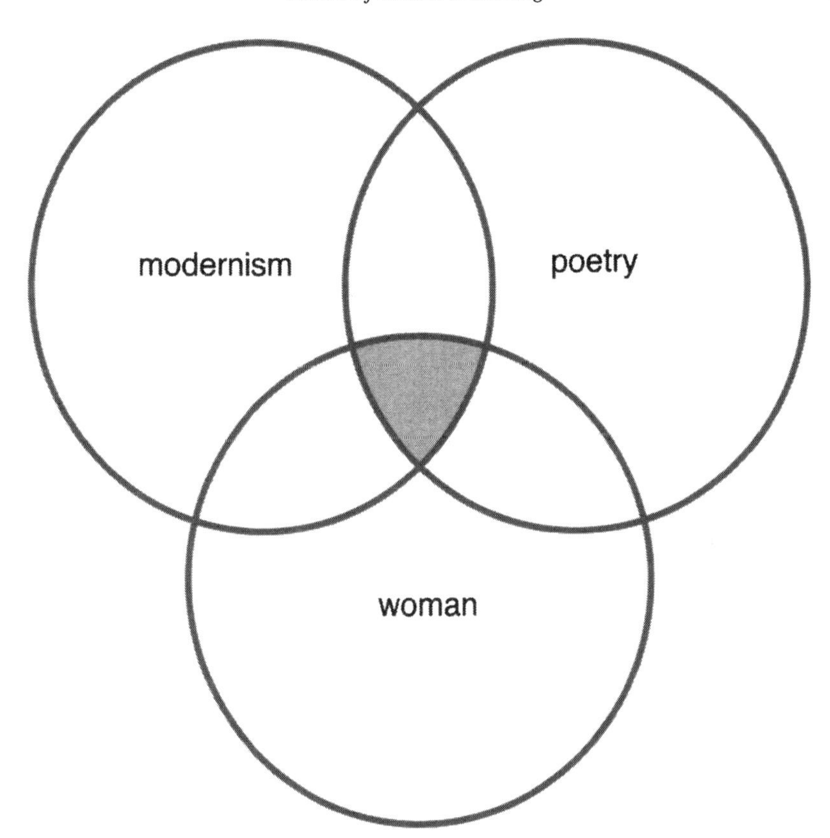

Figure 1.5. Boolean *and* search.

and requires that *all* terms listed be present in the results. Figure 1.5 shows a graphic illustration of the results of an *and* search. Use of the operator *or* broadens the search, retrieving results containing *any* of terms linked by this operator. Figure 1.6 shows the results of an *or* search. The operator *not* will exclude the terms specified by this operator. This particular command should be used with caution, as it is possible to exclude some useful results by accident. Figure 1.7 shows the results of a search integrating the *not* operator.

Truncation/Wildcards

Another way of broadening your search and saving time is the use of truncation and wildcards. Many search engines allow for these techniques in searching, although each one may use a different symbol for the same technique. Check the help screen or search tips page on the database you're searching for specific information relevant to this particular type of search. Probably the most common symbol used for truncation is the asterisk, *, although symbols such as ?,

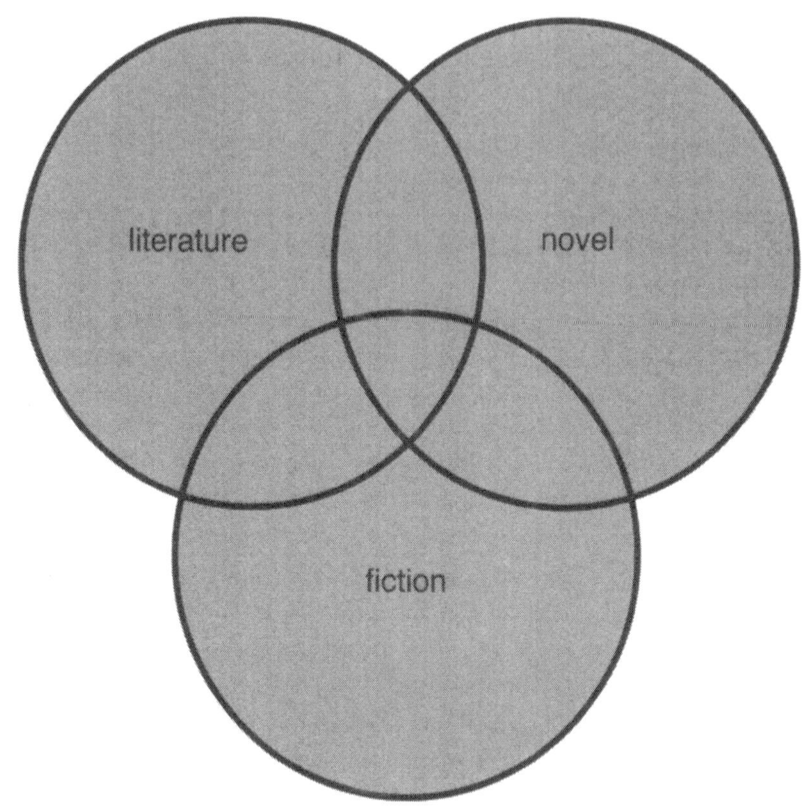

Figure 1.6. Boolean *or* search.

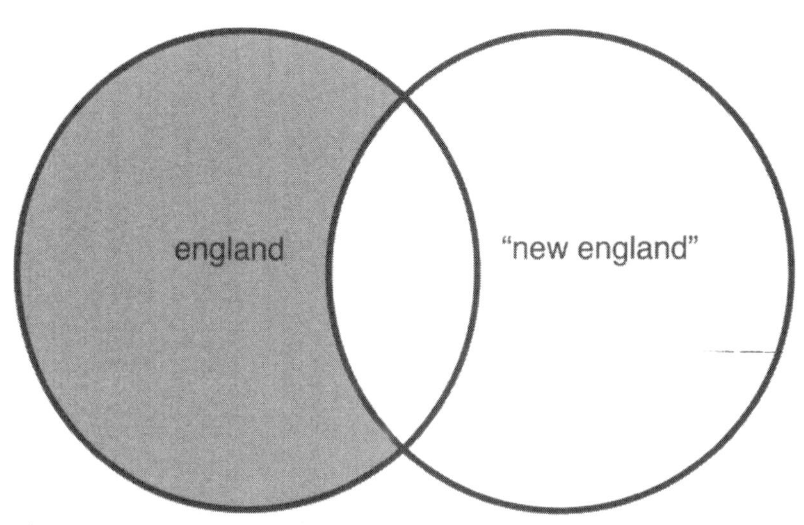

Figure 1.7. Boolean *not* search.

!, #, or others are sometimes used instead. The symbol is inserted at the end of a character string, and the search engine will search for those characters in that exact sequence, as well as those characters in sequence plus any additional ones immediately following without a space. So, for example, *modern** will return results for *modern*, *moderns*, *modernist*, *modernists*, *modernism*, and any additional permutation that might exist. Be careful not to truncate too far, however. A search for *mod** will return inappropriate results from 1960s culture such as *mod* and *mods*, not to mention other potentially irrelevant results such as *modest*, *moderate*, and so forth. Likewise, if you're looking for information on surrealists, a truncated search for *surrealist** will produce results for just that term and its plural, but it will leave out results more broadly focused on *surrealism*. In this case, *surreal** might be a better choice for truncation.

Wildcards are a similar technique to truncation, but the symbol allowing for variable results is inserted inside a character string rather than at the end. Thus, *wom?n* will return results for both *woman* and *women*. Wildcards are particularly useful for dealing with words that might have variant spellings in British and American English. For example, *lab?r* will return results for both *labor* and *labour*. Some databases are "smart" enough to search for both terms if only one is entered, but it's good to be aware of this technique in case you are missing out on the full range of materials available.

Nesting

Nesting is another technique that can help focus and speed your research. It generally uses parentheses as a way of grouping search terms together in a logical way. For example, if you were interested in finding information on modernist women writers of fiction, you might need to build a whole series of searches to cover this topic:

*Modern** **and** *wom*n* **and** *prose*
*Modern** **and** *wom*n* **and** *novel**
*Modern** **and** *wom*n* **and** *fiction*
*Modern** **and** *wom*n* **and** *short stor**

With the technique of nesting, however, you can collapse all these searches into one search:

*Modern** **and** *wom*n* **and** *(prose* **or** *novel** **or** *fiction* **or** *short stor*)*

This type of searching also has the advantage of eliminating duplicate records that might be encountered doing multiple, similar searches, because individual records will be returned only once, even if they contain multiple search terms within the *or* grouping.

Phrase Searching/Proximity Operators

Another useful search technique is phrase searching. Most search engines allow for phrase searching, which is generally accomplished by placing more than one word inside quotation marks. This causes the search engine to search for that series of words in that exact order. So, for example, while a keyword search for *James Joyce* without quotation marks might bring back an article co-written by James Smith and Joyce Jones; a keyword search for *"James Joyce"* in quotation marks would not. False hits are still a possibility, but the percentage of inappropriate returns should be lessened using this technique.

A related search technique is proximity searching, which will bring back results for terms found in proximity to each other, not necessarily as an ordered phrase. There are a number of permutations on proximity searching, and a variety of symbols that can be utilized. Again, it's best to consult the help screen or any search tips page provided by the search engine you're accessing to find out whether this technique is available and what conventions are being used. As an example of this type of searching, let's look at the *FirstSearch* search engine, which is familiar to many researchers because it hosts the popular bibliographic database *WorldCat* and is also one of the vendors for the *MLA International Bibliography. FirstSearch* allows for two types of proximity searching—*with* and *near*, which can be abbreviated as *w* and *n*. *With* requires that the terms be linked in the exact order stated; *near* allows the terms to be found in any order. Both terms can be used with digits to specify a number of intervening words between the terms. Thus, searching for *James w Joyce* is the same thing as performing a phrase search because it requires the term to be directly adjacent in the order stated. *Leonard w2 Woolf*, on the other hand, means that up to two intervening words may be present between the two terms, although they must occur in the order given. This search will return results for *Leonard Woolf* as well as for *Leonard and Virginia Woolf*. The use of *near* will allow the search to be broadened further by allowing the terms to appear in different orders. Thus searching for *Leonard n3 Woolf* will not only return all of the above results but will also pick up a hit for a record containing the phrase *Virginia Woolf and her husband Leonard.*

Relevancy Searching

Some search engines have an option for "relevancy" ranking of search results or may even return search results in relevancy order as a default. Again, each search engine that includes this service is different, and you should consult the documentation provided by the vendor in order to more fully understand a particular database's relevancy matrix. Generally, relevancy is determined by a combination of factors, such as these:

- The number of times the search terms appear in the record (high hit rate equals higher relevancy)
- The places where the search terms are located within the record (a search term appearing in the title, as a subject term, or in the first paragraph of the abstract all equate to higher relevancy)
- The proximity of the search terms to each other (if you are searching more than one term, the closer they appear to each other in the record, the higher the relevancy)
- The presence or absence of search terms (you may get hits for records with only some of your search terms, but they will be considered of lower relevancy)

Relevancy rankings are not foolproof; they cannot compensate for different uses or meanings of terms, nor can they intuit a particular researcher's unique interest in a topic. While relevancy searching does have flaws, it is anticipated that this type of searching will get "smarter" as programming and systems develop.

Limiting/Modifying

Many search engines will allow you to place limits on your search results or modify your search once you've received an initial set of results. For example, many multidisciplinary databases that cover a wide range of topics and index both scholarly and popular works provide an option for limiting the search results to those items appearing in scholarly publications (sometimes this option goes by other names, such as "peer reviewed"). This is a popular limit for undergraduates who have been instructed to find scholarly materials to support their arguments. For more advanced researchers or those using more specialized databases that contain only scholarly materials, other limitations may be useful. Two of the most widely available limitations are language and date. For databases including articles in many languages, some researchers find it useful to limit their results to English and/or another language they are proficient in reading. Researchers who follow a particular topic may want to limit their result to the most recently published materials, as they may already be familiar with prior research.

Once you've determined your search terms and their equivalents and settled on a search strategy using as many relevant techniques as necessary, you may still find yourself in the daunting situation of getting hundreds or even thousands of search results. If you find yourself in this position, the first thing to do is skim through your first few pages of results. Take a look at the materials returned and try to assess how relevant they are to your area of interest. If they all seem to be relevant, you may want to consider taking the time to page through all of them if you wish to complete a comprehensive literature review. If the results aren't all relevant, try to see whether any patterns are apparent. The false hits may give you a cluc for additional terms you need to use in your search or suggest a term to avoid, which would be appropriate for a *not* clause in your search. Many search engines allow you to go back to your search screen and add or modify the search terms and parameters without having to start from scratch. Other search engines may permit you to "search within the results" by adding additional search terms or phrases to allow you to further narrow and focus the results you've already obtained.

STEP FIVE: DATABASES VERSUS SEARCH ENGINES

Once you've brainstormed your topic, become aware of all the search strategies and techniques, and developed a tentative search plan, you will also need to become familiar with the particular search engine you'll be using and modify your search to fit its requirements. To do this, it's important to first understand the difference between a database and a search engine. For our purposes, a database is the collection of citations and associated information. It is what makes up the content that you will be searching. The search engine, on the other hand, is the means of accomplishing the search, the particular platform through which the content is made accessible. To return to the example of an electronic catalog of library holdings, the database is essentially the bibliographic data of all the library materials in the catalog. The search engine is the particular interface that the library uses to provide access to the bibliography. Many libraries have had to "migrate" their catalog information to a new system, or search engine, when their collection outgrows the previous system or they wish to work with a vendor offering additional services. The data being searched remains essentially the same, but the search interface changes.

Likewise, many bibliographic databases used by researchers are available on more than one search engine or platform. Access to a particular database will depend on which search engine a library has contracted with for services. Most scholarly bibliographic databases are proprietary—they are not available "free and on the Internet" but rather require a licensing agreement with a search engine vendor who charges subscription or access fees. For most college and university libraries, search engine subscription fees are based on the number of "full-time equivalents" or "FTEs" comprising their student body. In most cases, it is not affordable for an individual to purchase access to a scholarly database through a search engine vendor.

To further illustrate the database/search engine difference, let's consider the case of the *Modern Language Association International Bibliography* (*MLAIB*). This database is the largest and most widely used database of literature-related information. The bibliography is still available in print format, but more and more institutions are subscribing to electronic versions due to the increased efficiency in conducting a literature search. The information in the bibliography is collected and organized by the Modern Language Association (MLA), but a number of different vendors have developed their own search engines and market a search interface to the bibliography. Again, the access you have will depend on which licensing agreements your library has made. With the prevalence of "package" deals encouraged by many of the larger vendors, it's possible that you might have access to the *MLAIB* through more than one search engine. As of this writing, the *MLAIB* is available from the following vendors that provide the search engine interface: CSA, EBSCO, Gale, OCLC (*FirstSearch*), and ProQuest. Other databases are exclusively available through only one search engine vendor. In chapter 4, the most useful databases for literature research will be discussed. Contact information is included there for the creators of the databases rather than for the individual search engine vendors. Licensing agreements and access can change over time, and database producers are more than happy to direct you to where their products are currently available.

It's appropriate at this point to mention a couple of other new related technologies that many libraries are implementing that help scholars get what they need more quickly and with fewer steps when dealing with search engines. One is the advent of "federated search engines" or metasearching technology. Utilizing search strategies first developed by Web search engines such as *Google*, *WebCrawler*, and *Dogpile*, this technology has now been transferred to the library environment, where it has been adapted to do cross-platform searching on groups of proprietary databases all at the same time. These products (such as *WebFeat* and *MuseGlobal*) prevent the need to perform the same search multiple times in multiple search engines. They also remove duplicates from the search results, another task that researchers would normally have to perform themselves.

Another useful tool is open URL link resolvers. These tools (such as *SFX*, *WebBridge*, etc.) basically allow linking between different databases

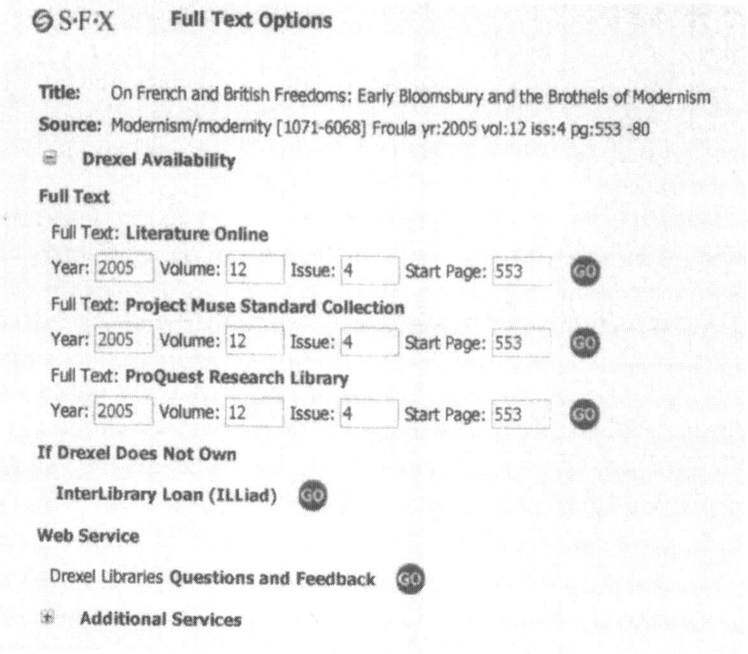

S·F·X Full Text Options

Title: On French and British Freedoms: Early Bloomsbury and the Brothels of Modernism
Source: Modernism/modernity [1071-6068] Froula yr:2005 vol:12 iss:4 pg:553 -80

Drexel Availability

Full Text

Full Text: **Literature Online**
Year: 2005 Volume: 12 Issue: 4 Start Page: 553 GO

Full Text: **Project Muse Standard Collection**
Year: 2005 Volume: 12 Issue: 4 Start Page: 553 GO

Full Text: **ProQuest Research Library**
Year: 2005 Volume: 12 Issue: 4 Start Page: 553 GO

If Drexel Does Not Own

InterLibrary Loan (ILLiad) GO

Web Service

Drexel Libraries **Questions and Feedback** GO

Additional Services

Figure 1.8. ***SFX*** **Screen for** ***Modernism/modernity*** **article.**

subscribed to by a particular library. Thus, if you find a useful citation while performing a search in one database, clicking on the link resolver can lead you to another database your library subscribes to that contains the full text of the article cited. If the full text is not present in any of the available databases, a library may use the link resolver to refer their patrons to interlibrary loan request forms, the library catalog, or other points of service. Again, such a tool helps prevent the need to perform multiple searches in multiple databases to find the material needed. Figure 1.8 shows an example of an *SFX* screen accessed via a record in the *MLAIB*. It shows links to possible full text in three other databases, as well as including a link to interlibrary loan and help services.

As exciting as these developments in electronic database searching are, a word of warning is still in order. These technologies are still very new and do not always work seamlessly. Due to the lack of standardization among various search engines, some products may not "work" with federated search engines or URL link resolvers, leading to gaps in access to databases to which your institution subscribes or the need to perform duplicate searching. Reference librarians and electronic resources librarians are useful sources of information regarding any unique aspects of the search technology used in your library, as well as providing you with guidance in performing electronic database searches. Searching technology continues to develop and improve, and librarians are often in contact with vendors to give feedback on search engine usability and researchers' needs. We can anticipate that electronic searching will continue to become better, easier, and faster.

STEP SIX: UNDERSTANDING *GOOGLE* SEARCHES

The Internet search engine *Google* has certainly helped usher in an era of fast and user-friendly navigation through the morass of information found on the World Wide Web. Because of its ease of use and the frequent usefulness of the results it produces, many undergraduate students consider *Google* the first (and sometimes only) tool of choice when conducting their academic research. Librarians and faculty members often have their hands full trying to persuade students that there are other, better ways of conducting serious research.

Two main critiques can be made of *Google* as a research tool. One is that *Google*'s results are presented in "rank" order, and the rank of any given site depends largely upon (1) the number of pages linking to the site and (2) the number of hits it receives. This is all well and good, and *Google* refers to its process as "democratic." However, "most popular" does not always translate into "best," especially in the context of academic research. *Google* also states that "Important, high-quality sites receive a higher PageRank," http://www.google.com/corporate/tech.html, but it does not precisely define what it means by "important" or "high quality."

The other controversial aspect of *Google* as a research tool is that "sponsored" (i.e., paid) links appear at the top of many search results pages. These are essentially advertisements embedded into the search results, occupying the prime real estate at the top of the page. Although *Google* does make an effort to distinguish these links by labeling them as "sponsored" and highlighting them, they can still mislead naive or inexperienced researchers to purely commercial sites.

Google, however, is ever on the cutting edge, trying to develop new products to address special needs and niche markets. It is in the process of developing *Google Scholar* (currently available in a beta version), which specifically searches for scholarly information. *Google Scholar* limits results to "peer-reviewed papers, theses, books, abstracts and articles, from academic publishers, professional societies, preprint repositories, universities and other scholarly organizations" (http://scholar.google.com/intl/en/scholar/about.html). It finds full text when available, as well as citations. The initial release of the product was particularly strong for providing access to science and technology information, but as it has developed, access to materials in the arts, humanities, and social sciences has significantly increased.

Many academic libraries, already seeing the writing on the wall, have been partnering with *Google Scholar*. *Google Scholar* allows libraries that use link resolvers (such as *SFX*, *WebBridge*, or others) to link their electronic journal holdings to *Google Scholar* search results for their patrons. They can also link to library catalog book records available through OCLC's publicly available version of the *WorldCat* database at http://www.worldcat.org/. Libraries must opt to be involved in these programs, and once they do, the direct linking function should be recognized throughout the computer network of the library's home institution. Library patrons at cooperating institutions can also choose to set the "Scholar Preferences" within *Google Scholar* on their home computers to have off-campus linking access to their library's materials. These services negate the need to perform duplicate searches on both *Google Scholar* and library resources and help avoid the possibility of researchers mistakenly paying for scholarly papers that are already held in their library's collections.

Google searching techniques are in many ways very similar to the database searching techniques already described, but there are differences. Phrase searching by enclosing groups of words in parentheses is supported. Use of the Boolean operator *or* is supported, but to exclude concepts from a search, you must use the minus sign rather than the operator *not*. *And* is implied in any *Google* search, so its use is not necessary. A number of words are excluded from *Google* searches by default (such as many single digits and letters, and even the words *how* and *where*), but you may specify their inclusion in a search by putting a plus sign in front of the term. The use of an asterisk in *Google* is basically the equivalent of proximity searching; a search involving an asterisk will find the search terms plus any intervening or continuing words. Truncation as such is not supported, but *Google* automatically performs what it calls "stemming," a technique that finds words related to those specified in a search. For example, a search for *women* will also return *woman* and *women's*. Features in *Google*'s advanced search function simplify some of these techniques by having a search box devoted to phrase searching and other search boxes essentially performing the tasks of the Boolean operators *and*, *or*, and *not*. The advanced search function also has the ability to easily limit results by language and date range as well as other more unusual limitations, such as to sites that have been updated within the past three months or to only those sites coming from an .edu domain.

Google searches, and *Google Scholar* searches particularly, can be of use to the scholarly researcher. It's imperative to realize the limitations of such searches, however, and to know that at this time they can supplement but not replace searching through available scholarly resources.

CONCLUSION

This chapter provided an introduction and overview of basic search techniques and best practices. It can serve as a place to start for understanding online searching on a deeper level, as well as a resource to return to if questions come up during the research process. The techniques outlined in this chapter should be useful for searching a wide array of electronic resources, from online library catalogs, to databases such as the *Modern Language Association International Bibliography*, to Web resources such as *Google*. Proficiency in electronic searching is now a required skill for researchers at any level. Don't be afraid to get your feet wet and practice these techniques. Happy searching!

Chapter Two

General Literary Reference Resources

In the initial stages of research, it can be useful to consult some general literary reference resources to obtain an overview or background of the time period, major figures, and literary schools or movements of the modern British era. General literary reference resources are the kind of tools typically found in a library's reference section, such as encyclopedias, dictionaries, handbooks, companions, and biographical resources. Today, more and more of these tools are migrating to an electronic environment, so in addition to browsing the print reference collection and consulting the library catalog, be sure to check your library's electronic reference sources as well. Libraries differ in the ways they provide access to both print and electronic materials, so consult with a reference librarian if you have any questions regarding where and how to access these tools. What follows are some representative tools that may serve as a starting point for your research.

GENERAL RESEARCH GUIDES

Bracken, James K. *Reference Works in British and American Literature*. 2nd ed. Englewood, CO: Libraries Unlimited, 1998.

Harner, James L. *Literary Research Guide: An Annotated Listing of Reference Sources in English Literary Studies*. 5th ed. New York: Modern Language Association of America, 2008.

Marcuse, Michael J. *A Reference Guide for English Studies*. Berkeley: University of California Press, 1990.

Harner's *Literary Research Guide* and Marcuse's *Reference Guide for English Studies* have long been the mainstays in research guides used by graduate students in English literature. They continue to be important resources and should be consulted by researchers for additional materials beyond what can be covered in this volume.

The ***Literary Research Guide***, published by the Modern Language Association, is generally a required text for graduate students in literary studies, but much here will be helpful to advanced undergraduate and professional researchers as well. Dubbed by *Choice* as "the standard in the field," Harner includes 1,059 entries for materials relevant to literary research, which also refer to 1,555 additional books, articles, and electronic resources and 723 reviews. The book is organized into sections, each designated by a letter of the alphabet, and each resource is assigned a unique number. Thus, the designation M2775 will lead the researcher to section M on English literature and the 2,775th overall resource, which is the *British National Bibliography*. Each lettered section focuses on general resources, a national literature, or particular topics and sources related to literature. Sections address topics under the following titles: "A: Research Methods;" "B: Guides to Reference Books;" "C: Literary Handbooks, Dictionaries, and Encyclopedias;" "D: Bibliographies of Bibliographies;" "E: Libraries and Library Catalogs;" "F: Guides to Manuscripts and Archives;" "G: Serial Bibliographies, Indexes, and Abstracts;" "H: Guides to Dissertations and Theses;" "I: Internet Resources;" "J: Biographical Sources;" "K: Periodicals;" "L: Genres;" "M: English Literature;" "N: Irish Literature;" "O: Scottish Literature;" "P: Welsh Literature;" "Q: American Literature;" "R: Other Literatures in English;" "S: Foreign-Language Literatures;" "T: Comparative Literature;" and "U: Literature-Related Topics and Sources." Each section is further divided in a fairly consistent pattern throughout the book.

Each entry begins with a complete citation for the resource and standard Library of Congress and Dewey library call numbers when available. Harner's detailed annotations give a general overview of the tool, its scope, organization, strengths and weaknesses, and comparisons with similar resources (as well as the *Guide* number of the other resource if it has an entry). Where appropriate, Harner provides "see also" references at the end of an item's description to other sections of the *Guide* or to broader or related tools covered in the *Guide*. The work has three useful indexes: one for individual names (of persons responsible for works cited in the *Guide*, but not for individual literary authors), one for titles of individual works cited in either a separate entry or an annotation (including former or variant titles), and one for subjects (as well as types of reference tools).

For the researcher of modern British literature, many of the tools in the general resources sections A through L and the special topics section U will be of interest. More specific resources will be found in the British national literatures sections M through P. Because of the international nature of modernism, items of interest may also be found in the non-British literature sections Q through T. Section M (entries 1310–2900), "English Literature," is the lengthiest section of the book and contains further subdivision by time period. Researchers in British modernism will especially wish to consult the subsection on twentieth-century literature, addressing histories and surveys; handbooks, dictionaries, and encyclopedias; bibliographies of bibliographies; guides to primary works; guides to scholarship and criticism; language; biographical dictionaries; and genres (fiction, drama and theater, poetry, and prose). Over one hundred items (entries 2755–2900) are listed in this section alone.

The fifth edition of Harner's work has more electronic resources than previous editions, focusing specifically on quality proprietary reference tools available by subscription, as well as those freely available over the Internet that are sponsored by professional organizations or universities. To make room for these new entries, the decision was made to delete entries for scholarly journals and background studies as well as the section on encyclopedias previously covered in the "Literature-Related Topics and Sources" division. The fifth edition is available both in print and electronically. The electronic version will continue to be updated over time; due to this fact, Harner will no longer post updates and revisions to the work on his website as he did for earlier editions.

Michael J. Marcuse's ***A Reference Guide for English Studies,*** while overlapping somewhat with the information in Harner, provides additional information in a slightly different format. Of particular interest is the inclusion of reference works devoted to individual authors, a category excluded by Harner. The resources included are current through 1985, with some additional materials available through 1989. Marcuse's work is also broken up into major sections designated by a letter of the alphabet. Each entry is numbered within its section, so there are no unique numbers but rather unique letter-number combinations. Thus, the *British National Bibliography* is item C-16—the sixteenth entry in section C, regarding national bibliographies. The sections in Marcuse are "A: General Works," "B: Libraries," "C: Retrospective and Current National Bibliography," "D: Serial Publications," "E: Miscellany," "F: History and Ancilla to Historical Study," "G: Biography and Biographical References," "H: Archives and Manuscripts," "I: Language, Linguistics, and Philology," "K: Literary Materials and Contexts," "L: Literature," "M: English Literature," "N: Medieval Literature," "O: Literature of the Renaissance and Earlier Seventeenth Century," "P: Literature of the Restoration and Eighteenth Century," "Q: Literature of the Nineteenth Century," "R: Literature of the Twentieth Century," "S: American

Literature," "T: Poetry and Versification," "U: The Performing Arts—Theatre, Drama, and Film," "W: Prose Fiction and Nonfictional Prose," "X: Theory, Rhetoric and Composition," "Y: Bibliography," and "Z: The Profession of English." The entries are of three types. The majority of the entries are listings of single scholarly reference works; Marcuse's useful annotations address the scope and content of the work, the principles of inclusion and arrangement, and any special features. Citations are supplied for other relevant materials on the same topic as well as cross-references to related materials contained in the *Reference Guide*. Other entries are selected scholarly journals in particular fields and a selection of frequently mentioned secondary works in particular fields. These are not annotated but stand on their own as helpful bibliographies of secondary sources. The work concludes with three indexes: an index of authors, compilers, contributors, and editors; an index of titles; and an index of subjects and authors-as-subjects.

While many of the sections will be of potential interest to the researcher of modern British literature, section M, "English Literature," and section R, "Literature of the Twentieth Century," will be the most germane. Section M, "English Literature," is further subdivided into categories covering "I: Bibliographies," "II: Literary Histories," "III: Handbooks and Reader's Encyclopedias," "IV: Biobibliographies," "V: Guides to Individual Authors," "VI: Scottish Literature and Scottish Studies," "VII: Anglo-Irish Literature and Irish Studies," "VIII: Anglo-Welsh Literature and Welsh Studies," "IX: Commonwealth Literature and World Literature Written in English," "X: Africa," "XI: Australia," "XII: Canada," "XIII: India," "XIV: New Zealand and the South Pacific," and "XV: West Indies." Among the authors included in subsection V are the major modernists Auden, Conrad, T. S. Eliot, Joyce, Lawrence, Woolf, and Yeats. Section R, "Literature of the Twentieth Century," is further subdivided into "I: Age of Transition," "II: General Bibliographies and Guides," "III: Biobibliographies and Handbooks," "IV: Poetry," "V: Drama and Theater," "VI: Prose Fiction," and "VII: Prose and Criticism." Browsing these sections as well as consulting the index of subjects and authors-as-subjects will provide an overview of the resources to consult for research in this area.

Bracken's ***Reference Works in British and American Literature*** is not as comprehensive as either Harner or Marcuse, but it helps fill an important gap, particularly since the new edition of Harner no longer covers scholarly journals. *Reference Works in British and American Literature* has citations and substantial annotations to various reference tools (including bibliographies, dictionaries, encyclopedias, handbooks, indexes, concordances, and periodicals) that relate specifically to individual authors. Both British and

American authors are considered, focusing on writers with entries in standard literary bibliographies. Thus all major British modernists and many minor writers of the period can be found in this work, although it contains more than 1,500 writers from all time periods. Entries are arranged alphabetically by the writer's last name, with tools subdivided by category. For example, the entry for D. H. Lawrence provides citations and descriptions of four bibliographies, five dictionaries, encyclopedias, handbooks, and three journals, all specifically devoted to Lawrence's work in general or some aspect of it, such as his poetry or drama. Bracken's work also features a chronological appendix, a nationality appendix, an author/title index, and a subject index (with useful chronological subdivisions such as "English Literature—20th Century").

MODERNISM PERIOD ENCYCLOPEDIAS, DICTIONARIES, AND COMPANIONS

Bradshaw, David, and Kevin J. H. Dettmar, eds. *A Companion to Modernist Literature and Culture*. Malden, MA: Wiley-Blackwell, 2006.

Harris, Laurie Lanzen, and Helene Henderson, eds. *Twentieth-Century Literary Movements Index: A Guide to 500 Literary Movements, Groups, Schools, Tendencies, and Trends of the Twentieth Century, Covering More Than 3,000 Novelists, Poets, Dramatists, Essayists, Artists, and Other Seminal Thinkers from 80 Countries as Found in Standard Literary Reference Works*. Detroit: Omnigraphics, 1991.

Henderson, Helene, and Jay P. Pederson, eds. *Twentieth-Century Literary Movements Dictionary: A Compendium to More Than 500 Literary, Critical, and Theatrical Movements, Schools, and Groups from More Than 80 Nations, Covering the Novelists, Poets, Short-Story Writers, Dramatists, Essayists, Theorists, and Works, Genres, Techniques, and Terms Associated with Each Movement*. Detroit: Omnigraphics, 1999.

Kemp, Sandra, Charlotte Mitchell, and David Trotter, eds. *Edwardian Fiction: An Oxford Companion*. New York: Oxford University Press, 1997.

Levenson, Michael, ed. *Cambridge Companion to Modernism*. New York: Cambridge University Press, 1999.

MacKean, Ian. *The Essentials of Literature in English, Post-1914*. London: Hodder Arnold, 2005.

Parker, Peter, ed. *A Reader's Guide to Twentieth-Century Writers*. New York: Oxford University Press, 1996.

Poplawski, Paul, ed. *Encyclopedia of Literary Modernism*. Westport, CT: Greenwood Press, 2003.

Rice, Thomas Jackson. *English Fiction, 1900–1950: General Bibliography and Individual Authors—A Guide to Information Sources*. 2 vols. Detroit: Gale Research Co., 1979–1983.

Serafin, Steven R., ed. *Encyclopedia of World Literature in the 20th Century*. 3rd ed. 4 vols. Detroit: St. James Press, 1999.

Stringer, Jenny, ed. *Oxford Companion to Twentieth-Century Literature in English*. New York: Oxford University Press, 1996.

The ***Encyclopedia of Literary Modernism*** is the only English-language encyclopedia devoted entirely to literary modernism. It focuses on the time period 1890 to 1939 and emphasizes British and American writing. The encyclopedia's full scope is definitely wider than this, providing insight into the international aspects of modernism (such as in Scandinavia and India) as well as important precursors and successors beyond the stated date range. Entries include major and minor writers of the period, literary movements such as surrealism and futurism, cultural concepts such as "The New Woman" and psychoanalysis, interdisciplinary studies such as "Film and Modernism," and critical terminology such as "Metaphor and Metonymy." Each of the several hundred entries, which range from a few paragraphs to more than a dozen pages, is written by an academic scholar and contains a list of citations for further reading. A general "Selected Bibliography" of materials related broadly to modernism can be found at the end of the work. The index is particularly useful for finding minor writers and topics not having their own entry; it refers the reader to additional areas of the work where a major figure or concept is also mentioned. Although occasionally uneven in its coverage, this work stands alone as a one-stop reference tool for literary modernism.

The ***Cambridge Companion to Modernism***, available in both print and electronic formats, critically considers the modernist movement of the late nineteenth and early twentieth century and places it within a larger cultural and political context. While the dominant focus of the book is literature, other art forms can be found here as well; and while British and American writers predominate, the influence of their Continental peers is also considered. The work begins with a chronology of modernism from 1890 to 1940, listing year by year the significant cultural events and literary works published. Nine scholarly essays follow, focusing on the metaphysics of modernism, the cultural economy of modernism, the modernist novel, modern poetry, modernism in drama, modernism and the politics of culture, modernism and gender, the visual arts, and modernism and film. A topically arranged list of selected works, primarily monographs, for further reading is also provided. The fairly detailed index facilitates quick access to materials related to particular persons, places, and concepts.

Similarly, ***A Companion to Modernist Literature and Culture*** looks at literature of the period while also venturing beyond to the wider cultural implications of modernism. Arranged in five parts, the work is made up of scholarly essays by academics specializing in modernism. Part 1, "Origins, Beginnings, and the New," contains essays on broad topics as they relate to modernism, including philosophy, religion, politics, technology, language, geography, and sexuality. Part 2, "Movements," addresses literary symbolism, dada, imagism, and literary impressionism. In addition to essays on the novel, poetry, and drama, part 3, "Modernist Genres and Modern Media," considers visual arts, film, music, photography, and more. Part 4 on "Readings" relates to major British and American writers, providing essays on Auden, Conrad, Eliot, Ford, Woolf, and Yeats. Each essay also has references and a list of works for further reading. The fifth part, "Other Modernisms," addresses contemporary critical concerns related to race, gender, sexuality, postcolonialism, globalization, and postmodernism.

Selected as an "Outstanding Reference Title" by *Choice*, the third edition of the ***Encyclopedia of World Literature in the 20th Century*** has been labeled "invaluable" as a resource. This extensive four-volume work is international in scope, covering some 130 national literatures. Lengthy essays consider British, Irish, Scottish, and Welsh literature. Essays on both major and minor figures include basic biographical information, a critical assessment of their work, and primary and secondary bibliographies of selected works. For major authors, there are also brief excerpts from significant critical appraisals. The encyclopedia's usefulness is increased by inclusion of entries on significant literary movements and techniques (such as stream of consciousness), as well as important historical events reflected in the literature of the period (such as the Spanish Civil War).

According to the editor's foreword in the ***Oxford Companion to Twentieth-Century Literature in English***, "the aim of this book is to present an overview of literature in English from 1900 to the present in a single volume." This title is international in scope, considering literature in English from the United Kingdom, Ireland, the United States, Australia, Canada, New Zealand, Asia, Africa, and the Caribbean. The bulk of the coverage is of the novelists, dramatists, and poets writing in English during the time period. Each concise entry has birth (and if appropriate, death) dates, nationality, and brief overviews of each author's biography, significant works, and influences, as well as an assessment of the writer's importance and impact. There are also entries for travel writers, critics, scholars, historians, and journalists of the twentieth century, as well as major philosophers, economists, and sociologists whose work influenced contemporary writers. Additional entries are for individual works, genres, critical concepts, periodicals, and literary groups and movements. Heavily cross-referenced, this work provides a firm basis for an initial exploration of the significant works and writers of the twentieth century, as well as the various connections between them and the wider culture.

Harris and Henderson's *Twentieth-Century Literary Movements Index* and Henderson and Pederson's *Twentieth-Century Literary Movements Dictionary* both have a subtitle almost as long as the massive reference works themselves and can be seen as companion tools. Each stands on its own and has a slightly different way of accessing information about modern literary movements. Taken together, they encompass a nearly comprehensive look at international literary movements of the twentieth century. Although the Harris and Henderson volume is most properly considered a bibliography, it is included in this section both because of its close association with Henderson and Pederson and the fact that it cites only other reference tools.

The ***Twentieth-Century Literary Movements Index***, as indicated toward the end of its subtitle, provides access to information about twentieth-century literary movements that is found in other standard literary reference works, such as *Benet's Reader's Encyclopedia* and the *Reader's Companion to World Literature*, as well as twenty-six additional sources. The *Index* volume leads to this information in two parts: the "Index to Movements" and the "Index to Authors." The "Index to Movements" lists each movement alphabetically and has short citations to articles on the topic found in the cited reference tools. The names of the major and minor authors associated with each movement can also be found here. The "Index to Authors" is an alphabetical index of authors' names, with short citations to articles about them appearing in the covered tools. The literary movement or movements with which each particular author is associated are also listed.

The ***Twentieth-Century Literary Movements Dictionary*** is more self-contained. It is arranged alphabetically by names of the literary movements; each entry has a brief description of the movement, an overview of any major writers associated with the movement, and a bibliography of materials for further reading. The work is international in scope; literary movements in Britain range from the realism of the 1850s–1890s to the feminist criticism of the 1960s–1990s. Included are both wide-ranging, amorphous groups, such as Freudian criticism and Marxist criticism, as well as smaller groups more specific to a particular time and place, such as the Bloomsbury Group, the Inklings, and Ireland's Abbey Theatre. Modernism receives particularly in-depth treatment as "at once the most singular and diverse of all multi-nation movements" (382). There is an overview essay of modernism in general followed by shorter individual essays, with author listings and suggestions for further reading, covering modernism as expressed in countries throughout Eastern and Western Europe, Scandinavia, and North and South America. The section

"British and Irish Modernism" cites the 1910s–1930s as the dominant time period and specifically notes Conrad, Eliot, Joyce, Lawrence, Pound, Woolf, and Yeats as the major figures. Appendixes in the *Dictionary* volume are "A Timeline of Literary Movements," "Chronology by Country," "Journals Cited," and "Web Sites." Indexes in this volume are "Movements Index," "Author Index," "Title Index," and "Country and Nationality Index."

Edwardian Fiction considers fiction published in Great Britain and Ireland between 1900 and 1914. The tool consists mainly of a single alphabetical listing of brief entries on people and topics related to the time period. The bulk of the entries concern over eight hundred individual authors, most of whom are British or Irish. Some representative Canadians, South Africans, Australians, New Zealanders, and a few Americans with strong British associations, such as Henry James, may be found here as well. Thematic topics such as "Marriage Problem Fiction" and "Empire," entries for significant individual works, and entries for important periodicals of the time period are also included. Of added value is a detailed chronology of the Edwardian era, giving a yearly time line of significant British fiction published, other important books and cultural events, and world historical events. A useful listing of pseudonyms and changes of name for authors of the period rounds out the work. This work was reprinted in paperback by Oxford in 2002. The authors are the same and the content is identical, but the title is slightly different: *The Oxford Companion to Edwardian Fiction.*

Ian MacKean's ***The Essentials of Literature in English, Post-1914*** has broad international coverage of English literature from the World War I period forward, but the emphasis is on British and American literature. Part 1 of the work consists of an alphabetical listing of major authors, with brief overviews of their life and work. Part 2 focuses on major themes in modern literature, such as "Critical Studies of Modern Literature," "Feminist Literature," "Modern Drama," "Postcolonial Literature," and "Postmodern Literature." Part 3 considers regional influences on modern literature: "American Literature," "Australian Literature," "British and Irish Literature" (which includes "A Survey of British Fiction and Poetry of the Twentieth Century," "The Poetry of the First World War," "The Bloomsbury Group," "British Writers of the 1930s," and "The Liverpool Poets"), "Canadian Literature," "Caribbean Literature," "Indian Literature in English," "Irish Literature," and "South African Literature." Part 4 provides useful reference materials, such as a glossary of terms, a listing of literary awards, prizes, and laureateships, and a time chart. An author index and a general index are found at the end of the work.

A Reader's Guide to Twentieth-Century Writers has one thousand entries for significant English-language writers producing important works in the twentieth century. Again, the geographic distribution is wide, although the majority of the writers considered are British, American, or Commonwealth authors. Each entry begins with a brief biographical and critical overview, which is followed by a bibliography of works. The bibliography is broken up by genre, with categories for "Fiction," "Poetry," "Edited," "For Children," "Collections," and so on. If a significant biography exists for the author, it is listed as well.

Rice's ***English Fiction, 1900–1950*** is an alphabetical listing of individual authors with citations to materials for further research into each. The first section of all entries is the primary bibliography, divided into five main sections: "1.1: Fiction," "1.2: Miscellaneous Writings," "1.3: Collected and Selected Works," "1.4: Letters," and "1.5: Concordances." The second section presents secondary publications, also divided into five sections: "2.1: Bibliographies," "2.2: Biographies, Memoirs, Reminiscences, Interviews," "2.3: Book-length Critical Studies and Essay Collections," "2.4: General Critical Articles or Chapters," and "2.5: Studies of Individual Works." The work has two volumes, the first covering Aldington to Huxley and the second, Joyce to Woolf. The first volume has author, title, and subject indexes; the second volume has an author index only.

GENRE AND GENERAL NATIONAL LITERARY ENCYCLOPEDIAS AND COMPANIONS

Cody, Gabrielle H., and Evert Sprinchorn, eds. *Columbia Encyclopedia of Modern Drama*. 2 vols. New York: Columbia University Press, 2007.

Drabble, Margaret, ed. *Oxford Companion to English Literature*. 6th ed. rev. New York: Oxford University Press, 2006.

Gonzalez, Alexander G., ed. *Modern Irish Writers: A Bio-Critical Sourcebook*. Westport, CT: Greenwood Press, 1997.

Hawkins-Dady, Mark, ed. *Reader's Guide to Literature in English*. Chicago: Fitzroy Dearborn, 1996.

Head, Dominic, ed. *Cambridge Guide to Literature in English*. 3rd ed. New York: Cambridge University Press, 2006.

Innes, Christopher. *Modern British Drama, 1890–1990*. New York: Cambridge University Press, 1992.

Jarman, A. O. H., and Gwilym Rees Hughes, eds. *A Guide to Welsh Literature*. 7 vols. Cardiff: University of Wales Press, 1992–2003.

Luckhurst, Mary, ed. *A Companion to Modern British and Irish Drama, 1880–2005*. Malden, MA: Blackwell, 2006.

Royle, Trevor. *The Mainstream Companion to Scottish Literature*. Edinburgh: Mainstream, 1993.
Serafin, Steven R., and Valerie Grosvenor Myer, eds. *Continuum Encyclopedia of British Literature*. New York: Continuum, 2003.
Stephens, Meic, comp. and ed. *New Companion to the Literature of Wales*. new ed. Cardiff: University of Wales Press, 1998.
Welch, Robert, and Bruce Stewart, eds. *Oxford Companion to Irish Literature*. New York: Oxford University Press, 1996.

The resources in this category are similar to the encyclopedias and other sources covered in the preceding section, but they focus specifically upon national literatures rather than the specific time period encompassing modernism. Thus, they place modernist British writers and writings within the context of British writing in general, or more narrowly within Irish, Welsh, or Scottish national literatures.

The *Oxford Companion to English Literature* and the *Cambridge Guide to Literature in English* each provide brief alphabetical entries in encyclopedia style. The ***Oxford Companion to English Literature*** has entries for people, works, characters, terms, places, and other concepts related to English literature of all time periods. Longer, two-page articles are interspersed throughout the work on special topics such as "Metre" or "Historical Fiction." The long entry on "Modernism" will be of particular interest, with its substantial cross-referencing to various entries throughout the work. The *Companion* also contains several useful appendixes, including a chronology spanning c.1000–2005 and lists of British poets laureate and winners of significant literary prizes such as the Nobel Prize in Literature, the Pulitzer Prize for fiction, the Library Association Carnegie medalists, and the Man Booker Prize for fiction.

The ***Cambridge Guide to Literature in English*** contains articles on a range of topics related to literature in English. Again, coverage is broad in terms of geographic areas and time periods. Entries fall into a number of categories: writers; individual plays, poems, novels, and other works; literary groups or schools (such as Bloomsbury); wider literary movements (such as modernism); critical schools or movements; literary genres; poetic forms and subgenres of drama and fiction; critical terms; rhetorical terms; theaters and theater companies (going back to the Globe); and literary magazines.

The ***Continuum Encyclopedia of British Literature*** also addresses British literature of all time periods. The bulk of the 1,200 brief entries concern British authors from the *Beowulf* poet to postmodern writers, including a number of major and minor modernists. Seventy topical entries concerning such matters as modernism, literary criticism before 1945, and war and literature are also presented. The work provides substantial cross-referencing in each article, easily leading the reader to related concepts and writers. Each article also has a brief bibliography, with citations for important works related to each author or topic.

The entries in the ***Reader's Guide to Literature in English*** analyze significant works of literary criticism on various topics connected to literature in English. Both the geographic areas and the time span are far ranging, although the focus is on British and American literature of all time periods. It is included here because of its significant coverage of modernism. Criteria for inclusion of a topic in the work are the existence of a significant body of critical work (particularly critical monographs) and evidence of current, continuing interest in the subject. Each entry begins with a list of citations of the scholarly works related to the topic; the significance and contribution of each is then discussed in the body of the article. Entries are arranged in one alphabetical listing. Those with similar headings progress from general to more specific, and from British, to American, and then to other national literatures. Thus the entries for poetry range from "Poetry: General" and "Poetry: Theory" to "Poetry: British," "Poetry: American," "Poetry: Canadian," and so on. There are also "Thematic Lists" that group the topics together by categories of interest, such as "British and Irish Literature: 20th Century," "Modernism," "Twentieth-Century Literature: Topics," and "Twentieth-Century Literature: Writers." In the back of the book is a "Booklist Index" that provides an alphabetical-by-author listing of all the works cited within the tool, with page number references. There is also a "General Index," which is an easy way of looking up all sections in the book that concern a specific person or topic. This is useful for major figures who are often discussed in multiple entries, as well as for minor figures who may lack their own individual entry. Overall, this is an excellent tool for gaining an overview of the classic and significant works on particular literature topics.

Christopher Innes's *Modern British Drama, 1890–1990* and Mary Luckhurst's *A Companion to Modern British and Irish Drama, 1880–2005* both analyze drama of the modernist and postmodernist eras. ***Modern British Drama, 1890–1990*** contains sections such as "Defining modernism: George Bernard Shaw," "Social themes and realistic formulae" (addressing Galsworthy, Lawrence, and O'Casey), and "The comic mirror—tradition and innovation" (covering Yeats, Priestly, Eliot, and Beckett). A checklist of major plays is given for each playwright, and a chronology is provided at the beginning of the work. ***A Companion to Modern British and Irish Drama, 1880–2005*** includes scholarly articles on a variety of topics and is broken into several parts: "Contexts," "Mapping New Ground, 1900–1939," "England, Class and Empire, 1935–1990," "Comedy," "War and Terror," and "Theatre since 1968." There is also an index to names of individual playwrights and plays.

In a similar vein, the ***Columbia Encyclopedia of Modern Drama*** is arranged alphabetically with entries for playwrights, directors, titles (such as *Waiting for Godot*), and movements (such as modernist drama). Each signed article is at least five hundred words long and contains a short bibliography for further reading. There are also a listing of "Selected Plays" for playwright entries and "see also" entries and cross-referencing from names and terms within the text. Coverage is international in scope, and the time period is focused on all of the twentieth century. At the end of the second volume, a synoptic outline of contents (organized by topics) enables greater access to the contents through entries such as "Countries," "Plays" (titles), "Playwrights," "Movements, Forms, Genres," "Companies, Groups, and Theaters," and "Concepts and Terms." An extensive index draws together information not found elsewhere. For example, the encyclopedia lacks an entry for the Abbey Theatre, but the index lists in one place all of the playwrights associated with it.

A number of resources are available that focus on national literatures within the British Isles other than the English, specifically Irish, Welsh, and Scottish. Similar to the *Oxford Companion to English Literature* listed above, the ***Oxford Companion to Irish Literature*** features brief articles on persons and concepts related to Irish literature. The scope of the work is earliest times to the present day, and it covers authors, significant works, movements, genres, folklore, religion, political figures, "the troubles," and more. Arranged alphabetically, most entries are brief with the occasional longer article for major writers such as Joyce and Yeats. Maps of Ireland and Dublin provide additional value. ***Modern Irish Writers: A Bio-Critical Sourcebook*** is more narrowly confined to Irish authors who published significant works in the twentieth century and thus contains more in-depth information than the *Companion*. Each essay is written by a scholar in the field and includes a brief biography, a discussion of the author's major works and themes, a review of the author's critical reception, and a bibliography of primary and secondary sources.

The ***New Companion to the Literature of Wales*** offers an excellent overview of a little-known national literature, from the sixth century to the twentieth. It has 3,300 entries on authors, major works, genres, periodicals, and poetic forms. The emphasis is on literature, but royalty, artists, clergy, and other important historical and cultural figures may be found here as well. Special features are a chronology of Welsh history and a listing of the winners of the Chair, Crown, and Prose Medal competitions in the National Eisteddfod, and its locations since 1861. The same publisher, the University of Wales Press, has published a series of seven volumes collectively entitled ***A Guide to Welsh Literature***. Each work is generally devoted to a particular time period, and taken together they cover this national literature in depth. The final two volumes will be of the most interest to the researcher in modern British literature. Volume 6, covering c.1900–1996, is edited by Dafydd Johnston (1998) and considers Welsh-language writing only. Chapters focus on poetry, drama, the novel, and the short story, as well as literature of World War I and the interwar period. Although English-language writing is not included, this work provides insight into a parallel literary tradition that may be relevant for some researchers. Volume 7, *Welsh Writing in English*, edited by M. Wynn Thomas (2003), also looks at literature primarily of the twentieth century, although it begins with a survey of English-language Welsh writing from earlier eras. Some of the major figures discussed are Rhys Davies, Dylan Thomas, Gwyn Jones, David Jones, and Alun Lewis.

The Mainstream Companion to Scottish Literature is a reprint of an earlier version of the same work published by Macmillan. It covers Scottish national literature of all eras. Entries devoted to individual authors contain biographical information, an overview of their work and career, and a list of primary and secondary sources. Also included are major works, genres, and political and cultural associations.

BIOGRAPHICAL SOURCES

Biography Resource Center. Farmington Hills, MI: Thomson Gale, 2007. www.gale.cengage.com/BiographyRC/.

Dictionary of Literary Biography. Detroit: Gale, 1978– . www.gale.cengage.com/servlet/ItemDetailServlet?region=9&imprint=000&titleCode=GAL15&type=4&id=110997.

Janik, Vicki K., and Del Ivan Janik. *Modern British Women Writers: An A-to-Z Guide*. Westport, CT: Greenwood Press, 2002.

Matthew, H. C. G., and Brian Harrison, eds. *Oxford Dictionary of National Biography* (in association with The British Academy: From the earliest times to the year 2000). 61 vols. rev. ed. New York: Oxford University Press, 2004. www.oxforddnb.com.

The *Dictionary of National Biography* (*DNB*), now officially referred to as the ***Oxford Dictionary of National Biography*** (*ODNB*), is *the* source of biographical information for those who have impacted the history and culture of Britain. The first editor of the original edition of the work was Sir Leslie Stephen, father of renowned modernist writer Virginia Woolf.

Originally published between 1885 and 1900, it was called "a monument to the Victorian age." The work has since undergone considerable revision and expansion, with enhancements such as the addition of more women, minorities, and non-English persons, as well as the inclusion of more contemporary modern figures. The current edition, published in 2004, ranges from prehistory to the turn of the twenty-first century comprises sixty volumes covering over 56,000 lives and a separate volume containing an index to contributors. Copiously illustrated, the *ODNB* provides basic biographical information for all its subjects, with essays ranging from a few brief paragraphs to longer (up to 35,000 words), more detailed essays for significant figures. Each entry also has a list of primary and secondary sources consulted in the writing of the biography. Criteria for inclusion in the *ODNB* are that the person had an impact on shaping British history and is no longer living. Both major and minor British modernist writers are included. The *ODNB* is now also available electronically, and many libraries subscribe to the electronic version in addition to, or instead of, owning the print volumes. Each January, approximately two hundred new biographies, written for persons who died in the previous year, are added to the electronic content. In March 2009, the first print supplement, with new entries for 2001 through 2004, was published. The *ODNB*'s associated website has a freely available searchable or browseable index to 55,000 entries in the work, a weekly selection of full-text sample biographies, and much useful free content related to biography and the history of the *ODNB*.

Gale's ***Dictionary of Literary Biography*** (*DLB*) has long been a standby of biographical information concerning writers. This award-winning reference tool has been named an "Outstanding Academic Book" four times by *Choice* and twice as an Outstanding Reference Source by the American Library Association's Reference and User Services Association (RUSA). Currently weighing in at 345 volumes, this ongoing series features themed volumes focused on particular genres, time periods, and/or nationalities. Each volume is arranged alphabetically by the last name of the authors under consideration and provides biographical and critical information concerning each author's life and career. Due to the broad scope of the *DLB*, only particular volumes will be of interest to researchers of modern British literature. These include volume 10, *Modern British Dramatists, 1900–1945* (two-volume set), volume 15, *British Novelists, 1930–1959* (two-volume set), volume 19, *British Poets, 1880–1914*, volume 20, *British Poets, 1914–1945*, volume 36, *British Novelists, 1890–1929: Modernists*, and volume 191, *British Novelists between the Wars*. There is some overlap in content between the volumes. A separate print index, updated regularly, allows researchers to ascertain which volume(s) have essays related to a particular writer. This index, in addition to covering the *DLB*, also indexes the contents of many other Gale series such as

Contemporary Authors, *Twentieth-Century Literary Criticism*, *Modern British Literature*, and *World Literature Criticism*. The index is also freely available online through the Gale website as *Literary Index* (http://www.galenet.com/servlet/LitIndex). The print and electronic versions of the index have the same content; the main differences between the two are that the electronic version is easier to read compared with the extremely small type size used in the print edition, and the electronic version enables the user to search by a portion of the name (such as only the first name), which is helpful in cases where a name is imperfectly remembered. The *DLB* itself is now available in electronic format, along with many of the other Gale literary series mentioned above, as part of the *Literature Resource Center* database.

Biography Resource Center is Gale's electronic equivalent to much of the content available in various Gale and associated publishers' biography series, such as *Contemporary Authors*, *Concise Dictionary of British Literary Biography*, *Encyclopedia of World Biography*, and *Feminist Writers*. The easy-to-use electronic search function and the convenience of the electronic format have made this a favorite biography tool for many libraries. Updates to news articles concerning biography subjects, living and dead, are available, as well as links to some full-text magazine articles and websites. *Biography Resource Center* is a comprehensive biography tool, covering all professions, time periods, and geographic locations, and modern British authors are well represented within it.

Janik and Janik's ***Modern British Women Writers: An A-to-Z Guide*** addresses British women writers active at some point (roughly) during the years 1900–1999. In-depth essays describe the careers and contributions of these modernist and postmodernist women writers, both major and minor. Of particular interest are essays on Dorothy Richardson, Virginia Woolf, Rebecca West, Edith Sitwell, and Dorothy Sayers.

CHRONOLOGIES

British Library. *Chronology of Modern Britain*. www.bl.uk/chronology/ (accessed 11 April 2009).

Cahalan, James M. *Modern Irish Literature and Culture: A Chronology*. New York: Maxwell Macmillan International, 1993.

Cox, Michael, ed. *Oxford Chronology of English Literature*. New York: Oxford University Press, 2002.

Chronologies are time lines that have information regarding the historical and cultural/social events of a given era, often including literary works published and events in the lives of writers. The items presented here all have particular relevance to modern British literature, and each describes itself as a chronology, although other information is frequently made available as well. Many general reference tools, such as some of those described above, also have chronological information, and many works dealing with individual authors give chronologies or time lines for their particular areas of focus.

The British Library's website (which is discussed in more detail in chapter 10) provides a ***Chronology of Modern Britain*** beginning at 1914 (as the first year of World War I) and continuing to the present time. Of most relevance to readers will be the year 1914 through the 1940s. Each year lists important historical, political, and literary events by date and is followed by a "Publications of the Year" section, which lists significant works published (along with their British Library call numbers or "shelfmarks"). Hotlinks in the chronology bring the reader to guides to collections of various authors, topical guides on subjects such as "Fine Presses," or other reference source guides. Additional interest is generated by reproductions of selected book covers, quotations from works, and links to sound files from the era.

Although focusing primarily upon the modern era, Cahalan's ***Modern Irish Literature and Culture: A Chronology*** actually considers Irish literature and culture from 1601 through 1992. Each annual entry has a brief synopsis of the important political or social events of the year, followed by subheadings covering relevant topics, if applicable, such as "Education," "Fiction," "Irish Language and Literature," "Periodicals," "Poetry," "Cultural Institutions," "Drama," "Music," "Prose Non-fiction," "Art," and "Literary Criticism." The introduction includes suggested works for finding bibliographical information on Irish fiction, poetry, drama, and other literary texts. There are also three dozen brief "Biographical Sketches of Recurrent Figures," such as W. B. Yeats, James Joyce, Frank O'Connor, George Moore, Flann O'Brien, Samuel Beckett, and others. Additional features are a list of "Secondary Works Cited" and a general index.

The ***Oxford Chronology of English Literature*** is the major chronology for "works originally written in English by British authors published in Britain." A massive scholarly undertaking, the scope of the chronology is from 1474 to 2000, and it addresses the works of some selected non-British authors (such as Henry James) who lived and worked primarily in Britain. This reference tool consists of two volumes, the first comprising the chronology itself, which is arranged by imprint date (or actual date of publication, if known) and then alphabetically by author's last name (and alphabetically by title if more than one work by the same author was published in a given year). The emphasis of the coverage is on fiction, poetry, and drama, but there is also consideration of nonfiction (travel writing, correspondence, criticism), scholarship on historical and literary topics, the Bible, and major reference works. Standard titles are assigned for works that are commonly known by a short form of a complicated title, a feature which will have little impact on researchers of British modernism but is useful for those interested in literature from earlier eras when books sometimes had unwieldy or variant titles. The years of greatest interest to researchers in British modernism span from the late 1870s (to identify influential works by Oscar Wilde, George Moore, and Thomas Hardy) to about 1950. The second volume of the work contains an author index, a title index, and an index of translated authors.

INDIVIDUAL AUTHORS AND GROUPS RESOURCES

Attridge, Derek, ed. *Cambridge Companion to James Joyce*. 2nd ed. New York: Cambridge University Press, 2004.

Becket, Fiona. *The Complete Critical Guide to D. H. Lawrence*. New York: Routledge, 2002.

Conner, Lester I. *A Yeats Dictionary: Persons and Places in the Poetry of William Butler Yeats*. Syracuse, NY: Syracuse University Press, 1998.

Goldman, Jane. *Cambridge Introduction to Virginia Woolf*. New York: Cambridge University Press, 2006.

Haule, James M., and Philip H. Smith. *A Concordance to the Novels of Virginia Woolf*. 3 vols. New York: Garland, 1991.

Markert, Lawrence W. *The Bloomsbury Group: A Reference Guide*. Boston: G. K. Hall, 1990.

McCready, Sam. *A William Butler Yeats Encyclopedia*. Westport, CT: Greenwood Press, 1997.

Reference works devoted to individual authors (or specific groups of authors) can take many forms, such as bibliographies, chronologies, companions, concordances, dictionaries, encyclopedias, guides, and handbooks. The items listed here are selected works by major publishers covering some of the most significant authors and groups of the modernist era. Researchers should also consult Bracken's *Reference Works in British and American Literature*, listed above, for standard reference tools and other resources related to individual authors.

Two series in particular bear mentioning in regard to modernist authors. Cambridge University Press has been publishing "companions" to various topics from philosophy and religion to music and literature (see the *Cambridge Companion to Modernism*, above). The ***Cambridge Companion to James Joyce*** is representative of an individual author title concerning a major

British modernist. Each volume usually has a brief chronology and a scholarly introduction, followed by various essays by specialist literary critics analyzing major and minor works, themes, influences, and biographical information concerning the author in question. The Joyce volume, for example, contains individual essays on both *Ulysses* and *Finnegans Wake* and one on "Joyce's Shorter Works," as well as "Joyce the Irishman" and "Joyce and Feminism," along with other topics. Other British modernist writers who have Cambridge companions devoted to them are Joseph Conrad, E. M. Forster, D. H. Lawrence, Virginia Woolf, and W. B. Yeats.

Cambridge University Press also publishes introductions to various literary genres or individual figures. The ***Cambridge Introduction to Virginia Woolf*** is one example. Written by a single author, these volumes provide overviews of the writer's life, works, context, and critical reception. In the Woolf volume, there are separate subsections covering the most productive decades of Woolf's life, her fiction, her nonfiction, and an overview of Woolf's critical reception from her contemporaries to the present day. Boxes interspersed throughout the work suggest sources for further reading. In addition, a bibliography of primary and secondary works along with an index concludes the volume. Other British modernist writers who have Cambridge introductions devoted to them are Samuel Beckett, Joseph Conrad, James Joyce, and W. B. Yeats.

The Complete Critical Guide to D. H. Lawrence is part of a Routledge series on major authors. At this writing, Fiona Becket's volume on D. H. Lawrence is the only modernist included in the series. Similar to Cambridge's *Introduction to . . .* series, these guides give a general overview of the author's life and career. The Lawrence volume consists of three parts: "I. Life and Contexts," "II. Work," and "III. Criticism." The guide also contains a scholarly preface, a chronology, an extensive selected bibliography, and an index.

Lester I. Conner's ***A Yeats Dictionary: Persons and Places in the Poetry of William Butler Yeats*** does not explicate Yeats's poetry, but rather helps the reader place his work in a better context by providing insight into the persons and places named in it. The dictionary covers character names used within the poetry; classical, historical, and Irish folklore figures mentioned; and poetic influences such as Dante and Donne. Also identified are real and mythological place names referred to in the poetry. Conner contributes a scholarly introduction, genealogical information about Yeats's maternal and paternal ancestors and immediate family, and an extensive listing of books consulted, which would serve as a useful starting point for Yeats scholarship in general.

At more than twice the size of *A Yeats Dictionary*, McCready's ***A William Butler Yeats Encyclopedia*** addresses similar subject areas with a bit more depth and breadth. Beginning with an introduction and chronology, the bulk of the work is made up of A-to-Z entries ranging from one paragraph to two pages in length, covering persons and places in Yeats's life and poetry. The work is wide ranging in scope and includes everyone from Lady Augusta Gregory, Yeats's contemporary and patron, to Lady Alice Kyteler, a fourteenth-century noblewoman accused of intercourse with an evil spirit and who is mentioned in Yeats's poem "Nineteen Hundred and Nineteen." Place names are found for both real and mythological areas, from Ravenna, a city in north-central Italy mentioned in the poem "Sailing to Byzantium," to Country-Under-Wave, a fairyland referred to in several of Yeats's plays, such as *The Countess Cathleen*. Each entry has short citations to further reading; full references can be found in the selected bibliography at the end of the work. Cross references are identified by boldface type throughout.

The bulk of ***The Bloomsbury Group: A Reference Guide*** consists of a chronological listing by year (from 1905 to 1989) of writings about the Bloomsbury Group, with usually brief annotations. Markert defines the Bloomsbury Group fairly broadly, starting with Leonard Woolf's definition of "Old Bloomsbury" as consisting of members of the Memoir Club, which was formed in 1920 and had as its members Leonard and Virginia Woolf, Vanessa and Clive Bell, Desmond MacCarthy, Adrian Stephen, Lytton Strachey, John Maynard Keynes, Duncan Grant, E. M. Forster, Saxon Sydney-Turner, and Roger Fry. This base definition is expanded to include others with links to the group, such as Karin Costelloe, Dora Carrington, Dorothy Brett, Mark Gertler, T. S. Eliot, Bertrand Russell, Vita Sackville-West, and D. H. Lawrence. Although not a comprehensive bibliography covering all of these figures, this work is useful in its focus on how each subject relates to Bloomsbury. An important strength of this work is the detailed index to personal names and concepts ("Aestheticism," "Cambridge," "World War I"), which makes it easy to track information about a particular person or subject in regard to Bloomsbury. Also provided are a preface and introductory essay by the author.

Haule and Smith's ***A Concordance to the Novels of Virginia Woolf*** is an impressive piece of scholarship, detailing the occurrence of all individual words in the nine full-length novels written by Woolf. The bulk of the three volumes is made up of the concordance, arranged alphabetically by keyword. The word *fate*, for example, is found twenty times in the novels. The entry for this word lists each occurrence in context, such as this partial line from *Orlando*: "At other times, and his **fate** perhaps was the most." The code for the novel title follows the quotation, as does the chapter, page, and line number for its exact location within the first American edition of the work. At the end of the third volume are two other useful features: an alphabetical list of all the keywords (called headwords here) without the citations, but giving the number of times the word appears; and a listing of the keywords arranged in order of frequency. Researchers can gain much insight into an author's work through a concordance, which quickly gives an impression of how important certain words and concepts are within the writings. If following a particular theme in the author's work, it will help to pinpoint the location of potentially relevant passages.

CONCLUSION

The general resources listed here serve as useful starting points for research. Many of them contain factual information such as publication dates, birth and death dates, life and historic event chronologies, and contexts for various authors' lives and works. Most also serve as a point for jumping off into deeper research on a particular author or topic, as they include listings of additional reference materials or bibliographies of critical monographs and articles that will lead to more detailed information. Once the necessary background information is obtained from an appropriate range of general resources, the search for more specific, focused works can begin.

Chapter Three

Library Catalogs

The library catalog is one of the most basic and ubiquitous tools for any research project you may be working on. This chapter presents an overview of the features of a typical academic library catalog as well as information concerning national union catalogs, catalogs of national libraries, and the *WorldCat* cooperative union catalog, which is readily accessible in some format to all researchers.

Occasionally, older researchers may feel nostalgia for the days of the library "card catalog" with its burnished wood exterior, nifty little drawers, and curious metal rods for holding the cards in place, but most currently active researchers have grown to love the convenience and additional features offered by the new electronic library catalogs. Located on the Internet rather than the library's main floor, these electronic catalogs take up less space and make searching for and acquiring library materials easier than ever before. Academic libraries often feature a simplified catalog search interface directly on their home page; lacking that, there should be a prominent link directing researchers to the library catalog's main page. Some libraries may refer to their electronic library catalogs as an "OPAC." This term is an acronym for Online Public Access Catalog. As such, the term *OPAC* qualifies as "library-speak," which is mystifying to most library researchers, and its use is being discouraged. Indeed, some academic library users, particularly undergraduates, may be confounded by the very term "catalog" itself. For this reason, many libraries have moved toward an even greater simplification of language to describe their resources. Looking for an area on the library home page promising to help "Find Books" should bear fruit.

In the old-fashioned physical card catalogs, the drawers were usually grouped into three areas, covering subject access, title access, and author access to the library's materials. Sometimes authors and titles were interfiled within one grouping of drawers. Current electronic library catalogs provide the same access to subjects, titles, and author indexes, and much more besides. Access points vary from library to library, but ones that are typically offered include the ability to search specifically for journal/serial titles, the ability to search by the unique international standard book or serial numbers (ISBN/ISSN) assigned to materials, and the ability to browse by call number or to limit one's search to a particular type of material (reference books, electronic resources) or collection within the library (archives, special collections). Particularly useful is the ability to search by keyword, which allows for a search across a number of fields such as author, title, publisher, subject headings, and notes, as described in chapter 1. Hyperlinks within certain fields in an individual catalog record can aid the researcher in quickly finding related materials. A hyperlinked subject heading, for example, will take you to a list of all library materials within the system sharing that heading, while a hyperlinked author name will take you to the list of many of the materials held by the library by that particular author (in the case of searching for materials by a particular author, a keyword search may turn up additional titles, such as works included in an anthology, that might not be shown in an author search).

Electronic library catalogs also offer a range of special features designed to make the life of the researcher easier. Most catalogs, for example, allow you to check off or mark records of interest. When your searching is finished, you can pull up a list of all marked items and print them, e-mail them to yourself, or download them to your computer or into a bibliography tool such as *RefWorks* or *EndNote*. Some library systems allow you to place an electronic hold on an item found in the catalog, activating the process of having the book pulled from the shelf and held for you to pick up at the circulation desk. If the book or other item is already checked out, placing a hold will put you in the queue for next available access to the item. For electronic books or reference materials your library may have access to, the library catalog record should contain a hyperlink leading you to the resource. Additionally, more libraries are starting to look at Amazon-like features to integrate into their library catalogs, such as cover images, the ability to electronically browse the table of contents and index, and the ability for users to rate or comment upon particular items. The card catalog of yesterday underwent a dramatic transformation into the electronic library catalog of today. All signs promise that the library catalog of the future may undergo a similar transformation into a tool that is much more interactive and customizable.

Specific features of the library catalog vary from institution to institution and partially depend on the type of software used for the catalog interface. Regardless of these variations, all catalogs offer several ways of searching the contents of the library catalog, and all produce results based on established principles and standards for organizing information. For libraries in the United Kingdom, North America, and Australia, as well as some other parts of the world, one of the main standards is the *Anglo-American Cataloguing Rules*, second edition, revised (*AACR2R*). The *AACR2R* has useful guidelines for cataloging librarians to follow in order to record information (such as author, title, publication information, and physical description) about books and other library materials in a consistent format.

The task of cataloging library materials also involves the application of controlled vocabulary to particular categories within the library record. These are standardized forms of description, such as officially sanctioned forms of author names, titles of serials, and titles of literary works for which there may be name variants. Not all records found in library catalogs, particularly those for older items, utilize the standardized forms of names and titles. For this reason, be aware that there may be inconsistencies within the catalog, such as differing forms of name for the same author. The other type of controlled vocabulary imposed on library records is the use of standardized subject headings. Subject headings are specific words, phrases, or combinations of words or phrases and dates, which are used to describe the subject matter of the work at hand. The most common system of subject headings is the Library of Congress Subject Headings (LCSH), used by most college and university academic libraries and research libraries in the United States. LCSH is also used by the British Library and many other research and academic libraries in the English-speaking world. Many libraries have print copies of the multivolume LCSH in their reference area or near catalog search computers to allow patrons the opportunity to focus and improve their catalog subject searching. While LCSH are increasingly the preferred standard for most libraries, be aware that other subject heading systems also exist. The two best-known systems after the LCSH are Sears subject headings, which are more general headings used primarily in school libraries, and MeSH headings, which were developed by the National Library of Medicine for use in medical libraries.

Once an item is cataloged and has had standardized forms of names, titles, and subjects applied to it, this information is arranged into the specific categories within the Machine Readable Cataloging (MARC) record, discussed in greater depth in chapter 1. MARC records, which are standardized electronic records, are readable across many software platforms, making them easy to migrate from one system to another or to share between libraries. This ability to share MARC records has simplified cataloging for librarians (allowing them to download records already input for an item held in common with another library), increased consistency of library records from one library to the next, and enabled greater access to library holdings worldwide. Since most electronic library catalogs are Internet-based, they are accessible to and fully searchable by any researcher, regardless of the home institution.

In spite of the many standardizations in place, there will be variations in records and functionality from one catalog to another. An understanding of basic Boolean search strategy is helpful for searching most electronic catalogs. Most catalogs also have links to "Help" pages and/or provide search tips on individual pages to guide you through the search process. Reference librarians can assist with additional guidance for online catalog searching. More and more frequently, reference consultations with librarians can be conducted electronically as well as in person.

What follows are suggestions outlining best practices for conducting various categories of searches in contemporary electronic library catalogs. These are general guidelines only and should be modified and fine-tuned based on the capabilities of the particular catalog being searched.

AUTHOR SEARCHES

A typical basic research need is to find out which books written by a particular author are held by your library. You may want to start by determining the Library of Congress authoritative heading for your author. You can do this by searching the Library of Congress Authorities at http://authorities.loc.gov/. By searching the name authority headings, we find that the authorized form of Virginia Woolf's name is "Woolf, Virginia, 1882–1941." The inclusion of birth and death dates in the heading is part of the standard format for personal names. Referral to the authorized form of Woolf's name is made from the unauthorized heading "Woolf, Virginia Stephen, 1882–1941," which includes her maiden name. Even within the Library of Congress catalog inconsistencies exist, as we see there are records using the more simplified unauthorized heading "Woolf, Virginia." This example shows that while the majority of records related to Woolf will be found using the authorized form of her name, in order to do the most complete and thorough search, unauthorized forms of her name will need to be searched as well.

Another complicating factor is the penchant of several high modernists for publishing under their initials. Library of Congress authorized name headings usually follow the pattern of the preferred form of the name used in publishing, with the full form of the name spelled out in parentheses, followed by the birth and death dates. Thus, the authorized form of name headings for D. H. Lawrence and W. B. Yeats are "Lawrence, D. H. (David Herbert), 1885–1930" and "Yeats, W. B. (William Butler), 1865–1939." As with Woolf, several variants on each of these names may exist in the same catalog.

If you don't have access to the Internet or time to search the authorities records on the Library of Congress website, you can fairly easily determine the correct author headings to use by doing an "author" category search in your online catalog, starting with your author's last name. Truncating your search will bring in the greatest number of results, allowing you the option to look at materials under that authorized form of the name as well as any variants in the catalog. Thus, if you are looking for D. H. Lawrence, doing an author search for *Lawrence, D* in the catalog will allow you to browse the author index in the correct general area. If you happen to know Lawrence's full name and search under *Lawrence, David* as an author, you will in most cases run across a "see" reference in the catalog, referring from the nonstandard form of the name to the authorized one, as in "Lawrence, David Herbert, 1885–1930—See Lawrence, D. H. (David Herbert), 1885–1930." A hyperlink should quickly connect you to the records for the correct form of the name. Of course, in the case of a common name such as David Lawrence, it is likely that there will be other authors with the same name who are not the modernist author. Consulting the birth and death dates or checking the full record should clarify which catalog entries are the ones of interest.

You can also conduct a search for your author's name as a keyword, which will possibly bring to light resources where the author's work is anthologized. This will happen only if content notes or subject tracings supply this information. This may be an especially useful technique for lesser-known authors, but the sheer number of results of a keyword search for a well-known and prolific author may prove overwhelming. When conducting this type of search, it would be best to do two separate keyword searches, one using the natural order of the name and the other using the inverted order of the name. This will ensure finding the natural-order name listed in titles or notes fields as well as the inverted order listing found in any subject or author tracings in the catalog record. For example, a natural-language keyword search for *Virginia Woolf* will reveal that her essay "Mr. Bennett and Mrs. Brown" is reprinted in the volume *Essentials of the Theory of Fiction*, edited by Michael J. Hoffman and Patrick D. Murphy. In this case, the essay is listed in the contents note, but Woolf does not have a separate author entry.

Once you've located the records for the materials written by your author that your library holds, you may find that more than one edition of a given work exists in the collection. For general reading and much undergraduate use, it is not terribly important which edition of a work is read or consulted. But for graduate and professional-level research, an effort should be made to locate the current standard edition of the work in question, which will be edited by a recognized scholar in the field and usually contain extensive notes on the text, as well as any variant passages. It is not always easy to determine what constitutes the current standard editions of texts within British modernism, as no centralized list exists and what is "standard" can shift based on new scholarly editions being printed. For example, Cambridge University Press has been issuing the series *The Cambridge Edition of the Works of D. H. Lawrence*, which is now generally considered to be the standard for Lawrence scholarship. Meanwhile, Scribner's has been publishing a series of *The Collected Works of W. B. Yeats*. If you're unsure which edition of a work is currently considered standard, consult the bibliography of a recent scholarly article or monograph referencing the work and see which version is cited. Lacking clear guidance, you should rely on common sense and knowledge of the reputation and reliability of the press publishing a given edition as well as the qualifications of any editor or scholar associated with the edition of the work.

Other forms of texts also can be useful for scholarly research. Some texts have been published in facsimile editions, to make available long out-of-print first editions or authorized versions of the work. Some manuscript versions of texts have been published in print format or made available as microforms, and more electronic versions are becoming available either via subscription or as scanned versions freely available on the Web. However, in order to do in-depth textual analysis of manuscript versions of works or to compare alternative versions of primary manuscripts, it will normally be necessary to travel to the library special collection or archives holding these unique items, and make special arrangements to do so. More on working with manuscripts collections can be found in chapter 9, while dealing with microforms and digitized collections is covered in chapter 8.

TITLE SEARCHES

A title search performed in a library catalog will lead you to all the copies of a particular work held by that library. As with the results of an author search, you will need to carefully assess the results to find the best version of the text for your purposes, based on knowledge of the publisher or editor, format, and other factors. Luckily, there are not as many issues with titles of works from the modern era as there were from previous time periods, when titles could be lengthy and complex or vary from one edition to another.

Some challenges are still involved in searching for works of modern British fiction by title. The Library of Congress also provides the ability to search for authority records for name/title entries in its catalog at http://authorities.loc.gov/. There you can find the official form of the title of a work, particularly as it varies by spelling or language of publication. Thus we find that a listing for "Lawrence, D. H. (David Herbert), 1885–1930. A propos of Lady Chatterley's lover" refers the researcher to the authorized form (with "Apropos" as one word instead of two), which is "Lawrence, D. H. (David Herbert), 1885–1930. Apropos of Lady Chatterley's lover," and that the Spanish-language form of a work such as "Lawrence, D. H. (David Herbert), 1885–1930. Amante de Lady Chatterley" directs the user to the English-language form of the title at "Lawrence, D. H. (David Herbert), 1885–1930. Lady Chatterley's lover. Spanish." Browsing the records in your library catalog after an initial search should help you gain insight into which works are held by a particular author and how successful the library has been at grouping different versions of a work under the same standardized title.

If the work you are looking for is shorter, such as a novella, essay, or short story, you might do best to perform a keyword search in the hope that the title may appear in the contents note of a catalog record where it has been collected or anthologized. For example, figure 3.1 shows a record retrieved through a keyword search for a short story entitled "No More Parades" by Ford Madox

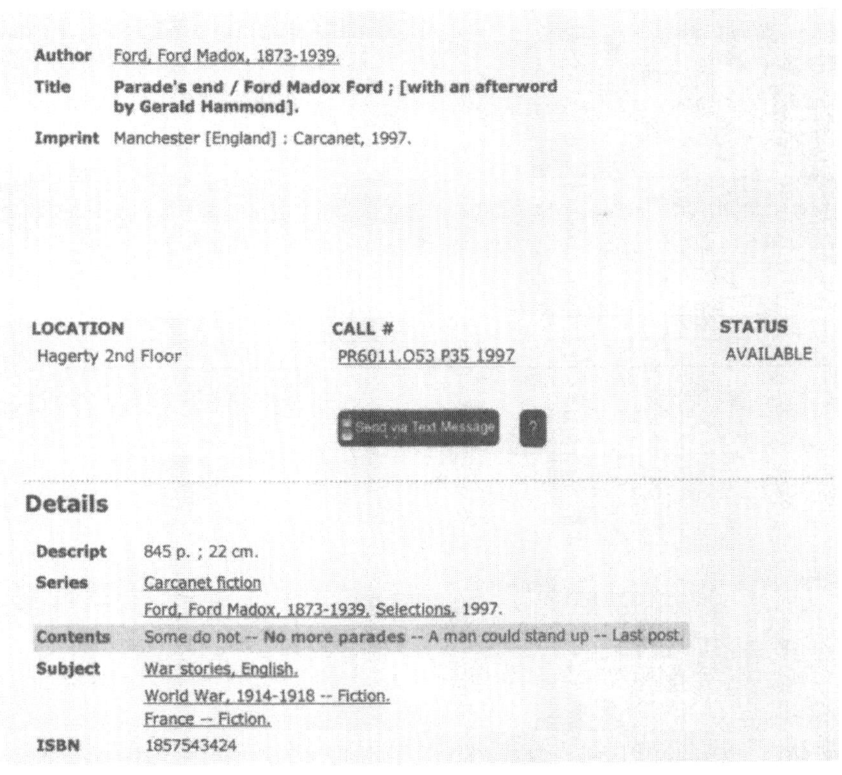

Figure 3.1. Story title found in contents note via a keyword search in library catalog.

Ford. The title of the story is located in the contents note and would not have been found through a title search. Works by lesser-known authors may prove to be particularly elusive, however, and may require going beyond the catalog in order to locate them. H. W. Wilson's *Short Story Index*, available in print or electronically, is extremely useful in tracking down where stories have been published, both in periodicals and in collections. Further information on the use of such indexes is covered in chapter 4.

In addition to locating books, the library catalog title search function can be used to see whether your library subscribes to a particular journal or serial publication. Again, depending on the software used by your library, the catalog functions can vary. Some library catalogs have the ability to search a separate subindex of journal and serial titles. If your library provides this service, it should be your first place to search for journal titles, although double-checking the general title index is a good idea if you fail to locate a journal title on your initial try. Once you've located the record for a journal title, it should supply you with additional useful information. For print journals held by your library, the record should include "holdings" information, a listing of actual volumes and issues of the title that are owned by the library. The record should make clear how far back in time the library's ownership of the title goes and identify any gaps or missing issues. More and more frequently, libraries are moving to journal access in electronic format. A catalog record for an electronic version of a journal should have a hyperlink to the electronic version of the journal itself or to the database or e-journal collection in which it resides. Many libraries restrict off-site access to electronic versions of journals to those who have passwords or institutional IDs, due to licensing agreements.

In addition to books and journals, the library catalog title search can also lead you to works held by your library in a variety of formats, such as films, DVDs, videos, maps, documents, databases, and unique materials in the institution's archives or special collections. Many libraries also catalog useful material found on websites, and a hyperlink in the catalog record will send you directly to the desired online resource.

SUBJECT SEARCHES

Subject searches help in locating materials that are *about* authors and their works, as well as other forms of literary criticism or historical or cultural analysis related to specific time periods, genres, literary movements, or theoretical approaches. As mentioned earlier in this chapter, most libraries use the Library of Congress Subject Headings (LCSH) standard. It will be useful to learn the particular LCSH related to your research interests so that you can routinely search for these in almost any library catalog you visit. You can check out your library's print copy of the LCSH, if available, or you can do trial searches in the online catalog to determine appropriate subject headings.

Since modernism is a broad concept and a movement that affected all art forms, there are a number of variations on "modernism" in the standard subject headings. An LCSH for "Modernism" alone exists, but it is most properly applied to general works about modernism. Perusing the titles under this heading may bring to light useful works that tie literary concerns into the broader agenda of modernism. Beyond the general subject heading, there are headings for "Modernism (Aesthetics)," which covers modernism broadly within the arts and is also worth looking at, and "Modernism (Art)," "Modernism (Literature)," and "Modernism (Music)." Each of these headings may be followed by a subheading for the particular country considered in the work (sometimes the subheading may be further subdivided to indicate a particular city or region). So "Modernism (Literature)" will be the most focused of the "modernism" subject headings for literary modernism, and works found under this heading may be of particular interest. But don't overlook the pertinent forms of the subject heading that are further geographically divided: "Modernism (Literature)—England," "Modernism (Literature)—Great Britain," "Modernism (Literature)—Ireland," "Modernism (Literature)—Scotland," and "Modernism (Literature)—Wales."

There is also an LCSH for "Literature, Modern," which, although inconsistently applied, can refer to any literature from the fifteenth-century Renaissance period forward. More specific will be the headings for "Literature, Modern—19th century" and "Literature, Modern—20th century." Additional subheadings can be found, such as "Literature, Modern—History and criticism" and "Literature, Modern—Women authors," among many others. Some headings and subheadings may be further subdivided geographically. Other LCSH begin with the national literature and then are divided by time period, such as "English literature—19th century" and "Scottish literature—20th century." Genre headings also exist, such as "English fiction—20th century" and "English poetry—19th century." To further confuse matters, there are also headings such as "Literature and history," "Literature and society," and "Women and literature," which may also be subdivided by "—Great Britain" or other country name, and by time period. Following is a selection of Library of Congress subject headings of relevance to modern British literature:

English literature—20th century
Modernism (Literature)—England—London
Modernism (Literature)—Great Britain—History—20th century

Modernism (Literature)—Themes, motives
Drama, Modern—Bibliography—Indexes
Poetry, English—20th century
Poetry—History and criticism, 19th–20th century
Poetry, Modern—20th century—Criticism and interpretation
Joyce, James, 1882–1941—Aesthetics
Lawrence, D. H. (David Herbert), 1885–1930—Biography—Psychology
Woolf, Virginia, 1882–1941—Characters—Women

You can also perform a keyword search, which will search across titles, notes, subject headings, and other fields in the library records. This is one way of possibly drawing together in one search many of the records for relevant items that may have been assigned different but related subject headings. There is not one magical "super search" that can be performed to obtain all the records you want and only the records you want. But by gaining familiarity with subject headings and their formats as well as the option for keyword searching, you will be able to fairly quickly find most of the materials that will be of interest. It's important to keep in mind that the assignment of subject headings is an art and not a precise science. The subject headings are assigned by human beings, not all of whom are specialists in the subjects under consideration. Therefore, remember that there are significant variations in how subject headings are applied, and realize that being willing to spend the time and energy to cast your net widely may yield hidden gems in unanticipated places.

UNION CATALOGS

Copac. www.copac.ac.uk (accessed 5 March 2009).

Library of Congress and the National Union Catalog Subcommittee of the Resources Committee of the Resources and Technical Services Division, American Library Association. *National Union Catalog, Pre-1956 Imprints: A Cumulative Author List Representing Library of Congress Printed Cards and Titles Reported by Other American Libraries*. 754 volumes. London: Mansell, 1968–1981.

WorldCat. Dublin, OH: OCLC. www.oclc.org/firstsearch.

Open Library. www.openlibrary.org.

Open WorldCat. Dublin, OH: OCLC. www.worldcat.org.

As adept as you may become at searching your own institution's library catalog or the online catalogs of other institutions, it's unlikely that any one library will hold all materials relevant to your subject. Eventually you will need to expand your searching to wider networks of libraries. When two or more libraries combine their holdings into a single searchable format, whether print or electronic, they form what is known as a union catalog. The advantage of the union catalog is that it enables "one-stop shopping" for library materials; it conserves your time and energy by enabling you to conduct your search in only one place rather than in multiple locations individually. Library networks that create union catalogs exist on local, regional, national, and international levels.

Some institutions may already share their catalog with other institutions in the same geographic area. An example of this is "Tripod," the online union catalog shared by three historically Quaker colleges—Bryn Mawr, Haverford, and Swarthmore—located in the Philadelphia suburbs. Searching Tripod reveals titles held by all three colleges, and researchers associated with any one of the institutions can request delivery of items held by any of the member institutions. Other libraries may be part of a regional library consortium, such as PALCI (the Pennsylvania Academic Library Consortium, Inc.), which formed in 1996 as a federation of thirty-five academic libraries and is currently made up of sixty-eight public and private college and university libraries in Pennsylvania, New Jersey, and West Virginia. Such consortia allow their members to access a range of services, usually including "interlibrary loan"—cooperative borrowing and lending of books among member libraries. PALCI, for example, provides its members with access to "E-Z Borrow," a service that allows patrons to electronically search a union catalog of all member libraries' holdings and submit online requests for books or other library materials from any other member. Ask a librarian at your home institution about which options are available for extended services from consortia or other libraries in your area.

Larger union catalogs that exist on national and international levels, such as *WorldCat*, *Copac*, and the *National Union Catalog*, have shown themselves to be extremely useful tools for a wide variety of researchers. They are particularly effective for tracking down out-of-print items and all extant editions of an author's work, as well as identifying the locations where these items are held. *WorldCat* and *Copac* have the added advantage of being available electronically so that they can be searched from your desktop. All three tools have extremely large numbers of records, representing holdings from many institutions.

WorldCat is the union catalog from the OCLC (Online Computer Library Center). It holds over ninety-eight million catalog records from sixty thousand member libraries in over one hundred countries and territories worldwide, as of this writing. Holdings include not only books but serial publications such as journals and newspapers, archival materials, visual materials, maps, sound recordings, computer files, and even some individual articles. The worldwide holdings, combined with the ability to limit your search by language, is useful for tracking down foreign-language editions of the work of British modernists. However, in spite of the enormous number of records held in this union catalog, the largest in the world, no tool is utterly comprehensive. The records available are for only the holdings that have been reported by the member libraries to OCLC, not necessarily everything contained in their collections.

Access to the full version of the *WorldCat* union catalog is available only by subscription. If your institution subscribes to the database, it comes via the *FirstSearch* interface, which provides a wealth of searching parameters, particularly in "advanced search" mode. You can search by typical catalog record elements such as author, title, subject, keyword, ISBN or ISSN, series title, publisher name or location, and material type. A number of search limitations are available, such as the ability to specify a date range for searching, a particular language, or a subtype of material such as fiction or nonfiction. Combining search elements can lead to fruitful information about the publication habits of British modernists. For example, combining an author name with a publisher name will illuminate a writer's relationship with a particular publisher over time. Combining a title with a publisher location and a time period may help clarify the publishing history of British and American editions of a particular work.

There are some subtle nuances to be aware of in order to develop the best search strategy. For example, there is a difference between searching a name in the "Author" field and searching the same name in the "Author Phrase" field. Searching for *Lawrence, D. H.* in the "Author" field results in 10,339 records, while the same search in the "Author Phrase" field nets 6,522 records. The author phrase search returns only those records that contain the name "Lawrence, D. H." in the author or "named person" fields. All of these are presumably works authored by the British modernist of that name. On the other hand, the author search draws in many more records, some of which are "false hits." Because the author search does not search the complete name as a phrase, it can return records that have "Lawrence" in one name and "D" in another. On the other hand, the author search on Lawrence's name finds some materials that are missed by the author phrase search, primarily stories and poems by Lawrence that are found anthologized in works written or edited by other authors. This is because the author search peruses the "contents" field while the author phrase search does not.

As with any other catalog, especially one made up of contributed records from myriad libraries around the world, there are some inconsistencies in the manner in which names in particular are represented. The index icon next to the drop-down menu for search fields will allow you to search a particular index to find out exactly what terminology exists in a particular field. For example, if I choose to browse the author phrase index for *Lawrence, D. H.*, I get the results depicted in figure 3.2. The entry for "lawrence, d h" returns slightly fewer than the 6,522 results obtained in the initial author phrase search for Lawrence's name. The three entries following that are variations on the entry for Lawrence's name, all of them being actually closer to the official LCSH that searchers may already be familiar with. All return records for materials authored by the British modernist, in spite of the fact that the author entries are inconsistent with the main entry. However, it will be noted that the majority of records returned from searches for the "irregular" forms of Lawrence's name refer to foreign-language editions of his work. A researcher wanting to perform the most thorough search possible or a researcher particularly interested in translations or the author's foreign publishing record will do well to browse the author phrase index and track down any nonstandard forms of the author's name.

WorldCat also includes some other useful features that advanced researchers will appreciate. One is a field on the item record called "More Like This" which is essentially a hyperlink to other records containing the same author

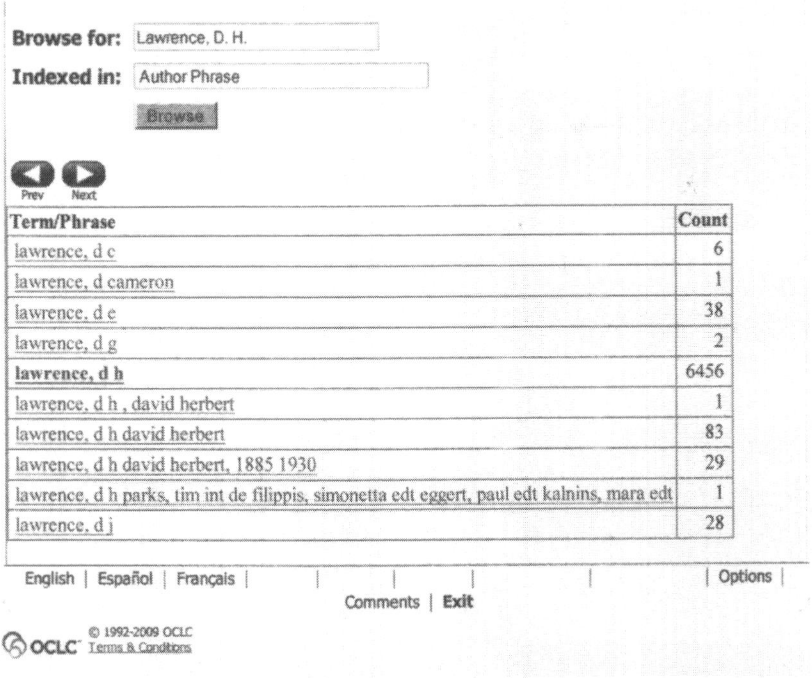

Browse for: Lawrence, D. H.
Indexed in: Author Phrase
Browse

Prev Next

Term/Phrase	Count
lawrence, d c	6
lawrence, d cameron	1
lawrence, d e	38
lawrence, d g	2
lawrence, d h	6456
lawrence, d h , david herbert	1
lawrence, d h david herbert	83
lawrence, d h david herbert, 1885 1930	29
lawrence, d h parks, tim int de filippis, simonetta edt eggert, paul edt kalnins, mara edt	1
lawrence, d j	28

English | Español | Français | | | | | | Options |
Comments | Exit

OCLC © 1992-2009 OCLC Terms & Conditions

Figure 3.2. Results for browsing author phrase in *WorldCat*.

and title. Alternately, you may choose to go to the "Advanced options" screen to do a focused search for similar items based on other fields (such as publisher, series, or material type), either alone or in combination. Even more useful are the features that allow access to the full text of the work itself, found under the heading "Get This Item." The "Access" link, when available, links to additional material concerning the work, such as a synopsis, a link to the official Library of Congress catalog record, or even sample pages to peruse. The latter is available for those materials in the public domain or for which publishers have given permission for access. Also under "Get This Item" is a link that takes the viewer to a list of "Libraries worldwide that own item" and another link that takes viewers to the catalog of their home institution. If the item is not readily available at their home institution, they can quickly find out whether another library in their area holds a copy, as results are usually returned in order of geographic proximity to the subscribing institution. Finally, the links found in the category of "External Resources" facilitate direct access to approved online booksellers, the library's interlibrary loan page, or a page of sample citations for the work in various citation styles.

The other major online union catalog in the United States was the Research Libraries Group's *RLG Union Catalog*, which older researchers and librarians may remember as "RLIN"—the Research Libraries Information Network. Similar to OCLC's *WorldCat* but on a much smaller scale, RLG provided a union catalog to the 150 member academic libraries, archives, museums, and other cultural institutions. In June 2006, the RLG membership voted to combine forces with OCLC, entailing the integration of all RLG union catalog records into *WorldCat*. Record importation began in July 2006 and was completed a little over a year later. This merger has been a boon to researchers, who now have only one database to search instead of two and access to a wider range of data from a greater variety of resources.

At the time of its merger with OCLC, RLG had successfully initiated a freely available, Internet-based version of some 120 million of its union catalog records through the *RedLightGreen.org* service. After the merger, *RedLightGreen* was discontinued and rolled into the ***Open WorldCat*** initiative, freely available on the Internet as *WorldCat.org*. All *WorldCat* records are searchable via *WorldCat.org*, but holdings are displayed only for those libraries that subscribe to *WorldCat* through *FirstSearch*; this represents approximately 80 percent of the content of the full *WorldCat* database. For researchers who do not have access to the *FirstSearch* version of *WorldCat*, *WorldCat.org* is a great free alternative.

The search interface for *WorldCat.org* is very different from the *FirstSearch WorldCat* interface, and it probably comes down to a matter of taste in deciding which one is "better." Younger, Web-savvy researchers often prefer the more user-friendly interface of *WorldCat.org*, while librarians and other "power searchers" often prefer the ability to do more nuanced searches in *FirstSearch*'s advanced search mode. *WorldCat.org* also offers both a simple and an advanced search screen, although they function differently from the *FirstSearch* version of the database. Catalog records have tabs available that allow you to quickly move to other records that share the same subject headings or are different editions of the same book. Searchers can identify their locations by submitting their zip code or city/state/country. *WorldCat.org* will then list holding information for libraries in that geographic vicinity. Users who register with *WorldCat.org* (for free) can also create their own lists of materials they search for and can either make those lists private or share them with others.

Copac is in many ways the British equivalent of *WorldCat*. Found online at http://www.copac.ac.uk/, it provides free searchable access to the combined catalogs of almost fifty major academic and special collection libraries in the United Kingdom and Ireland. It began as a project of the Consortium of University Research Libraries (CURL), a collaborative initiative similar in purpose to the Research Libraries Group (RLG) in the United States. (CURL is now known as Research Libraries UK, or RLUK.) Included in *Copac*'s approximately thirty-two million records are the online holdings of the British Library, the National Library of Scotland, the National Library of Wales/Llyfrgell Genedlaethol Cymru, Oxford, Cambridge, Edinburgh, and Trinity College Dublin. Some specialized collections within the database are the online holdings of the Natural History Museum, the Royal Academy of Music, the School of Oriental and African Studies (SOAS), and the Victoria & Albert National Art Library. *Copac* continues to add contributing libraries to its collective and to add additional records from current member libraries. At this time, holdings go back as far as 1100 AD, with about one-third of the materials published post-1980. There is interest in adding additional older records to the union catalog, as these items are often not found elsewhere and are potentially of great interest to scholars. Although most records are for English-language items, materials in over three hundred languages can be found in *Copac*. As with *WorldCat*, contents of *Copac* do not represent all the holdings of each member library, only those that are currently available electronically. For details regarding what else may be found in the holdings of the member libraries, follow the links to each library's website from the *Copac* records.

Copac offers three search interfaces on its website. The first is the "Quick Search" option, which allows for fast searching by author, title words, and/or keywords. The "Main Search" page adds the ability to search by publisher, ISSN/ISBN, and subject headings. The search can be further limited by publication date, publication place, material type, and language. You can also restrict your search to the holdings of a particular library. One of the peculiarities of *Copac* is that some member libraries have electronic records that use Library of Congress subject headings, while others use subject headings and terminology that is more specifically British. This means that users will often need to perform more than one subject search in order to retrieve records using British spelling and those using American spelling, or those using British terminology ("railways") as well as those using American terminology ("railroads"). The third search option available in *Copac* is "Map Search," which additionally allows searching by scale, either "fuzzy" or exact.

A search in *Copac* results in a list of short citations, arranged in alphabetical order by title and then by date for author or title searches. A drop-down menu allows you to reorder the list in a number of ways. For subject or keyword searches, results are ranked by relevancy, with no option for reordering. Each title in the short citation list is a hotlink that will take you to the full record for the item. As with many other catalogs, *Copac* provides hotlinks in various fields, so one can quickly perform an author, title, or subject search that pulls up all records that match the same field in the original record. *Copac* also has hotlinks in the "Location details" field, which will bring you to a page displaying the short citation again and the location, shelfmark (call number), status (due date or available), and any notes for the library that holds the item. In the case of an item being held by more than one institution, there are links to separate listings for each library. The full catalog record for the item also includes a button labeled "Find a Copy" that will connect researchers from member institutions to options for obtaining a copy of the listed work.

Copac is fairly intuitive and easy to search, and it functions very similarly to *WorldCat.org*. For researchers in North America, identified items related to British modernism usually can be found closer to home. *Copac* can be a useful starting point for finding more unique items that may be available only in Britain or Ireland. Check *WorldCat* first for libraries that may hold the item in question, and if it is not available more locally, then inquire about the possibility of interlibrary loan services. It is usually best to go through the interlibrary loan office of your home institution rather than contacting a foreign library directly, as most libraries are willing to honor loan requests to other institutions but not to individuals.

While we are on the topic of electronic union catalogs, it's worth mentioning a recent initiative that may provide either enhancement or competition to *WorldCat* and *Copac* in the future. The ***Open Library*** initiative has the ambitious goal of making "all the published works of humankind available to everyone in the world." It is currently featuring high-quality scanned copies of works in the public domain as part of an open source project of the *Internet Archive*, http://www.archive.org, a nonprofit group facilitating free access on the Internet to moving images, live music, audio, and text. The *Internet Archive* also hosts the popular *Wayback Machine*, which allows searching for archived versions of web pages no longer currently in use. As part of its project, the *Open Library* has developed new means of storing the massive amounts of data resulting from the digitization efforts, as well as other technological features to enhance the functioning and aesthetics of its library. The *Internet Archive* has been in discussion with OCLC regarding the possibility of linking *Internet Archive* and *Open Library* materials to *WorldCat* records. No agreements have yet been reached, but it will be interesting to watch this project as it develops.

Until such time as "all published works" have electronic catalog records available, serious researchers wanting to conduct a thorough search for all works and editions of works by a particular author, particularly those from the modern era who are less well known, it will still be necessary to consult the massive print edition of the ***National Union Catalog, Pre-1956 Imprints*** (*NUC*) in addition to resources like *WorldCat* and *Copac*. Beall and Kafadar reported that, at the time of their research, almost 28 percent of the NUC records were not found in *WorldCat*.[1] Their results were confirmed in a follow-up study by DeZelar-Tiedman who, using a different dataset, still found roughly 25 percent of the records searched for missing from *WorldCat*.[2] The oversized NUC volumes contain photocopies of the actual catalog cards from the Library of Congress's catalog. The items included were published prior to 1956, so the initial publishing period of the British modernists is covered. Entries are arranged alphabetically by the author's or editor's name or else by title for anonymous works and some edited works (which are referred to by "see" references from the editor's name). In addition to the Library of Congress, other major libraries in the United States and Canada, such as Yale University, the University of Texas at Austin, and the New York Public Library, contributed records to this catalog. Codes at the bottom of the cards indicate which library or libraries hold copies of an item. This information was correct at the time it was produced, but you should double-check with the library in question before assuming that it still owns the item. Occasionally, there are duplicate records for a particular work if contributing libraries had significantly varying catalog records. Many libraries have been discarding their copies of the NUC as more information is becoming available via *WorldCat* and other Internet-based resources. Most major research libraries, however, recognize the importance of retaining these print volumes until such time as they are truly obsolete.

The *National Union Catalog of Manuscript Collections* (NUCMC) is another important national catalog, part of which is available online and part of which is still available only as a print catalog. It is discussed in more detail in chapter 9, "Manuscripts and Archives."

NATIONAL LIBRARY CATALOGS

British Library *Integrated Catalogue* at http://catalogue.bl.uk/ (accessed 4 April 2009).

British Library *Manuscripts Catalogue* at www.bl.uk/catalogues/manuscripts/INDEX.asp (accessed 4 April 2009).

Library of Congress Online Catalog at http://catalog.loc.gov/ (accessed 4 April 2009).

National libraries fill an important role in the intellectual life of a nation, particularly for researchers. Although the Library of Congress is not technically the national library of the United States but rather the library supporting the functioning of Congress, in many ways it does indeed function as a national library. Both the British Library in London and the Library of Congress in Washington, D.C., provide substantial, deep, wide-ranging collections. Although there may be some restrictions on use, materials are generally available to any approved researcher. Both have also made great strides in automating access to their various library catalogs, enabling researchers from around the world to easily gain awareness of their holdings.

The ***Library of Congress Online Catalog*** currently has approximately fourteen million records for books, manuscripts, maps, music, serials, sound recordings, and visual materials. The main catalog web page presents several choices to the user: you may proceed to either a "Basic" or a "Guided" search, or you can choose to go to a more specialized catalog, such as the one for photographs and prints or the one for sound recordings. The "Basic" search option consists of one box for inputting terms of interest and a drop-down menu to choose the type of search you'd like to perform, including title, author, subject, keyword, call number, ISSN, and several other choices. Some of the choices also allow you to place limitations on the search, such as specifying a date or date range, language, type of material, location within the library, and place of publication. "Basic Search Tips" are located below the search boxes, giving explanations and examples of each type of search. "Guided" searching has two search boxes and the ability to link terms with Boolean operators, as well as the limitations listed earlier. Step-by-step instructions are provided on the guided search page, just below the search boxes. The Library of Congress's collections of British literature are rated at the research or comprehensive levels according to the RLG Conspectus for Linguistics, Languages, and Literatures.[3] Although its holdings in British modernism are not among the Library of Congress's greatest strengths, the rare book and manuscript collections have some significant holdings for minor modernists such as Rudyard Kipling, Hugh Walpole, W. Somerset Maugham, and A. E. Housman.

The British Library serves as the official depository library for the United Kingdom and Ireland, and as such its collection holds 150 million items, with an estimated three million new items added annually. The British Library ***Integrated Catalogue***, which serves as the main catalog for the British Library collections, contains records for fourteen million books plus serials, printed music, and maps. There are also five other major online catalogs, eighteen "specialist" online catalogs, and a number of specialized print-only catalogs. For researchers of modern British literature, however, the *Integrated Catalogue* will be the most useful starting point. The search interface for the catalog has four options for beginning a search. The first two options are the basic and advanced search screens. The default is the "Basic search," which provides one box for entering a term or terms of interest, a drop-down menu allowing you to select "any word" (keyword), word from author, word from title, publication year, publisher, subject, subject heading (Library of Congress), ISBN, ISSN, or shelfmark (call number), and a choice of "yes" and "no" radio buttons for searching exact phrases. Searches can be performed adequately in this basic mode, but since the number of holdings in the catalog is so great, many researchers prefer to refine their strategy using the "Advanced search" option. This interface has three search boxes of the type found in the basic search option, which can be used to combine terms from various fields. Results display the number of records found for each term individually as well as for the combined search. The advanced search screen also allows you to limit materials found by language, publication year or range of years, and format.

The other two search options from the main page of the integrated catalog are the "Catalogue subset search" and "Browse." The subset search allows for searching certain subgroups of the integrated catalog, either alone or in combination. An important concept for researchers in modern British literature to be aware of is that the subset search is the only place that the British Library's newspaper collection can be searched; it is not included in the main, integrated catalog. By choosing "Newspapers" from the list of links in the subset page, you will be transferred to the newspaper catalog, where you can then do a basic or advanced search within this particular collection. The search results are catalog records for the newspapers as units, not individual issues or articles; the records provide place of publication, any title changes, and dates for the holdings of this particular title. The catalog does not index individual articles within the newspapers. The "Browse" option can be found on both the main page for the integrated catalog and on the subset search screens as well. This option allows you to search the alphabetical indexes for authors, titles, series, publishers, and a number of other categories. "Browse" may be the best place to start a search, in order to locate the official forms of names or titles for which you may be interested.

The other main online catalog from the British Library that researchers of British modernism may be interested in is the ***Manuscripts Catalogue***. It has records for items ranging in date from the pre-Christian era to the present day, which the library acquired from 1753 to the present. Not all of the manuscript catalogs have been automated, and to get the complete picture of the manuscript holdings of the British Library, one would have to consult additional print catalogs as well. The *Manuscripts Catalogue* has a very different interface from that of the *Integrated Catalogue*. It allows for two types of searching: index searching and descriptions searching. This type of searching is far less intuitive than most online catalogs; however, a plethora of search tips are provided that will help guide the way of even the most inexperienced searcher. This catalog is also described more in depth in chapter 9, "Manuscripts and Archives."

CONCLUSION

With the advent of the Internet and the technologies making electronic library catalogs possible, we have entered a new era for literature researchers. Unlike a few short years ago, it is now possible to research holdings in libraries across town and around the world without ever leaving the comfort of our homes or offices. The number of library material records available to us through national catalogs, union catalogs, and individual catalogs searchable on the Internet has grown exponentially since libraries started going online. We do, however, live in a hybrid time when both print and electronic catalogs and searching aids are needed. It's tempting to think that everything we need could be found online, but this is really not yet true for the serious literature researcher. While we will continue to move closer and closer to 100 percent electronic access for catalog records, there will continue to be the gritty legwork of double-checking print catalogs for older, more unique, or more obscure resources.

NOTES

1. Jeffrey Beall and Karen Kafadar, "The Proportion of NUC Pre-56 Titles Represented in OCLC WorldCat," *College & Research Libraries* 66, no. 5 (September 2005): 431–35.
2. Christine DeZelar-Tiedman, "The Proportion of NUC Pre-56 Titles Represented in the RLIN and OCLC Databases Compared: A Follow-up to the Beall/Kafadar Study," *College & Research Libraries* 69, no. 5 (September 2008): 401–6.
3. Library of Congress, "Collection Overview: Anglophone/Commonwealth Literature" (2008), www.loc.gov/acq/devpol/colloverviews/anglophone.pdf, p.1 (21 May 2009).

Chapter Four

Print and Electronic Bibliographies, Indexes, and Annual Reviews

Scholars are probably most familiar with bibliographies that they create themselves or ones they find at the end of a book or article they've been reading. This is the list of materials that have been referred to in the work at hand, and it can lead to "backward chaining" for finding additional useful resources on the topic under consideration. But bibliographies as stand-alone research tools, separate listings of works on a particular topic or area of study, are important scholarly resources as well. The bibliographies considered in this chapter are all relevant to researchers of modern British literature. Some are broader, more general literature bibliographies that contain materials on British modernism; others are focused on modern British literature or some particular aspect of it. Many of the bibliographies have references to primary materials (original writings by a particular British modernist, which can take the form of manuscripts, first and subsequent editions of published works, or even personal writing such as letters or diaries), while others are devoted entirely to secondary materials (criticism or reviews of particular creative works, which can include scholarly monographs, journal articles, book reviews, dissertations, etc.).

A number of bibliographies attempt to be comprehensive, as in a listing of all first editions of published works by a now-deceased author. Bibliographies devoted to primary materials are the most likely to have the goal of comprehensiveness. There are, however, no comprehensive general bibliographies of British modernism primary materials. Most bibliographies are by necessity selective, limiting themselves to only certain types of materials or those published in a particular time period. For example, Janet Grimes's *Novels in English by Women, 1891–1920: A Preliminary Checklist* strives to be comprehensive, but only within the stated parameters of language, gender, genre, and time period. Even the largest bibliography in this category, the *Modern*

Language Association International Bibliography (MLAIB), which covers all modern languages and literatures from the earliest times to the present day, is selective in spite of (or perhaps because of) its extremely large scope. In the case of the *Year's Work in English Studies* (*YWES*), where selectivity is the hallmark of the brand, entries are limited to those considered to be of the highest quality by its contributors.

A specialized form of bibliography is the annual review, which normally looks at the secondary materials published on a given subject during a particular year. The emphasis is on scholarly articles and books, but many also include dissertations, reviews, new scholarly editions, anthologized materials, or reference works. The *Year's Work in English Studies* is a good example of a separately published annual review. Annual reviews of particular authors or genres are often published in journals or by scholarly societies. The International Virginia Woolf Society's annual *Bibliography of Woolf Studies* is an example of the latter. It is important to be aware of the time lag involved in the production of such annual reviews; there is usually a gap of a year or two before materials published in a particular year are presented in bibliographies. This is due both to the challenge of tracking down relevant materials and the production time involved in moving the bibliographic work to print. Annual reviews published in journals tend to be made available more quickly than those that are separately published, although the degree of comprehensiveness sought will also affect the time frame.

Another category of bibliography is the index, a tool that provides access to materials found in specific journals or selected monographs or other materials, usually by author, title, and subject matter. Sometimes these tools also have abstracts or short summaries of the contents of the individual work, in which case they might be titled "abstracts." Libraries often group these tools together under a category such as "abstracting and indexing tools." The two largest bibliographies considered here, the *MLAIB* and the *Annual Bibliography of English Language and Literature* (*ABELL*), both act as indexes to the materials covered in them. Each contains not only citations for useful secondary materials found in scholarly journals, books, book chapters, and dissertations, but also the ability to retrieve this material by author or title and by means of specialized controlled vocabulary subject headings. This subject-level access is what makes indexes particularly valuable to researchers who are trying to pinpoint items of interest in a large selection of potentially relevant items. Full-text databases such as *JSTOR* and *Project Muse* are electronic collections of full-text articles from selected print journals; they also act as searchable indexes to the more limited selection of materials found in them.

Many bibliographies are available exclusively in print format, some consisting of multiple volumes. Other bibliographies may have begun in print format but have subsequently migrated to electronic format. Electronic versions of bibliographies are often found on library websites under the more confusing moniker of "databases"—this is a grab-bag term encompassing any electronic resources that can lead a researcher to information on specific topics. They are, however, usually divided up by subject areas so that those focused on literature can be located fairly quickly.

The two major literature indexes, *MLAIB* and *ABELL*, are both available in electronic formats. The electronic versions have a number of additional access points beyond the author, title, and subject indexes of the print versions. For example, the online *MLAIB* can also be searched by series title, journal title, publisher, publication year, ISBN/ISSN, keyword or controlled vocabulary descriptors and, sometimes, by full text. Additionally, results can be limited to a particular year or range of years, publication type, and language. Most vendors providing access to the database also make it possible to link to the full text of articles held electronically by the host institution and also to the institution's library catalog.

Electronic versions of *MLAIB* and *ABELL* are particularly useful to scholars. In addition to the wider range of access points available for searching, as described above, searching in the electronic environment eliminates the need for paging through multiple volumes of the print indexes. Additionally, there is the convenience of being able to access the indexes not only in the institutional library but through any networked computer on campus and often from off-campus as well, via the use of institution-specific user IDs and passwords. Most researchers appreciate the ability to search these indexes from their homes or offices. Some of the electronic versions also have the ability to save user-generated searches or even to automatically run searches at selected intervals and e-mail the results to the user. Not to be overlooked is the currency of electronic databases. Print bibliographies are usually issued once a year, whereas most electronic versions of the *MLAIB*, for example, are updated ten times a year. All of these features combine to make for faster, easier, and more timely searching experiences for the modern researcher.

There is, however, a downside to the increased electronic availability of bibliographies and indexes. If the institution you are affiliated with does not subscribe to the index you need, this may make it essentially inaccessible. In the past, when indexes were exclusively in print format, it was usually possible to visit the library of an institution that subscribed to a particular index and use it there if your home institution did not subscribe. Print indexes were normally made available in a special area of the library that was publicly available to anyone who had gained entrance to use resources in-house. However, electronic databases are often limited to the population of the subscribing institution and may require a log-in and password to access them, even from computers within the library. Unless the researcher can locate a library within reasonable distance that still subscribes to the print version of the index needed, the information may remain inaccessible. This is particularly a problem for independent scholars who may not be formally affiliated with any academic institution but who still need access to the information in the indexes in order to effectively pursue their research.

The good news is that more public library systems are becoming aware of the need for broader public access to electronic indexes and other databases. Some may subscribe to a specialized database such as the *MLAIB*, but many more will provide access to general databases such as *Expanded Academic*, *Ebscohost*, *InfoTrac*, or some of the Wilson databases such as *Humanities Index*, all of which index selected journals devoted to literary criticism. Additionally, there are increasing numbers of quality websites, most produced by academics and hosted by educational institutions, available on the World Wide Web. These sites contain bibliographic information and other relevant materials on British modernism. Selected examples of these are discussed more in chapter 10, "Web Resources."

Whether you consult a print or an electronic bibliography, it will save time and effort if you first familiarize yourself with both the coverage and the arrangement of the work at hand. For print indexes and bibliographies, first take a look at any available front matter in the work. Often there is an introduction or an explanatory essay at the beginning, written by the author or editor, that gives insight into the scope of the work. For electronic indexes, there is usually an "About" link that will take you to a separate page explaining the use of the work and the nature of its contents. In either case, the explanatory matter should provide details concerning which formats (books, articles, dissertations, etc.) are included, which time limits are in place (works published only after a certain date, for example), and any other limitations such as nationality of the writers, geographic area, time period, and so on. Usually there is also an explanation of the arrangement of items, the elements within the individual records, and any "exceptions to the rules" or other inconsistencies within the work. For electronic indexes and those print indexes that are published on a regular, ongoing basis, some sense should be given of the frequency of updates or publication. A single-issue print bibliography normally notes its relationship to other works, particularly if it is an update, revision, or continuation of an earlier work.

Print bibliographies are most often arranged by author name, subject, time period, or some combination of these. It is usually fairly easy to determine the sections of greatest interest for your research topic; however, don't fail to consult any available indexes at the end of the work. Taking this step will help ensure that nothing was overlooked or missed while consulting a particular work. In most electronic indexes, you can consult a subject index or thesaurus that will give you insight into both the subjects included and the appropriate controlled vocabulary to use in your searching. There should also be a help link leading to an area that gives specific information and examples of how to best formulate a search strategy in that tool. Search tips for specific literary databases addressed in this chapter are discussed in their descriptions. For immediate how-to questions concerning the use of a print or electronic bibliography, consult the reference librarian.

It should be obvious from the descriptions here that a wide range of indexes is available, with varying foci and coverage. Depending upon your goals, it may be more appropriate to consult one particular bibliography rather than another. For example, if you are looking for primary works by a particular author, it may be best to start with a work such as the *New Cambridge Bibliography of English Literature* or Mellown's *A Descriptive Catalogue of the Bibliographies of 20th-Century British Poets, Novelists, and Dramatists* in order to determine which primary bibliographies are available and which are the most comprehensive. If you are interested in the concept of literary modernism in general, Davies' *An Annotated Critical Bibliography of Modernism* would be a useful starting point. If you are particularly interested in poetry or drama, one of the specialized tools focusing on those genres might provide more in-depth information about the topic than a more generalized tool. For students embarking on dissertation research or for any researcher seeking a comprehensive literature review, consulting both the *MLAIB* and *ABELL* will be required. On the other hand, if you already have a good grasp of the literature of your particular research interest and only want to stay on top of what is new, the *Year's Work in English Studies* may be the most appropriate tool to consult.

Following is an overview of some of the standard bibliographies for finding primary works and secondary criticism on modern British literature. Because the time frame for what constitutes "modernism" is so fuzzy, and because modernism was an international movement, very few of these resources can be said to exclusively address British modernism as we have defined it here. There is often overlap with other national literatures or a focus on British literature from a shorter or longer time period. Frequently reference books will take the twentieth century as a defining timeframe, although by our definition this leaves out important modern work from the late nineteenth century and frequently includes postmodern literature of the late twentieth century. In spite of these drawbacks, all of the works cited are useful in researching modern

British literature to some degree. There are four basic categories of materials. The first is general bibliographies, which are those works that consider literature broadly, often of many time periods, and are so comprehensive and/or so ubiquitous that they will naturally be consulted by students of English literature whatever their topic or time period. The second category consists of works that focus on British literature but that cover several time periods, including the modern era. The third category is bibliographies for British literature (although some may address other literatures as well) during roughly the modern era, give or take a few years on either side of our definition. The fourth category contains bibliographies for individual British modernists.

GENERAL LITERATURE BIBLIOGRAPHIES

Annual Bibliography of English Language and Literature (ABELL). Leeds: Maney Publishing for the Modern Humanities Research Association, 1921–. Annual. See www.il.proquest.com/products_pq/descriptions/abell.shtml.

JSTOR: The Scholarly Journal Archive. New York: JSTOR, 1995–. www.jstor.org/.

Modern Language Association International Bibliography of Books and Articles on the Modern Languages and Literatures (MLAIB). New York: Modern Language Association of America, 1922–. Annual. Available online through various vendors. Check www.mla.org/bib_dist_comparison for a list and comparison of online vendors.

Project Muse. Baltimore, MD: Johns Hopkins University, 1993–. muse.jhu.edu.

Short Story Index. New York: H. W. Wilson, 1900–.

Year's Work in English Studies. Oxford: Published for the English Association by Oxford University Press, 1921–. Annual. ywes.oxfordjournals.org/.

The largest bibliographic index for literature studies is the ***Modern Language Association International Bibliography of Books and Articles on the Modern Languages and Literatures*** (***MLAIB***). It is produced on an annual basis by the Modern Language Association (MLA), the major professional association for teachers of literature and modern languages in higher education. In fact, the *MLAIB* began its life in 1926 as a section of *PMLA*, the journal published by the association. In 1969, the bibliography began to be printed separately, and about ten years later, the first electronic version became available. In the beginning of electronic access, records went back only to 1963; thanks to more recent retrospective conversion efforts, the bibliography now provides electronic access to content going all the way back to 1926. The *MLAIB* currently contains over two million records and adds more than 66,000 records annually. It covers materials related to literature from around the world, language, linguistics, folklore, literary theory and criticism, dramatic arts, and the history of printing and publishing. Materials related to the college-level teaching of language, literature, or composition and rhetoric have been included since 1998. Over four thousand journals are indexed (the current master list of periodicals is forty-six pages long: http://www.mla.org/bib_sources), as are critical monographs and book collections, reference works, working papers, and citations to dissertations from *Dissertation Abstracts International*. Masters theses, reprints, book reviews, and individual articles from encyclopedias and dictionaries are excluded. The print version of the *MLAIB* is available by subscription to libraries or individuals through the MLA. The electronic version of the bibliography is currently available through EBSCO, Gale, OCLC, and ProQuest-CSA. Most electronic versions also make access available to the names and subjects thesauri of controlled vocabulary for the *MLAIB*, as well as the MLA's *Directory of Periodicals*, which is a useful tool for scholars to obtain contact information, scope of content, and submission guidelines for more than five thousand scholarly journals.

The ***Annual Bibliography of English Language and Literature*** (***ABELL***) is the other major bibliographic index for literature. *ABELL* is produced on an annual basis by the Modern Humanities Research Association (MHRA), an international scholarly association based in Britain. All aspects and periods (going back to Anglo-Saxon times) of English language and literature are covered, including British, American, and Commonwealth writings. Source materials, such as monographs, journal articles, critical editions, book reviews, essay collections, and published doctoral dissertations, are international in scope. *ABELL* is available through MHRA as print volumes and can also be obtained through the vendor Chadwyck-Healey on CD-ROM or in electronic format, either as a stand-alone product or as part of the *Literature Online (LION)* database. Some 900,000 records can currently be found in the electronic version of *ABELL*, which provides content from volume one (1920) to the present and is updated monthly. The electronic version now also contains additional retrospective indexing for materials from 1892 through 1919. There are major areas of overlap between *ABELL* and *MLAIB*, although each has its own unique content, such as with smaller, regional publications. Book reviews, not found in the *MLAIB*, can be located in *ABELL*. Most scholars agree that a thorough search of literature resources would require consulting both indexes.

Recently *LION*, one of the means of obtaining electronic access to *ABELL*, has entered into an agreement to market the *MLAIB* as an add-on subscription to its database. Institutions subscribing to *LION* and the *MLAIB* add-on thus have access to the largest and most comprehensive combined electronic bibliographic index in the field of literature. Through the *LION* interface, *ABELL* and the *MLAIB* can be searched together or separately. When searched together, a number of duplicate records are sometimes returned, but the distraction of this is outweighed by the convenience of being able to search both bibliographies at the same time. *LION* also has a number of other services packaged together, including full-text access to thousands of works of English and American poetry, drama, and prose in the public domain; access to 212 full-text literature journals that link to their articles from citations found in the database; and the ability to link to full-text articles in *JSTOR* and *Project Muse* if your institution subscribes to them.

Both ***JSTOR*** and ***Project Muse*** might more properly be called "searchable electronic journal collections" rather than bibliographies as such. However, due to the fact that these collections are searchable by author, title, and keywords or subjects, they do function as bibliographic indexes to the particular titles within the collection. Because they are widely available in academic libraries, they are included here as special examples of electronic databases that contain full-text articles from a significant number of literature-related journals. *JSTOR* is a nonprofit organization that started in 1995 with the idea of creating a product to help libraries deal with the space constraints imposed by long runs of print academic journals. Making these materials available as high-quality PDF electronic documents would serve the needs of researchers while conserving space for libraries. Starting as a pilot project at the University of Michigan, *JSTOR* now has over 4,600 subscribers around the world. Over one hundred titles are currently found in the "Literature & Language" category of the database. *JSTOR*'s strength is providing deep back issues of scholarly journals, usually starting with volume 1 of a title's run. Often the most recent issues of a journal are not accessible; publishers may select a "moving wall"—the time lag between an item's publication and its availability in *JSTOR*—between zero and ten years, with most opting for a three- to five-year wall. When searching in *JSTOR* in either basic or advanced mode, it is possible to limit the search to only the titles in the "Language & Literature" category. In basic mode, you can also add other discipline categories to your search as a group. You can do the same in advanced mode, but here you can also "explode" each discipline category and select individual journal titles upon which to focus your search. There is also an "Article locator" search function, which allows a researcher to easily search for a known item by article title, author, and journal title.

Project Muse is in many ways a complement to *JSTOR*. It, too, is a nonprofit enterprise featuring full-text versions of a range of scholarly journals, including over one hundred titles in its "Literature" category. It began at

Johns Hopkins University (JHU) as a collaboration between the university press and the Milton S. Eisenhower Library, the main research library at JHU. In 1995, electronic versions of JHU publications were made available, and the database now contains over four hundred journals from almost one hundred nonprofit publishers. Instead of specializing in deep back issues, however, *Project Muse* focuses on current volumes and recent back issues. Many journals have back issues in *JSTOR* that meet the more current volumes in *Project Muse*, and many others are working on filling in any gap in coverage between the two. In addition to being able to search by author, title, and full-text keywords, *Project Muse* also allows users to search by Library of Congress subject headings, previously described in chapter 3, "Library Catalogs." As with *JSTOR*, the advanced search mode in *Project Muse* allows you to limit your search by category, which means you can choose to search only those titles in the "Literature" category. You can also pick and choose individual journals upon which to focus your search. The advanced search modes in both *JSTOR* and *Project Muse* also enable some limited cross-searching between the two. While access to either or both of these electronic collections will not ensure a thorough literature search by any means, they will go a long way toward satisfying the need of any researcher to quickly obtain copies of a number of relevant articles. In fact, a quick search on just the word *modernism* produces several hundred results in both databases.

The ***Year's Work in English Studies*** **(*YWES*)** is very different from the bibliographies discussed here so far. It is an annual review and has an unusual format in that it is arranged in a series of narrative essays that strive to evaluate "all work of quality in English Studies published in a given year." Given this emphasis on "quality" work, it is not a comprehensive tool but rather a subjectively selective one. *YWES* covers all aspects of English literature from Old English to the twentieth century. British literature (including that from all of Ireland) is emphasized, but American literature is also found here, as is English literature from other areas of the world (Africa, Australia, Canada, the Caribbean, India, New Zealand, and the South Pacific). Researchers in British modernism can turn their attention directly to the chapter entitled "Modern Literature," which is exclusively focused on twentieth-century British and Irish literature. The chapter is divided into sections concerning general works and individual genres and time periods, such as poetry prior to 1950 or fiction after 1950. Each section is written by an expert in the field, and while the emphasis is on important books that were published during the year, there is also some inclusion of scholarly periodicals as well. Indexes at the back of the work provide comprehensive access to all authors, critics, and subjects mentioned. A particularly useful feature is the bibliography at the end of each chapter, listing all of the works discussed therein. Because of the highly selective nature of the *YWES*, this tool serves only as a starting point for research on any given subject or a means of keeping up to date. More comprehensive resources need to be consulted in order to get a fuller picture of the scholarship available and to identify materials dealing with more obscure topics or those not meeting the highest standards of the volume's contributors but that still may be useful.

YWES is also available electronically; check with your library to see whether your institution has access. The review's website has tables of contents for all volumes from January 1919 to the present. Although the full text of the articles can be accessed only by subscribers, the search function provided can help pinpoint chapters that address a particular topic or a work. A brief context for the search terms is given in the results, which will help to determine the potential relevancy of the cited section. For researchers not affiliated with a subscribing institution, personal short-term access to the entire content can be purchased at a nominal rate.

The ***Short Story Index*** is yet another type of general index. Like *YWES*, it focuses on monographs, in this case anthologies and collections of short stories, although there is some journal content as well. The index essentially locates where particular short stories have been published. Author, title, and limited subject indexing are all available. While short stories by most major writers are easily accessible through their collected works, there are occasional stray pieces that may have escaped notice or items not chosen for "selected" collections. This index is even more important for locating the works of more obscure authors for whom collected works are not available. The *Short Story Index* is available electronically, but its retrospective contents go back only to 1984. For this reason, many libraries retain their print copies of the index, which provides coverage back to 1900.

BIBLIOGRAPHIES INCLUDING BRITISH MODERNISM

Alexander, Harriet Semmes. *American and British Poetry: A Guide to the Criticism, 1925–1978*. Athens, OH: Swallow Press, 1984.

Beene, Lynn. *Guide to British Prose Fiction Explication: Nineteenth and Twentieth Century*. New York: G. K. Hall, 1997.

Bell, Inglis F., and Donald Baird. *The English Novel, 1578–1956: A Checklist of Twentieth-Century Criticism*. Denver, CO: Alan Swallow, 1959.

Cavanagh, John. *British Theatre: A Bibliography, 1901 to 1985*. Mottisfont, Romsey, Hampshire: Motley, 1989.

Howard-Hill, Trevor Howard. *Bibliography of British Literary Bibliographies*. 2nd ed. Oxford: Clarendon Press, 1987.

———. *Index to British Literary Bibliography*. 9 vols. Oxford: Clarendon Press, 1969–1999.

Kuntz, Joseph M., and Nancy C. Martinez. *Poetry Explication: A Checklist of Interpretation since 1925 of British and American Poems Past and Present*. 3rd ed. Boston: G. K. Hall, 1980.

Martinez, Nancy C., Joseph G. R. Martinez, and Erland Anderson. *Guide to British Poetry Explication: Victorian–Contemporary*. Boston: G. K. Hall, 1995.

Palmer, Helen H., and Anne Jane Dyson. *English Novel Explication: Criticisms to 1972*. Hamden, CT: Shoe String Press, 1973.

Shattock, Joanne, ed. *Cambridge Bibliography of English Literature, Volume 4: 1800–1900*. 3rd ed. New York: Cambridge University Press, 2000.

Watson, George, ed. *New Cambridge Bibliography of English Literature*. 5 vols. New York: Cambridge University Press, 1969–1977.

The ***New Cambridge Bibliography of English Literature*** is the successor to the earlier *Cambridge Bibliography of English Literature*. The latter work, while still useful in some circles, covers only English literature to 1900 and so is of limited value to researchers interested in modernism. The *New Cambridge Bibliography* is divided into four volumes by periods; of interest here is volume 4, edited by J. R. Williston, concerning the period 1900–1950. This volume is broken up into sections and subsections, with particular authors highlighted for the major genres. The first section is the "Introduction," which has two subsections on general works (such as literary histories and literary memoirs) and book production and distribution (including authorship and distribution). The second section is on poetry and contains two subsections: "General Works" and "Individual Poets." The highlighted authors here are Eliot, Graves, Auden, and Thomas. If the author worked in additional genres, materials related to those genres may also be found in the initial listing here. Following the highlighted authors are listings for lesser-known writers or those for whom fewer materials are available. Section 3 focuses on "The Novel" and is divided into three subsections concerning general works, individual novelists, and children's books. The highlighted novelists here are Conrad, Wells, Bennett, Forster, Joyce, Woolf, Lawrence, and Greene, again followed by others of their peers. Section 5 broadly considers prose writers of all genres, including critics, historians, philosophers, and scientists. Section 6 is devoted to "Newspapers and Magazines" as well as little magazines and those periodicals related to particular genres. Listings for authors within the work have bibliographies for both primary and secondary works. Volume 3 of the *New Cambridge Bibliography*, edited by George Watson, looks at the period 1800–1900 and may also be of interest, particularly the sections on late nineteenth-century poetry, prose, drama, and the novel. There is also a section on Anglo-Irish literature that particularly highlights the work of Yeats and Synge. Cambridge is currently putting out the successor to the *New Cambridge Bibliography*, which again will be called ***Cambridge Bibliography of English Literature***, 3rd edition. So far, the only volume published is volume 4 (edited by Joanne Shattock), the update of the *New Cambridge Bibliography*'s volume 3, concerning the time period 1800–1900. It has hundreds of new entries, many of which reflect a special effort to fill in gaps for women writers and noncanonical writing, although only a portion of this may be of interest to the researcher of British modernism. Volume 5 of the *New Cambridge Bibliography* is the index for all four of the proceeding volumes and is useful for pinpointing all materials related to a particular author.

Howard-Hill's impressive series, grouped together under the series title ***Index to British Literary Bibliography***, basically consists of bibliographies of bibliographies. Volume 1, ***Bibliography of British Literary Bibliographies***, is probably the best known and most widely available of the current nine volumes. It was originally published in 1969, but a second edition, revised and expanded, was published in 1987. It specifically cites other bibliographies written in English that list the printed works of British writers or works published in Britain from 1475 forward. Some English-language subject bibliographies are included as well. The publications addressed are limited to works published after 1889, with a few exceptions. Of greatest interest to scholars of modern British literature will be the references for period bibliographies from 1901 to the late twentieth century, which are mainly bibliographies of modern British authors and "contemporary" writings of the twentieth century. Additionally, the "Authors" section of this work lists bibliographies devoted to individual writers, many of which are related to the major modernists such as Lawrence and Woolf. The regional bibliographies (focusing on Scotland, Ireland, England, and Wales) and various subject bibliographies may also be of use, depending upon one's research interests. All works are arranged chronologically within the major categories, and most cited works have brief annotations or reviews attached. There are two indexes for names and subjects. Volume 2 of the *Index* is devoted exclusively to Shakespeare bibliography, and volume 3 (which was never published in print but resides on the Bibliography Society of America's website at http://www.bibsocamer.org//BibSite/HowardHill/index.htm) is on British books and the book trade up to 1890, so both are of little interest to scholars of British modernism. Volumes 5 through 9 update the original volume 1, with volumes 8 and 9 bringing the coverage forward to 1989.

Several bibliographies are available that more narrowly consider a particular genre of literature and that include British modern writers to some degree. Alexander's ***American and British Poetry: A Guide to the Criticism, 1925–1978***, considers English and American poetry from all eras (Donne and Marvell to Jong and Updike). Secondary literature published from 1925 through 1978, such as criticism from scholarly journals, book chapters, and book sections, are cited, but not books as a whole. The scope of the work is limited to poems of one thousand lines or fewer, and criticism must be of an entire work and more than four lines in length. Both major and minor poets are covered, so in addition to material on poets such as Eliot and Yeats, you will also find critical works on Housman, Hopkins, Cummings, and C. D. Lewis. The work is arranged alphabetically by author last name and within each listing by the title of individual works. There are "see also" references to material on the poet's work more generally and cross-references for materials that relate to more than one poem or work.

Kuntz and Martinez's ***Poetry Explication: A Checklist of Interpretation since 1925 of British and American Poems Past and Present*** also covers British and American poetry of all time periods, and the criticism is roughly from the same time period, 1925 to 1978. Several limitations are imposed here as well. First, only criticism of poems five hundred lines or fewer is cited. Excluded are works of criticism dealing solely with metrics or paraphrase, those dealing with sources or circumstances of composition, and criticism from books dealing with the work of a single author. The book is arranged alphabetically by the poet's last name, with the titles of poems listed alphabetically underneath. Criticism is presented by the critic's last name under the title of the poem considered. Complete citations are given for journal articles and most books, except for those considered "main sources," which are works of criticism containing a wealth of explication of more than one poet. These items are listed at the end of the book, and the citations within the work refer to them by author's last name, short title, and page numbers.

The series of guides to British and American poetry subsequently published by G. K. Hall is meant to expand and continue the work of *Poetry Explication: A Checklist.* A two-volume set on American poetry was issued in 1989. The *Guide to British Poetry Explication* comprises four volumes, each focusing on a time period from Old English to contemporary. Of interest to scholars of British modernism is volume 4, ***Guide to British Poetry Explication: Victorian–Contemporary*** by Martinez, Martinez, and Anderson. The new guides drop some of the limitations of the earlier *Checklist.* Now included are explications for poems of all lengths and criticism from volumes considering the works of a single author. All works from the original *Checklist* relevant to the period and nationality are retained, but the expanded scope of coverage and extending the period forward to 1993 means that the number of citations has almost tripled, from fewer than 3,000 in the original volume to more than

8,500. The layout of the work is essentially the same as the original—poets are arranged alphabetically by last name, their poems are listed alphabetically below, and the citations to the criticism are cited under each poem title by author's last name. A bibliography of main sources is given at the end of the work and provides citations for periodicals that often print bibliographies of poets from Victorian times forward.

British Theatre: A Bibliography, 1901 to 1985 contains lists of bibliographies of secondary critical works related to British and Irish theater of all eras that were published between 1901 and 1985. The emphasis here is on theater as performance, as opposed to the play as literature. The works cited will serve as useful context for any researcher focused on drama. The work is broken up into four sections: "A: Theatre," "B: Drama," "C: Music," and "D: Indexes" (subject and author). The sections of most interest to those studying British modernism are A.5.7, "Theatre—History—1881–1985" and B.15.9, "Drama—History—1881–1985." The citations in these sections also include works focused on earlier periods, but all works related to modern British theater are contained here. The bibliography also cites general works, reminiscences of persons associated with the theater, writing relevant to specific theaters in London, and works by and about named persons significant in the field, such as actors, directors, dramatists, designers, and so on.

Lynn Beene's ***Guide to British Prose Fiction Explication: Nineteenth and Twentieth Century*** contains citations to secondary works explicating prose by major writers of the nineteenth and twentieth centuries. Because this guide includes authors whose creative output was accomplished prior to our main period of concern, such as Dickens, as well as authors who came later, such as Fowles, it is useful for placing British modernism within the context of the larger continuum of British writing. All major British modernists can be found here, such as Conrad, Joyce, Lawrence, and Woolf. A bibliography of "Main Sources Consulted," listing the most important source material used for compiling the bibliography, is another helpful feature.

Bell and Baird's ***The English Novel, 1578–1956: A Checklist of Twentieth-Century Criticism*** covers twentieth-century secondary criticism of English novels from all time periods. The volume begins with a scholarly introduction, which is followed by the checklist, arranged in alphabetical order by the novelists' last names and subdivided by titles of individual novels. Citations for individual critical works are provided, along with a brief explanatory note. There are no indexes, but the volume ends with a list of sources—those monographs and journals where the criticisms were located. Bell and Baird's work is supplemented by Palmer and Dyson's ***English Novel Explication: Criticisms to 1972***, updating the work with criticisms found through 1972. Additional supplements have been published, continuing to expand the work. The most recent, and presumably the last, is *Supplement VI*, edited by Christian J. W. Kloesel (2002), which updated the criticisms through the first months of 2001. Supplements 5 through 7 were published by Archon Books, an imprint of Shoe String Press.

BRITISH MODERNISM BIBLIOGRAPHIES

Cassis, A. F. *The Twentieth-Century English Novel: An Annotated Bibliography of General Criticism*. New York: Garland, 1977.

Davies, Alistair. *An Annotated Critical Bibliography of Modernism*. Totowa, NJ: Barnes & Noble, 1982.

Grimes, Janet. *Novels in English by Women, 1891–1920: A Preliminary Checklist*. New York: Garland, 1981.

Mellown, Elgin W. *A Descriptive Catalogue of the Bibliographies of 20th-Century British Poets, Novelists, and Dramatists*. 2nd ed. rev. Troy, NY: Whitston, 1978.

———. *A Descriptive Catalogue of the Bibliographies of 20th-Century British Writers*. Troy, NY: Whitston, 1972.

Nicoll, Allardyce. *English Drama, 1900–1930: The Beginnings of the Modern Period*. New York: Cambridge University Press, 1973.

Rice, Thomas Jackson. *English Fiction, 1900–1950*. 2 vols. Detroit: Gale Research, 1979–1983.

Schlueter, Paul, and June Schlueter. *The English Novel: Twentieth Century Criticism*. Vol. II. Athens, OH: Swallow Press, 1982.

Alistair Davies's ***An Annotated Critical Bibliography of Modernism*** is uniquely focused on literary modernism. Because modernism was an international movement, the book is not limited to British literature specifically but by necessity contains information on American and Continental writers as well. The first section comprises an annotated list of major books and articles concerning literary modernism, which seek to describe the characteristics of modernism, explain both its origins and influences, examine its techniques, consider its political, social, and philosophical underpinnings, and look at its relationship to other arts. Entries are arranged chronologically within sections, and the first item listed in the work is Edmund Wilson's 1931 seminal *Axel's Castle: A Study in the Imaginative Literature of 1870–1930*, which relates modernism to its roots in the symbolist movement and is considered a classic in the field. This first section, dealing with modernism in general, is of great value for the range of materials presented and their focus on modernism. It is broken down into ten subsections covering "Theory of Modernism,"

"Modernism and Its Literary Context," "Modernism and Poetry," "Modernism and Fiction," "Modernism and Drama," "The Critique of Modernism," "Modernism: The Problem of Critical Reception," "Anthologies of the Key Documents of Modernism," "Guides to Modern Writing and to Modernism," and "Literary Modernism and the Other Arts." Davies's annotations are particularly useful in explaining the significance of each item and often offer descriptive quotations taken directly from the original works.

An Annotated Critical Bibliography of Modernism also has four other sections, each considering an individual author: W. B. Yeats, Wyndham Lewis, D. H. Lawrence, and T. S. Eliot. No explanation is given for why these four particular authors were chosen for study. Certainly Yeats, Lawrence, and Eliot are considered "major" modernists almost universally; the inclusion of Lewis here is somewhat more perplexing. In any event, each of the individual author bibliographies contain subsections devoted to bibliographic information (such as available primary and secondary bibliographies for the author's work), memoirs and biographies, and political and social thought. Other categories are included as appropriate for the given author. Lewis's section is the shortest, and Lawrence's section is the longest, with subsections covering various individual novels, the poetry, the drama, and the criticism, in addition to topical categories such as "Lawrence and women." Other special subsections relevant to the particular author are provided; for example, Yeats's section has a subsection on full-length studies of his relationship to the occult. There is also an author index for the books and articles cited as well as a subject index. Both indexes are divided into five sections corresponding to the general modernism and author sections of the main work, described above.

Mellown's ***A Descriptive Catalogue of the Bibliographies of 20th-Century British Poets, Novelists, and Dramatists*** is the second edition, revised and enlarged, of his ***A Descriptive Catalogue of the Bibliographies of 20th-Century British Writers*** (1972). The earlier work was extremely broad in scope, attempting to catalog works related to all British writers (those working in the social sciences and sciences as well as the humanities) born after 1840 who published the majority of their work in Britain or Ireland after 1890 and for whom there were bibliographies available. The new edition of the work used the same criteria, expanding the coverage to include those works published from 1972 to 1977, but limiting the authors to "imaginative" writers, as the title change suggests. The catalog is selective, attempting to present only the most comprehensive and authoritative bibliographies available for each author. This makes it an excellent tool for quickly determining the highest-quality bibliographies for a range of major and minor modern British writers. The work begins with a listing of nineteen general bibliographies that broadly consider twentieth-century creative writers. Following that are alphabetical listings of individual authors with their birth and death dates and any pseudonyms used. "See" references are made within the alphabetical listings from the pseudonym to the official form of the name. For each author, where applicable, there are three categories of bibliographies: "Primary," for those works regarding the writings by the author; "Secondary," covering those works about the author; and "General," referring to the general bibliographies listed in the beginning and indicating which ones relate to the author in question. Within categories, items are arranged chronologically. For each listing there is a brief descriptive and critical annotation, often with an excerpt from a review of the work. In instances in which more than one bibliography is available, an attempt is made to explain any differences between them. An index to the names of the authors of the secondary works cited within the main body of the text may be found at the end of the work.

Grimes's ***Novels in English by Women, 1891–1920: A Preliminary Checklist*** was written with the goal of providing the most comprehensive listing available of novels written by women in English (and published in Britain and the United States) between the years of 1891 and 1920. Since this time period covers the first part of the era we are here defining as modernism and because a significant number of British writers are included, this work may be of interest, particularly in its consideration of many overlooked or little-known women writers. The work is divided into three series. Each series is arranged alphabetically by the author's last name and then by titles of the novels (each of which is individually numbered). In some cases, brief excerpts from a review are quoted to give a sense of the quality and content of the work. The first series is the largest and features citations to all of the English-language novels written by women during the stated time period, which have been verified by the author. The second series has citations to works that were published anonymously, pseudonymously, or under a gender-neutral name, and for which research has not been able to determine the gender of the author. The third series contains citations to works that were discovered via various review sources but that the author has been unable to verify. At the end of the work is an inclusive title index.

Rice's ***English Fiction, 1900–1950*** covers general bibliographies and individual author bibliographies for English fiction from the first half of the twentieth century. Coverage ranges from major authors (Conrad, Lawrence) through "second-echelon" writers (Ford, Forster, Huxley, Maugham) to minor authors (Lehmann, Munro, Powys, Richardson). The first volume of this work focuses on general bibliographies and bibliographies on individual authors from Aldington to Huxley. The second volume contains the entries for individual authors from Joyce to Woolf. The general bibliographies start with primary bibliographies and then move to those on literary history, critical studies of modern English fiction, theory of fiction, studies of major types (crime fiction, political fiction, religious fiction, and science fiction, fantasy, and utopian fiction), histories and memoirs, and the related arts of art, film, and music. The individual author bibliographies begin with bibliographies of primary works devoted to fiction, miscellaneous writings, collected and selected works, and letters. Bibliographies of secondary works follow, including general bibliographies, biographies and interviews, general criticism, criticism of individual works, and miscellaneous writing about the author. Each listing provides a brief description of its content. Volume 1 has author, title, and subject indexes; volume 2 has an author index only.

Schlueter and Schlueter's second volume of ***The English Novel: Twentieth Century Criticism*** deals exclusively with twentieth-century criticism of twentieth-century English novelists. The first volume of this work, edited by Richard J. Dunn, covers twentieth-century criticism of earlier English novels, from Defoe through Hardy, and so is of more limited interest to students of British modernism. Part 1 of the second volume is arranged alphabetically by authors' names; for each writer there are bibliographic listings for general bibliographies, interviews, special issues of journals, general studies, and criticism of individual works. Modern novelists included are Conrad, Durrell, Ford, Forster, Graves, Greene, Huxley, Joyce, Lawrence, Maugham, Moore, Orwell, Richardson, Sayers, Waugh, Wells, West, and Woolf. More contemporary writers such as Murdoch, Spark, Pritchett, and Lessing can be found here as well. The second part of the volume has a list of all the books cited as well as a general bibliography.

The Twentieth-Century English Novel: An Annotated Bibliography of General Criticism by Cassis is also concerned with twentieth-century criticism of twentieth-century English novels, but its emphasis is on general criticism of the novel rather than on specific novelists. It cites some 2,800 books, book chapters, journal articles, dissertations, and important review articles written between 1900 and 1972 that analyze more than one author or that are concerned with the techniques of the twentieth-century novel. Some late nineteenth-century works are included in the criticism because of the starting date and because some major writers such as Joseph Conrad and Henry James produced significant works on either side of the turn of the century. A master list of the sources drawn from and the abbreviations used to identify them are listed at the beginning. The first section of the work consists of bibliographies and checklists of both primary and secondary works. The second section, dealing with criticism, is divided into two parts: books and articles. The third section covers dissertations and theses concerning the twentieth-century English novel. Each entry has an individual number associated with it, and most also contain descriptive annotations detailing more information about the scope and content of the work. Two indexes are also provided; the first is for individual authors whose work is known to be addressed in listed items, and the second focuses on selected topics and themes. Those interested in the modern British novel will find fairly comprehensive coverage of the topic by using this volume in conjunction with the Rice and the Schlueter and Schlueter works.

Nicoll's ***English Drama, 1900–1930: The Beginnings of the Modern Period*** is not technically a bibliography, although the second half of the work acts as a specialized form of one. Nicoll's work is a follow-up to his impressive *A History of English Drama, 1660–1900* (Cambridge, 1952–1959), which was a six-volume work concerning English drama from the Restoration to the late nineteenth century; a short-title catalog of plays produced or printed in England during that period was also provided. In *English Drama, 1900–1930*, he covers the history and development of English drama in the early twentieth century, including its influences, patterns, and forms, from regional dramas to general drama found on the London stage. This is excellent background (as is volume 5 of *A History of English Drama*, which looks at English drama 1850–1900) for those interested in modern drama. The second half of the work is a handlist of all plays produced in England during this thirty-year period, arranged alphabetically by the playwright's name. This painstaking compilation was taken from the records of the Lord Chamberlain's Office and other sources and in spite of its bulk (almost six hundred pages) is necessarily incomplete. Regardless of any gaps, this work is extremely useful not only for understanding the production history of the works of major modern playwrights but also for tracking down the works of minor or forgotten writers, particularly women playwrights of the period. References are made to *A History of English Drama* for those writers whose works span the nineteenth and twentieth centuries.

BRITISH MODERNISM AUTHOR BIBLIOGRAPHIES

Cowan, James C., ed. *D. H. Lawrence: An Annotated Bibliography of Writings about Him*. 2 vols. De Kalb: Northern Illinois University Press, 1982–1985.

Deming, Robert H. *A Bibliography of James Joyce Studies*. 2nd ed. Boston: G. K. Hall, 1977.

Kirkpatrick, Brownlee Jean, and Stuart N. Clarke. *A Bibliography of Virginia Woolf*. 4th ed. Oxford: Clarendon Press, 1997.

Majumdar, Robin. *Virginia Woolf: An Annotated Bibliography of Criticism, 1915–1974*. New York: Garland, 1976.

Roberts, Warren, and Paul Poplawski. *A Bibliography of D. H. Lawrence*. 3rd ed., rev. New York: Cambridge University Press, 2001.
Slocum, John J., and Herbert Cahoon. *A Bibliography of James Joyce: 1882–1941*. Westport, CT: Greenwood Press, 1971.

Scholars working on individual authors will do well to begin by consulting resources such as the *New Cambridge Bibliography of English Literature*, Mellown's *A Descriptive Catalogue of the Bibliographies of 20th-Century British Poets, Novelists, and Dramatists*, and Howard-Hill's *Bibliography of British Literary Bibliographies*, all of which are described above. These give one an idea of both available and recommended author bibliographies. Other relevant bibliographies included in this chapter can be consulted as well, depending upon one's research focus. Newer bibliographies not covered in these resources can be found by searching a union catalog such as *WorldCat*, described in chapter 3. A quick keyword search such as *Lawrence* and *bibliography* can be conducted, but this will unfortunately call forth too many false hits, such as every item record that lists a bibliography in one of its notes fields and that has the name "Lawrence" anywhere associated with it. A better strategy would be to use multiple search boxes in an advanced search and look for *Lawrence* as a subject and *bibliography* as a subject. While this will still bring up some false hits (such as a bibliography for Lawrence Durrell), the results will be much more focused as the author's name and the genre of bibliography are necessarily found in the subject field for works of this kind.

Bibliography production is a labor-intensive endeavor, but luckily there are bibliographies available for all of the major British modernists and many of their minor counterparts. No printed secondary bibliography can be considered entirely up to date, as work continues to be published on modern British writers at an impressive pace. Because of this, additional research in tools such as *MLAIB*, *ABELL*, and *YWES* will be required in order to find the most recent critical works on any particular author. Additionally, journals and professional societies are great resources for keeping abreast of new publications related to a particular author. For example, the *James Joyce Quarterly* and the *D. H. Lawrence Review* publish annual checklists of Joyce and Lawrence scholarship, respectively, and the International Virginia Woolf Society produces an annual *Bibliography of Virginia Woolf Studies* for its members. Primary materials do not change so rapidly, however, so for this type of material older works will maintain a much longer shelf life. On the other hand, it is interesting to note that two of the three primary bibliographies referred to in this section have gone into multiple updated editions. This is both because new scholarly editions of works by these authors continue to be published and because new manuscript materials such as letters or unpublished essays still occasionally come to light. Consulting author-specific journals, such as those listed in chapter 5, is a way of keeping informed of new publishing initiatives as well as a way of discovering any previously unknown manuscript materials. In this section, we'll take a look at some representative examples of high-quality bibliographies of primary materials and secondary materials for three major British modernists: James Joyce, D. H. Lawrence, and Virginia Woolf.

Slocum and Cahoon's ***A Bibliography of James Joyce: 1882–1941*** is still considered the standard primary bibliography of James Joyce's work. It is based on Slocum's personal collection of Joyce materials, which are now part of the Beinecke Rare Book and Manuscript Library at Yale University. It covers an extensive array of works written by Joyce and published through the year 1950. Certain sections, particularly the one related to foreign-language translations of Joyce's writings, are known to be incomplete; and certainly the provenance of many of the privately held manuscript materials is no longer current. The sections of the bibliography are A. books and pamphlets by James Joyce; B. books and pamphlets with contributions from James Joyce; C. contributions by James Joyce to periodicals and newspapers; D. translations of works by James Joyce; E. manuscripts of James Joyce; F. musical settings of works by James Joyce; and G. miscellany. Using standard bibliographic format, the sections focused on books have separate entries for each edition of a work, with a transcription of the title page, a complete physical description, and copious notes concerning publishing history, variations in different printings, and other useful and interesting information. The index provides access to the bibliographic entries via personal and proper names, including publishers, titles of periodicals, and titles of Joyce's works.

Deming's ***A Bibliography of James Joyce Studies*** is now in its second edition, having been revised and enlarged; Mellown called the first edition of this work the "most important listing of bibliographical information for material published before December, 1961" (193). It is now updated through December 1973 in its present edition. In addition to twelve years' worth of new materials being added, some 770 items from 1961 and earlier have been added retrospectively. A total of 5,555 entries are now available for a wide range of materials. Unfortunately, because of space limitations, most of the annotations from the first edition have been dropped from the second. The work is divided into three sections. The first section focuses on bibliographical, biographical, and general treatments. This section is divided into subsections consisting of A. bibliographical studies; B. biographical studies (including milieu studies on modernism, the 1920s and 1930s, and comparisons to other works); C. general studies; D. comprehensive studies of Joyce's works; E. reviews of Joyce's works; F. dissertations; and G. musical settings, theatrical productions, radio and television broadcasts, and records. Section 2 covers studies of separate works by Joyce and is broken down by genre and titles of works. There are separate listings for works specifically addressing individual episodes of *Ulysses*. The third section is the smallest, containing a few items that have been categorized as "uncategorized" or "unverified." The work also includes a combined index of names of authors, editors, translators, and reviewers of the items presented, as well as listing unsigned reviews and articles by title.

Warren Roberts's ***A Bibliography of D. H. Lawrence***, first published in 1962, has long been considered the most authoritative primary bibliography of D. H. Lawrence materials available. Now in a revised third edition, Paul Poplawski continues this scholarly work following Roberts's death in 1998. The book is divided into six parts, the first five concerning work written by Lawrence: A. books and pamphlets; B. contributions to books; C. contributions to periodicals; D. translations; and E. manuscripts. A sixth section, F. books and pamphlets about D. H. Lawrence, is a selected bibliography of more than seven hundred secondary works about Lawrence. Each entry is identified by section letter and number (such as A1 for Lawrence's first novel, *The White Peacock*) and a lowercase letter designating the particular edition. A transcription of the title page of the work is provided, followed by a complete physical description, including any variations in subsequent printings of the edition. Where applicable, such as in the case of a collection of short stories, complete contents are listed as well. A particularly nice feature of the current edition is the inclusion of twelve color plates of the original dust jackets from early editions of Lawrence's work. There are also three appendixes. The first covers parodies and sequels written by others of *Lady Chatterley's Lover* and piracies and forgeries of *Lady Chatterley's Lover*. The second contains listings of other "spurious works," and the third lists periodicals with some connection to Lawrence and his works. There is also a combined author/title index at the end of the work. This remains the definitive guide to Lawrence's works for scholars, book collectors, and booksellers alike.

As for secondary bibliographies of Lawrence, James Cowan's two-volume ***D. H. Lawrence: An Annotated Bibliography of Writings about Him*** is the most ambitious and most complete. It covers scholarly research, biography, comparative studies, introductions to primary and secondary works, criticism, bibliography, reviews, adaptations of Lawrence's work to other media, news items, letters to the editor, imaginative writing, and doctoral dissertations. Each volume begins with a checklist of the primary works cited or referred to within the volume. The bibliography is arranged chronologically. Volume 1 begins with comments written in 1909 about Lawrence's earliest published work—four poems published in the *English Review*—and goes through materials published through 1960—2,061 citations to works in all. Volume 2 begins with material from 1961 and goes through 1975, with a total of 2,566 citations. Each volume is divided into six parts, concerning writings about Lawrence's work by genre: I, fiction; II. poems; III. plays; IV. nonfiction prose, including essays, travel books, and letters; V. translation; and VI. paintings. The first four parts are divided into subsections focused on separate works and collected editions. Each item listed in the bibliography is individually numbered and contains a complete citation and short abstract of the work. Both volumes also feature individual indexes covering authors, titles of secondary works, periodical and newspaper titles, foreign languages, and titles of primary works.

Turning to Virginia Woolf, Mellown called the 1967 revised edition of Brownlee Jean Kirkpatrick's Woolf bibliography "the authoritative bibliography" for primary works. Now in its fourth edition (1997) and co-authored by Stuart N. Clarke, ***A Bibliography of Virginia Woolf*** remains the authoritative source for Woolf's primary materials. There was a publishing glut of Woolf materials (due in part to British copyright concerns) after the publication of the third edition of the work in 1980. Since the early 1980s, Woolf's diaries and letters have been published in multivolume sets, previously unknown letters have surfaced, and numerous scholarly editions of her work have been published. The current volume covers the following areas of Woolf's writings: A. books and pamphlets; AA. composite editions (a new category for the fourth edition, for multiple works printed in the same binding); B. contributions to books and pamphlets, and books translated by Virginia Woolf; C. contributions to periodicals and newspapers; D. translations into foreign languages; E. foreign editions in English and miscellaneous printer material; F. books and articles containing uncollected letters and extracts from uncollected letters; and G. manuscripts. The largest section is section A, arranged chronologically, starting with Woolf's first published novel, *The Voyage Out*, in 1915. Items are assigned letters and numbers within their categories, with lowercase letters assigned to various editions. Thus, A1a is the first edition of the previously mentioned novel. A transcription of the title page is given as well as a complete physical description, including notes regarding the history of the publication and any variations in printing. Most other sections provide more modest citations and descriptions. There is also a combined name/title index at the end of the work.

Robin Majumdar's ***Virginia Woolf: An Annotated Bibliography of Criticism, 1915–1974*** is the most comprehensive secondary bibliography of criticism and writing about Woolf. Each item included has a complete citation and, in most cases, a useful annotation. The work is divided into seven parts:

I. books on Virginia Woolf; II. articles, essays, and chapters on Virginia Woolf; III. introductions and prefaces by editors in selections from Virginia Woolf; IV. memoirs, obituary notices, and articles; V. correspondence, letters to the editor, and interviews; VI. general studies that contain observations on Virginia Woolf's work; and VII. book reviews. The section on book reviews covers reviews in major newspapers and journals, both British and American, for Woolf's fiction, but British sources only for her nonfiction. There are also a bibliography and two indexes, one for the names of critics and reviewers cited in the main body of the text, and the other for titles of Woolf's works discussed or referred to in the cited entries.

CONCLUSION

Because of the international character of modernism and because of the fuzzy nature of the time frame for its definition, there really are no available bibliographies focused specifically on British literary modernism. However, there is a range of bibliographies available that cover some aspect of British literary modernism by genre and/or time period or that include it within a larger context. As this chapter illustrates, there is no shortage of both general and specific bibliographies to which a scholar of British modernism can refer, whatever the topic of research might be. One advantage of studying this era is that the materials, both primary and secondary, are closer to us in time and therefore easier to access. More sources are becoming available in electronic format, thus cutting down on travel and research time. The standard general indexes are now widely available in electronic versions, enabling researchers to more quickly and thoroughly conduct an initial search and to subsequently remain up to date. Combining use of these general indexes with the most relevant print bibliographies available will give researchers a nearly comprehensive overview of the history and availability of the previous work in their area of interest.

Chapter Five

Scholarly Journals

Although research has shown that scholars in the humanities tend to favor monographs for the bulk of their research, scholarly journals are still of major importance.[1] Monographs can provide an in-depth treatment of a subject that journal articles can't aspire to, but journals do have the advantage of being published more quickly and frequently. Thus they serve as a means of facilitating timely access to information and trends in the field. Scholarly journals are also used by researchers as sources of book reviews, calls for papers, and conference announcements and reports. This chapter gives information about scholarly journals covering modern British literature. The journals are broken up into three general categories: those that are specifically related to literary modernism, those that are devoted to particular modernists, and a selected group of general journals that have more than one period of literature and/or more than one national literature as their scope but that include British modernism to some degree. Each discussion gives details about the types of articles published, the number and length of essays in each issue, and titles or topics of recent relevant articles. If the journal has a Web presence, particularly one that posts tables of contents, article abstracts, or other useful information, the URL is listed in the bibliography at the head of each section.

Journals specifically dealing with the literature of the modernist time period started to come into existence in the mid-twentieth century. *Twentieth Century Literature: A Scholarly and Critical Journal* and *MFS: Modern Fiction Studies* both began publishing in 1955. The *Journal of Modern Literature* followed in 1970. Without exception, these journals are aware of the international nature of the literary enterprise during the modern era. While writers from most time periods have had at least some influence exerted on them from countries and literary traditions other than their own, this is especially true of the modern era in the West, with its increased interaction through communication and travel. British writers of the modern era had a great deal of interaction with North American and Continental writers and were influenced by culture and writing from the British colonies as well. So, while a book like this one can choose to focus on British literary modernism, the reality is that these parameters are artificial; as such, there is no journal specifically devoted to modern British literature.

Modernist Studies: Literature & Culture, 1920–1940, publication of which has now ceased, published between 1974 and 1982. This journal did not limit its coverage to literature but started to branch out into wider cultural concerns related to modernism. In 1994, the Modernist Studies Association (MSA) began publishing *Modernism/modernity*. Now published by Johns Hopkins University Press, it remains the official journal of MSA. It self-consciously considers all aspects of modernism, including literature. The editorial policies of both of these journals reflect the growing recognition that literature itself is inseparable from other forms of art and culture.

Beginning in the late 1960s and early 1970s, a number of journals and reviews began to spring up devoted to particular modernist writers. This seems to be an effect of greater specialization within the field of literature and a growing "critical mass" of scholars focused on major figures. Societies devoted to major figures got their start and began to publish journals devoted to their particular interests. Thus, in 1963, the *James Joyce Quarterly* began publication, and the *D. H. Lawrence Review* got its start in 1968. Journals devoted to Woolf, Yeats, and Eliot appeared in the 1970s.

Certainly other, more generalized literature journals also publish articles on British modernism. *Publications of the Modern Language Association (PMLA)* is the premiere general literature journal and frequently carries articles related to British modernism. Other general journals discussed here are *Critical Inquiry*; *ELH: English Literary History*; *MLQ: Modern Language Quarterly*; *Novel: A Forum on Fiction*; and *The Review of English Studies*. Some more specialized journals also carry work concerning British modernists, such as *Tulsa Studies in Women's Literature* and *Victorian Studies*.

All of the journals discussed in this chapter are available in the traditional print format. Many of them also have electronic versions available. The bibliographic listings below give the International Standard Serial Numbers (ISSN) for the print version of the journal and for the electronic version as well, if available. Indexing to most of these journals is available through one or both of the major literature bibliographies, the *Modern Language Association International Bibliography (MLAIB)* and the *Annual Bibliography of English Language and Literature (ABELL)*. Full text of many of these journals can also be found in one or more of the electronic journal collections available by subscription, including the nonprofit *JSTOR* and *Project Muse* collections, and for-profit services such as *Academic Search Premier* and *Ingenta.* Additionally, many journal publishers provide tables of contents and article abstracts on the Web as well as author's guidelines and subscription information. *Project Muse* also allows free access to tables of contents for many titles and full-text articles for those affiliated with subscribing institutions. It's always a good idea to be a regular reader of at least two or three journals relevant to your area of interest; this helps you stay abreast of any trends or developments in the field. Additionally, periodic searching of major bibliographies such as *MLAIB* and *ABELL*, as described in chapter 3, will turn up materials from sources you do not regularly read.

Many electronic databases and indexes also give users the ability to set up alerts or receive current awareness services. An example of such a service is saving a canned search for articles on certain topics or written by certain authors, which is then automatically run on a set schedule with the results e-mailed directly to you. Taking advantage of this type of technological innovation can help you stay aware of current publishing trends with a minimum investment of time and energy.

LITERARY MODERNISM

English Literature in Transition, 1880–1920. Robert Langenfeld. 1957–. Quarterly. ISSN: 0013-8339. E-ISSN: 1559-2715. www.uncg.edu/eng/elt/.

Journal of Modern Literature. Indiana University Press. 1970–. Quarterly. ISSN: 0022-281X. E-ISSN: 1529-1464. www.iupjournals.org/jml/.

MFS: Modern Fiction Studies. Johns Hopkins University Press. 1955–. Quarterly. ISSN: 0026-7724. E-ISSN: 1080-658X. www.press.jhu.edu/journals/modern_fiction_studies/index.html.

Modernism/modernity. Johns Hopkins University Press. 1994–. Quarterly. ISSN: 1071-6068. E-ISSN: 1080-6601. www.press.jhu.edu/journals/modernism_modernity/index.html.

Modernist Studies: Literature & Culture, 1920–1940. University of Alberta. 1974–1982. Irregular. ISSN: 0316-5973.

Twentieth Century Literature: A Scholarly and Critical Journal. Hofstra University. 1955–: Quarterly. ISSN: 0041-462X. www.hofstra.edu/Academics/HCLAS/EAS/EAS_engspot_tcl.cfm.

The titles in this category all specifically address modern literature or twentieth-century literature, including what is defined here as British modernism.

English Literature in Transition, 1880–1920 (*ELT*) is unique in that it does *not* publish articles on the "major" modernists such as Conrad, Joyce,

Lawrence, Woolf, or Yeats unless these writers are "linked to less-prominent authors of the era." Formerly (1957–1963) titled *English Fiction in Transition, 1880–1920* (ISSN: 0364-3549), the journal was initiated by former editor Hal Gerber at Purdue University. Gerber resisted straight chronological divisions of literary study and was interested in the transitional era of late Victorian and early twentieth-century writing. He also encouraged interest in so-called minor figures of the time period, such as Kipling, Wilde, Ford, Pater, and Maugham. *ELT* typically contains three to four lengthy scholarly articles and at least a dozen book reviews (which can focus on major modernist figures only). It also occasionally publishes surveys of research or annotated bibliographies of works on minor modernists or topics of interest, as well as previously unpublished writings by these figures. Some examples of recent articles are "Rupert Brooke's Celebrity Aesthetic" and "Brief Encounter: Richard Aldington and the *Englishwoman*." The journal's website provides tables of contents for the current volume as well as an index for articles and book reviews appearing in all volumes going back to volume 26 (1983). *ELT* has recently entered into an agreement with *Project Muse*, which will be carrying tables of contents from volume 50 (2007) forward, as well as full text for subscribers.

The ***Journal of Modern Literature*** is devoted to twentieth-century literature. Coverage initially focused on British and American modernism, although in recent years this focus has expanded considerably. It now considers world literature outside of Britain and the United States and has expanded in time to all literature written in the twentieth century. Currently, each quarterly issue is edited by one of the four standing editors, who writes an introductory essay to the issue. Issues typically have between eight and ten critical essays and between zero and three reviews of books related to modern literature. Recent articles have included consideration of Julia Kristeva's psychological theories as applied to Virginia Woolf's *The Waves*, the composition practices exhibited in E. M. Forster's *Passage to India*, and urban impressionism in works of Joseph Conrad and Ford Madox Ford. The journal's website has tables of contents going back to volume 21 (1997/1998). Tables of contents for volumes 22 (1998/1999) to the present are available from *Project Muse*.

MFS: Modern Fiction Studies, as the title suggests, focuses exclusively on works of fiction. The scope is broader in terms of time and place, however. In addition to works from the modern era, more contemporary twentieth- and twenty-first-century fiction are considered as well. The main emphasis has been on British and American writers, but Continental and colonial/postcolonial authors have been increasingly covered. *MFS* is published quarterly and occasionally features thematic issues that focus on the work of a particular author or a particular movement or milieu. Normally between seven and eleven critical articles are contained in each issue. *MFS* also publishes longer review essays that consider recently published books and their themes in a scholarly fashion, and shorter book reviews (usually over a dozen in an issue) that briefly consider new works. The book reviews tend to be placed in categories, which give some insight to the journal's range of interests: "The Americas"; "British, Irish, and Postcolonial Literatures"; "Comparative Studies"; and "Theory and Cultural Studies." Checklists of selected criticism on a particular author or theme are usually found in the first and third numbers of each volume. Recent critical articles focusing on modern British literature have addressed sexuality and self-authorship in Virginia Woolf's *Mrs. Dalloway* and the idea of snobbery and cultural capital in works by James Joyce. Tables of contents from volume 31, number 1 (1985) and forward are available through *Project Muse*.

Modernism/modernity is the official journal of the Modernist Studies Association. The Association "is devoted to the study of the arts in their social, political, cultural, and intellectual contexts from the later nineteenth- through the mid-twentieth century." Thus the time period considered is roughly equivalent to our current definition of modernism, but the journal is far more international and interdisciplinary in scope. British modernist literature is well represented in the journal's pages, as many of the critical articles and book reviews reflect upon major British modernists and their works. A typical recent issue of *Modernism/modernity* has six to thirteen critical articles, one to three scholarly review essays, and more than a dozen shorter book reviews. A bibliography of "Recent Books of Interest" provides citations for additional books received that are related to modernism but not reviewed in the journal. An occasional translation of a short work is also published. Recent articles have covered such topics as the presentation of churchgoing in modern novels by Joyce and Woolf and bridging aesthetics and history in Joyce's *Ulysses*. Tables of contents going back to the first volume are available through *Project Muse*.

Modernist Studies: Literature & Culture, 1920–1940 was published irregularly by the University of Alberta in Calgary between 1974 and 1982 and has now ceased. Articles on British and North American modernist writers made up the bulk of the journal, but occasionally pieces were about Continental writers. Although this can no longer be considered a potential publishing venue for scholars, many of the articles in the journal will still be of interest to researchers. Articles on major British modernists such as Woolf, Yeats, Lawrence, Conrad, and Forster can be found here as well as more general articles on subjects such as "Modern Literature and Iconography" and 1930s English proletarian fiction.

Twentieth-Century Literature covers all aspects of twentieth-century literature, including major and minor British and American modernists, as well as more contemporary writers and works in languages other than English. Each issue typically contains five or six scholarly articles running approximately twenty to twenty-five pages, but no book reviews. Recent articles have focused on topics such as Joyce's epiphanic mode and the pseudo-Homeric world of Woolf's *Mrs. Dalloway*.

SPECIFIC MODERN FIGURES

Auden Studies. Oxford University Press. 1990–. Irregular. ISSN: 1366-056X. www.oup.com/us/catalog/general/series/AudenStudies/?view=usa.

Conradiana. Texas Tech University Press. 1968–. 3/yr. ISSN: 0010-6356. www.ttup.ttu.edu/JournalPages/Conradiana.html.

D. H. Lawrence Review. State University of New York, Geneseo. 1968–. 3/yr. ISSN: 0011-4936. www.geneseo.edu/~dhlr.

D. H. Lawrence: The Journal of the D. H. Lawrence Society. The Society. 1976–. Annual. ISSN: 0308-7662.

James Joyce Quarterly. Academic Publications, University of Tulsa. 1963–. Quarterly. ISSN: 0021-4183. www.utulsa.edu/jjq/default.htm.

Joyce Studies Annual. University of Texas Press. 1990–2003. Fordham University Press. 2007–. Annual. ISSN: 1049-0809. E-ISSN: 1538-4241. www.utexas.edu/utpress/journals/jjsa.html and www.fordham.edu/academics/programs_at_fordham_/joyce_studies_annual/index.asp.

Virginia Woolf Bulletin. Virginia Woolf Society of Great Britain. 1999–. 3/yr. ISSN: 1465-2579. www.virginiawoolfsociety.co.uk/vw_bulletin.htm.

Virginia Woolf Miscellany. Southern Connecticut State University. 1973–. 2/yr. ISSN: 0736-251X. www.home.southernct.edu/~neverowv1/www/Miscellany/vwm.html.

Virginia Woolf Quarterly. Aeolian Press. 1972–1980. Quarterly. ISSN: 0090-4546.

Woolf Studies Annual. Pace University Press. 1995–. Annual. ISSN: 1080-9317. http://appserv.pace.edu/execute/page.cfm?doc_id=2372.

Yeats: An Annual of Critical and Textual Studies. University of Michigan Press. 1983–. Annual. ISSN: 0742-6224.

Yeats Annual. Palgrave Macmillan Ltd. 1982–2002. Irregular. ISSN: 0278-7687.

Yeats Eliot Review. Murphy Newsletter Services. 1974–. 2/yr. ISSN: 0704-5700.

All of the periodicals in this category deal specifically with a major modernist writer or writers. Most are published by small societies interested in the particular author and as such are less likely to have their materials available in electronic format. All are indexed in at least one of the major abstracting and indexing tools, *MLAIB* and/or *ABELL*. Some of the publications are also associated with websites providing additional content of interest to the scholar.

Auden Studies is an irregularly published serial that has appeared three times between 1990 and 1996. It focuses on the career of W. H. Auden and publishes previously unpublished primary material such as poetry, prose, and letters. Also included are scholarly articles related to the theme of the volume, such as Auden's early works and works after 1940.

Conradiana is published three times a year and focuses on the work of the Polish-born English writer, Joseph Conrad. A typical issue has five to eight scholarly articles related to Conrad and his work. Examples of some recent articles are "Conrad and Ambiguity: Social Commitment and Ideology in *Heart of Darkness* and *Nostromo*" and "Going Beyond Limits: De-Territorialization in Conrad's Novels." Tables of contents going back to volume 39, number 1 (2007) are now available through *Project Muse*.

D. H. Lawrence Review is the official journal of the D. H. Lawrence Society of North America. Published three times a year, it typically contains three to five scholarly articles related to Lawrence as well as a number of book reviews of titles related to Lawrence, his circle of friends and acquaintances, and his milieu. There are also occasional bibliographies of scholarship on Lawrence, news tidbits related to Lawrence called "Lawrenciana," and announcements and reports of conferences. "Strange Gods Beneath the Post-War Rubble in *Kangaroo*" and "The Radical Individualism of D. H. Lawrence and Max Stirner" are some examples of recent scholarly articles.

D. H. Lawrence: The Journal of the D. H. Lawrence Society is now published annually by the D. H. Lawrence Society, a literary society based in the Nottingham area in England. The journal publishes news and information about events related to Lawrence as well as some scholarly articles. The title is selectively indexed in the major bibliographic databases. Examples of scholarly articles appearing in the journal are "Editing *Sons and Lovers*" and "Pastoral and Industrial Themes in Lawrence."

James Joyce Quarterly is published by the University of Tulsa Press. A typical issue has an introductory essay by the editor called "Raising the Wind," firsthand reports of conferences, classes, and other activities called "Perspectives," four to eight scholarly articles, several short "Notes/Entertainments," letters to the editor, a checklist of publications related to Joyce, and a number of reviews of books related to Joyce and his milieu. Examples of recent scholarly articles include "Joyce's Use of Mathematics in 'Ithaca'" and "Stephen Dedalus's Fantasies of Reality: A Zizekian View." The journal's website provides indexes to the journal going back to volume 35 (1997), lists of books received, the current checklist of articles on James Joyce, and archives of certain materials.

Joyce Studies Annual was published from 1990 to 2003 by the University of Texas Press. It published information on new Joyce manuscripts, reports of conferences, and scholarly articles related to Joyce's work. Back issues of the annual are still available, and the website has tables of contents available for the complete run. Scholarly articles covered such topics as "The Oxymoron of Fidelity in Homer's *Odyssey* and Joyce's *Ulysses*" and "Issy's Mimetic Night Lessons: Interpellation and Resistance in *Finnegans Wake*." In 2007, the annual was picked up by Fordham University Press, which has so far published two volumes (2007 and 2008) of the work. Tables of contents for these volumes can be found on the Fordham University Press website.

The ***Virginia Woolf Bulletin*** is the official newsletter of the Virginia Woolf Society of Great Britain. Its stated purpose is to provide "a forum for all varieties of common readers, many of whom lack the opportunity to be heard." Each issue contains five or six short scholarly pieces, generally less than ten pages in length. Also included are book reviews of new publications concerning Woolf, her work, her circle, and her milieu, and announcements of conferences or other events related to Woolf. The society's website has tables of contents for all issues, going back to number 1. Examples of recent scholarly pieces are "Bloomsbury and the Literature of Empire: Virginia Woolf and her *Voyage Out*" and "A Simple Darting Melody: Birds in the Works of Virginia Woolf."

Virginia Woolf Miscellany is a biannual publication appearing in spring and fall. It may be received as part of the membership benefits of belonging to the International Virginia Woolf Society or may be subscribed to separately. The *Miscellany* typically publishes two or three brief articles of eight hundred to two thousand words as well as reviews of books related to Woolf, illustrations, news items, and conference updates. Some representative recent articles are "Virginia Woolf's Pacifist Narrative Structure" and "The Value of *Three Guineas* in the Twenty-First Century."

The ***Virginia Woolf Quarterly*** has currently suspended publication. It was produced quarterly in 1972, 1973, 1975, and 1980. Special features were sometimes included, such as bibliographies of Hogarth Press titles and the Monks House library, as well as book and film reviews and scholarly articles on Woolf, her work, and her circle. Examples of scholarly articles are "Moments of Vision in Virginia Woolf's Biographies" and "Mr. Forster and Mrs. Woolf: Aspects of the Novelist as Critic."

Woolf Studies Annual has been published yearly since 1995 by Pace University Press. Each volume contains three to nine scholarly articles, each approximately twenty to thirty-five pages in length, that pertain to Virginia Woolf and her milieu. Each *Annual* also has roughly a dozen reviews of new books and a guide to library special collections of interest to researchers. Occasionally, edited transcriptions of previously unpublished manuscripts are presented. The *Annual*'s website posts tables of contents for all volumes.

Yeats: An Annual of Critical and Textual Studies was published through volume 17 in 2003. Each issue would have a number of scholarly essays on the poet W. B. Yeats as well as book reviews, an international bibliography of scholarship on Yeats, and abstracts of recent dissertations concerning Yeats. The final volume includes an index to the articles and book reviews found in all seventeen volumes. Examples of scholarly articles published in this annual are "Yeats: Cast-offs, Non-starters and Gnomic Illegibilities" and "Visits and Revisits: W. B. Yeats at the Municipal Gallery, Dublin."

The similarly titled ***Yeats Annual*** has published sixteen volumes somewhat irregularly between 1982 and 2005. Each of the recent numbers has a special focus, such as "Poems and Contexts," "Yeats' Collaborations," and "Yeats and the Nineties." Each contains full-length scholarly articles, short notes, and reviews. Currently edited by Professor Warwick Gould of the Institute of English Studies at the University of London, available back issues can be obtained through the publisher, Palgrave Macmillan.

The ***Yeats Eliot Review*** generally publishes four to seven scholarly articles, each running five to ten pages long, concerning the lives and works of W. B. Yeats and T. S. Eliot. Short notes and review articles may also occasionally be published. Recent articles have covered such topics as Yeats's vision and the metaphor of chess in Eliot's *The Waste Land*. The journal was formerly titled *T. S. Eliot Review* (ISBN:0318-6342; until 1977) and the *T. S. Eliot Newsletter* (ISBN:0315-1174; until 1975). It is now published semiannually.

GENERAL LITERATURE

Critical Inquiry. University of Chicago Press. 1974–. Quarterly. ISSN: 0093-1896. E-ISSN: 1539-7858. www.journals.uchicago.edu/CI/.

ELH: English Literary History. Johns Hopkins University Press. 1934–. Quarterly. ISSN: 0013-8304. E-ISSN: 1080-6547. www.press.jhu.edu/journals/english_literary_history/index.html.

MLQ: Modern Language Quarterly. Duke University Press. 1940–. Quarterly. ISSN: 0026-7929. E-ISSN: 1527-1943. http://mlq.dukejournals.org.

New Hibernia Review. 1997–. Center for Irish Studies, University of St. Thomas. Quarterly. ISSN: 1092-3977. E-ISSN: 1534-5815. www.stthomas.edu/irishstudies/nhr.htm.

New Literary History. Johns Hopkins University Press. 1969–. Quarterly. ISSN: 0028-6087. E-ISSN: 1080-661X. www.press.jhu.edu/journals/new_literary_history/index.html.

Novel: A Forum on Fiction. Brown University, Department of Literature. 1967–. 3/yr. ISSN: 0029-5132. www.brown.edu/Departments/English/publications/novel.html.

PMLA: Publications of the Modern Language Association of America. Modern Language Association. 1884–. 6/yr. ISSN: 0030-8129. www.mla.org/pmla.

The Review of English Studies. Oxford University Press. 1925–. 5/yr. ISSN: 0034-6551. E-ISSN: 1471-6968. http://res.oxfordjournals.org/.

Tulsa Studies in Women's Literature. University of Tulsa. 1982–. 2/yr. ISSN: 0732-7730. www.utulsa.edu/tswl/.

Victorian Studies. Indiana University Press. 1957–. Quarterly. ISSN: 0042-5222. E-ISSN: 1527-2052. http://inscribe.iupress.org/loi/vic.

Yale Journal of Criticism. Johns Hopkins University Press. 1987–2005. 2/yr. ISSN: 0893-5378. E-ISSN: 1080-6636.

A number of high-quality scholarly journals that cover a wide range of topics and more than one time period also publish articles and information of interest to scholars of modern British literature. Most are published by university English departments in the United States or Britain, and many have their back issues available electronically in *JSTOR*, *Project Muse*, or *Literature Online (LION)*. This list is not to be considered comprehensive, and certainly a thorough search of the *MLAIB* and other appropriate search engines is necessary for doing a complete literature review on any topic.

Critical Inquiry has been published by the University of Chicago since 1974. It is an interdisciplinary journal, including critical articles on all aspects of the arts and humanities. It normally contains between eight and twelve scholarly articles of fifteen to twenty-five pages in length as well as book reviews and critical responses to previous articles. Recent articles of possible interest to modern British literature scholars are "Redeeming Value: Obscenity and Anglo-American Modernism" and "In Praise of the Novel." Tables of contents are available on the website. Several of *Critical Inquiry*'s special issues, such as *Literature and Social Practice* and *"Race," Writing, and Difference*, have been enlarged and republished as books.

ELH: English Literary History is a well-established journal published since 1934 by Johns Hopkins University. Its main emphasis is on major works in British literature from Chaucer forward, but it also reflects upon American literature as well as some world literature and theory. A typical issue contains approximately eight to ten critical essays, each running between twenty and fifty pages long. Recent articles, such as "'Doing Business with Totalitaria': British Late Modernism and the Politics of Reputation" and "Talking with the Dead: Leo Africanus, Esoteric Yeats, and Early Modern Imperialism," may be of interest. *ELH* also occasionally publishes bibliographies of works by significant writers or critics.

MLQ: Modern Language Quarterly focuses on literary history from the Middle Ages to the present. Each issue has four or five scholarly articles between twenty and forty pages long and six or seven review articles running three to five pages in length. Recent articles of possible interest to scholars of British modernism include "T. S. Eliot and the Lost Youth of Modern Poetry" and "Putting the House in Order: Virginia Woolf and Blitz Modernism." The journal occasionally produces special themed issues such as recent ones focused on "Genre and History," "Postcolonialism and the Past," and "Feminism in Time." Electronic full text for volumes 61–65 (1999–2004) is available through *Project Muse*; more recent issues are available through Duke's electronic journals program.

A relative newcomer on the scene, ***New Hibernia Review*** began publishing in 1997 as a multidisciplinary journal of Irish studies, based in the Center for Irish Studies at the University of St. Thomas. The journal concerns itself with Irish life and culture very broadly, both at home and in the diaspora. A typical issue presents eight to ten articles, a selection of new poetry from an Irish author, and two to five book reviews. Because of the flourishing of arts and literature in Ireland during the modernist period, the journal regularly publishes articles of interest to scholars of British modernism. Recently published titles are "Joyce and Yeats: Easter 1916 and the Great War," "Flann O'Brien's Bombshells: *At Swim-Two-Birds* and *The Third Policeman*," and "Louis MacNeice's Struggle with Aristotelian Ethics." Tables of contents for this journal are available electronically from 2001 forward in the *Project Muse* collection.

New Literary History from Johns Hopkins University Press focuses broadly on "theory and interpretation—the reasons for literary change, the definitions of periods, and the evolution of styles, conventions, and genres." The journal usually publishes between eight and fifteen critical articles between ten and thirty pages long. Themed issues are frequent, and a list of "Books Received" is published regularly, although book reviews are not. Titles of articles of possible interest to scholars of British modernism are "Cinecriture: Modernism's Flicker Effect," "Nemo: George Yeats and Her Automatic Script," and "'Rats' Alley': The Great War, Modernism, and the

(Anti)Pastoral Elegy." Tables of contents for this journal are available from 1995 through the present from *Project Muse*.

Novel: A Forum on Fiction publishes specifically on the genre of the novel without regard to geography or time period. It contains both scholarly articles and review articles. Scholarly articles run approximately fifteen to twenty-five pages long, and normally five are printed in each issue. Eight to ten review articles are also included, running one to three pages long. Some issues are special thematic issues; two recent ones of note are "Modernisms" and "Postcolonial Modernisms." Though articles are published on a wide range of topics, some recent examples related to British modernism are "Joyce, the Propheteer," "'New Forms for Our New Sensations': Woolf and the Lesson of Torts," "Seeing the Animal: Colonial Space and Movement in Joseph Conrad's *Lord Jim*," and "Suburbia, Ressentiment, and the End of Empire in *A Passage to India*."

PMLA: Publications of the Modern Language Association of America is the official journal of the Modern Language Association, the leading professional organization for professors of literature and modern languages. This highly regarded publication presents a wide range of articles on all periods and all literatures, although there is a greater preponderance of articles dealing with English literature due to the bulk of the membership practicing in that field. Published six times per year, the January, March, May, and October issues have scholarly essays on literature and language topics (generally twelve to twenty pages long) as well as essays on theory and methodology, the state of the profession, a letters forum, and news items of interest to the readership. The September issue of *PMLA* is the membership directory of the organization, and the November issue is the program issue for the annual convention, which takes place in late December. Recent scholarly essays in *PMLA* specifically dealing with British modernism are "1939–40: Of Virginia Woolf, Gramophones, and Fascism," "The Decomposing Form of Joyce's *Ulysses*," and "T. S. Eliot and the Cultural Divide."

Taking a distinctly historical perspective, ***The Review of English Studies*** covers English literature from the earliest period up to today with a strong focus on historical scholarship rather than interpretive criticism. This is an approach that has fallen somewhat out of favor in academic circles, making this perspective all the more valuable. Published five times a year by Oxford University Press, the journal contains both articles (four to six per issue, running approximately twelve to twenty pages long) and book reviews (twenty to thirty-five per issue, approximately one to three pages in length). Occasionally a special "Note" or slightly longer review article is also published. Articles of potential interest to scholars of British modernism include "Orwell, Tolstoy, and *Animal Farm*," "The Best of Companions: J. W. N. Sullivan,

Aldous Huxley, and the New Physics," and "The British Communist Novel of the 1930s and 1940s: A 'Party of Equals'? (And Does That Matter?)."

Tulsa Studies in Women's Literature focuses on women's writing from all time periods and all languages, although English-language literature seems to predominate. Male authors are also occasionally covered, but only in relation to a woman's writing. Each issue has five or six scholarly articles varying from twelve to twenty-five pages. An occasional "Archives" article is published, in the form of a bibliography or a report of archival research. Five to eight book reviews, two to five pages in length, are presented concerning books of interest to women's studies scholars. A list of "Books Rcccivcd" is also found in each issue. Some recent articles of potential interest to scholars in modern British literature are "Moving Dangerously: Mobility and the Modern Woman," "Revisiting Woolf's Representations of Androgyny: Gender, Race, Sexuality, and Nation," and "'Like a Hook Fits an Eye': Jean Rhys, Ford Madox Ford, and the Imperial Operations of Modernist Mentoring." The *TSWL* website features an index for volumes 1 through volume 27, number 1 (1982–2008).

While it's obvious from its title that ***Victorian Studies*** focuses on an earlier era than the one under consideration here, it's important to remember that chronological boundaries in literature are somewhat artificial and that the influences of earlier generations can be of great importance for understanding the literature of a given time period. Thus, *Victorian Studies* publishes much of interest to the scholar of British literature in the modern age. For example, recent articles have included "The Rival Ladies: Mrs. Ward's *Lady Connie* and Lawrence's *Lady Chatterley's Lover*," "'Natural Evolution' in 'Dramatic Essences' from Robert Browning to T. S. Eliot," and "'Something Highly Contraband': Woolf, Female Sexuality and the Victorians." *Victorian Studies* publishes two to six scholarly articles per issue, each generally running between fifteen and thirty-five pages in length. The journal's website has tables of contents for volumes 42 (1998/1999) to the current issue. *Project Muse* also provides access to tables of contents from volume 42, number 2 (1999/2000) to the present.

The ***Yale Journal of Criticism*** unfortunately ceased publication after volume 18 in 2005. It published high-quality essays on all aspects of the humanities, with a particular emphasis on literary studies and literary theory. Many articles available in their back issues would be of interest to those researching British modernism, such as "Posters, Modernism, Cosmopolitanism: *Ulysses* and World War I Recruiting Posters in Ireland," "Writing and Conversion: Conrad's Modernist Autography," and "Thinking Race in the *Avant Guerre*: Typological Negotiations in Ford and Stein." Each issue normally carried six to thirteen scholarly essays ranging from fifteen to thirty pages long.

Some issues had a special focus on a particular person or topic of cultural significance. *Project Muse* carries tables of contents and archival full text (for subscribers only) for volumes 9 (1996) through 18 (2005).

CONCLUSION

This chapter has highlighted some of the journals that will be most useful to researchers of British modernism, including general titles as well as those specific to the era or to particular modernist authors. Although literature scholars tend to gravitate toward book-length monographs, a knowledge of the journal literature of the field is imperative for anyone doing serious research. Journals are published more quickly than monographs, and it is in these publications that new research is often first published. Journals are also an important means of keeping up to date concerning new books published on topics of interest, calls for papers for conferences or edited volumes, news items, and information and reports on conferences or special events. Regularly reading a selection of relevant journals will help you to remain informed on current trends in scholarship and gain familiarity with others working in the field.

NOTE

1. See, for example, John Budd, "Characteristics of Written Scholarship in *American Literature*: A Citation Study," *Library and Information Science Research* 8 (1986): 189–211; Rebecca Watson-Boone, "The Information Needs and Habits of Humanities Scholars," *RQ* 34, no. 2 (1994): 203–16; and Jennifer Wolfe Thompson, "The Death of the Scholarly Monograph in the Humanities? Citation Patterns in Literary Scholarship," *Libri* 52 (2002): 121–36.

Chapter Six

Contemporary Reviews

One of the advantages of being a scholar of modern British literature is that the modernists lived and worked in an age not too far removed from our own, and so at least some of the landmarks of that time are still familiar to us. This is particularly true when it comes to reviews. If we were to look at what most people would consider the top English-language review sources today, the list would look very similar to those with which the modernists would be familiar. The *Times* (London) and the *Times Literary Supplement* (*TLS*) in Britain and the *New York Times* and *New York Times Review of Books* in the United States would top the list on both sides of the Atlantic, then and now. Of course, reviews appeared in a range of contemporary newspapers and standard periodicals during the time the British modernists were writing. Add to the mix the variety of little magazines (small, privately produced, often short-lived literary and political journals) that were publishing reviews as well as creative work during this period, and you get a sense of how well covered any newly published work could be. The nearness to our own time period also helps to ensure that copies of most of these review sources remain extant and at least somewhat accessible.

When it came to criticism and reviewing, there was a bit of an incestuous quality among the modernists. Many of them were friends or at least acquaintances, and they often published one another's writing in their magazines and through their presses. Most of them were critics as well. To give one example of the importance of reviewing to a writer's career, we can look at Virginia Woolf. Some of her earliest published writing efforts as a young woman were book reviews published in women's magazines. As she became more established as a writer, she also became a fixture as a reviewer at *TLS*. She reviewed, and was reviewed by, other major writers of the period. This doesn't mean, however, that they were uncritical of one another for fear of offense. To the contrary, there has been some debate on the level of objectivity these writers could hold toward one another. The general consensus is that they were often harshly critical, seeing the other's work through the lens of their own ideas of the modernist project. Virginia Woolf was cautious and somewhat tenuous in her praise of James Joyce's *Ulysses*, while her friend T. S. Eliot often undervalued her work because it fell outside of his own brand of modernist literary innovation. Eliot certainly became highly regarded as a literary critic in his own right, and both he and Woolf are still read today for their criticism as well as their literary pursuits. In one sense, modernism can be seen as a collaborative effort between writers and critics, each side of the equation influencing the other and bringing new forms and ideas to the table.

INDEXES TO CONTEMPORARY REVIEWS FOR BRITISH MODERNISM

Book Review Digest. 1905–. New York: Wilson, 1905–. www.hwwilson.com/NewDDs/wn.htm.

Book Review Digest Retrospective: 1905–1982. New York: Wilson. www.hwwilson.com/databases/brdig_retro.htm.

Farber, Evan I., ed. *Combined Retrospective Index to Book Reviews in Humanities Journals, 1802–1974*. 10 vols. Woodbridge, CT: Research Publications, 1982–1984.

New York Times Book Review Index, 1896–1970. 5 vols. New York: Arno Press, 1973.

New York Times Index for the Published News. 1851–. New York: New York Times, 1913–. New York: R. R. Bowker, 1966–.

Official Index to the Times. London: Times Publishing Co., 1914–1957.

Palmer's Index to the Times Newspaper. London: Samuel Palmer, 1868–1943.

ProQuest Historical Newspapers. Ann Arbor, MI: ProQuest. www.proquest.com/products_pq/descriptions/pq-hist-news.shtml.

Sader, Marion, ed. *Comprehensive Index to English-Language Little Magazines, 1890–1970*. 8 vols. Millwood, NY: Kraus-Thomson, 1976.

Times Digital Archive. Gale. www.gale.cengage.com/DigitalCollections/products/Times/.

Times Literary Supplement Index, 1902–1985. 6 vols. Reading, England: Research Publications, 1978–1986. www.tls.psmedia.com/default.htm.

Book Review Digest is one of the premier indexes for literature-related reviews. Started in 1905, it provides access to reviews of English-language books (including fiction, published plays, and collections of poetry) published or distributed in the United States. The digest is arranged alphabetically by author's last name and then by title of the work reviewed. A short synopsis of the work is presented, followed by short citations for reviews of the work. There are usually brief excerpts republished from the reviews so that the reader can get a sense of the flavor of them, such as whether they are favorable or negative. Indexes to titles of works reviewed and general subjects make it easy to locate works if the author is not immediately known. *Book Review Digest* indexes major review sources such as the *Times Literary Supplement* (*TLS*), the *New York Times Book Review* (*NYTBR*), *Booklist*, and *Bookman*, as well as respected periodicals and reviews such as the *Dial*, *New Republic*, *Nation*, *North American Review*, *Weekly Review*, and *Yale Review*. Currently the *Book Review Digest* is published ten times per year, but for the years covering contemporary reviews of the works of British modernist writers, most libraries will have retained only the annual cumulative volumes. If the approximate year of publication for a work is known, this will make it fairly easy to home in on particular volumes that contain reviews of it. Generally speaking, the *Book Review Digest* does not include reviews published more than eighteen months after the initial release of the book reviewed.

H. W. Wilson, the publisher of *Book Review Digest*, now offers an electronic version of the index as well as the traditional print volumes. *Book Review Digest Plus* offers the advantage of linking to the full text of the review when available electronically. The contents of this database go back only to 1983, however. Of more interest to those seeking contemporary reviews of modernist literature is the Wilson product ***Book Review Digest Retrospective: 1905–1982***, which takes the retrospective coverage back to the first volume of the work. It has information concerning more than three hundred thousand books that were reviewed in over five hundred popular magazines, newspapers, academic journals, and library review media. It also allows the user to link to the full text of reviews, when available.

The ***Combined Retrospective Index to Book Reviews in Humanities Journals, 1802–1974*** was intended not to duplicate *Book Review Digest* but rather to expand and supplement it. It provides access by title to more than 500,000 reviews from 157 humanities journals, including many more scholarly titles than those covered in *Book Review Digest*. Since the content goes back to the early nineteenth century, this ensures the inclusion of reviews of books written by British modernist writers in the latter half of that century. Volumes 1 through 9 contain the author index, arranged alphabetically by author's last name. Under each name, titles of the author's works are arranged alphabetically, with short citations for the review sources under each. Unlike the *Book Review Digest*, no summaries or excerpts are reproduced. What the *Combined Retrospective Index* lacks in this regard is compensated for by the fact that it is more compact and that there is only one area to consult for a given author's work. Volume 10 is the title index for all works and refers the reader to the correct author's name to consult for reviews of that particular work. A "Quick-Reference User's Guide" can be found at the front of each volume for additional guidance in the use of the tool. Obviously for works published prior to 1905, the *Combined Retrospective Index* is the correct tool to consult; for modernist works published after that date, both the *Combined Retrospective Index* and the *Book Review Digest* should be used.

The ***Times Literary Supplement Index*** and the ***New York Times Book Review Index, 1896–1970*** are the two most prestigious book review sources on either side of the Atlantic. Because of their prominence, both are included in many review indexes. However, some scholars may find it useful to have easy access to all the materials reviewed in these two sources. Luckily, the five volumes of the *New York Times Book Review Index, 1896–1970* and the six volumes of the *Times Literary Supplement Index* handily cover the majority of the time period we have defined as British modernism. Each volume of the *New York Times Book Review Index, 1896–1970* contains a separate index. Volume 1 is the author index, providing an alphabetical listing of the authors of the works reviewed; volume 2 is the title index, for titles of the works reviewed; volume 3 is the byline index, for authors of the reviews themselves; volume 4 is the subject index; and volume 5 is the category index, allowing access to reviews by literary category, such as poetry or short stories. At the beginning of each volume is an introduction and an abbreviation key to aid the researcher in using the work and interpreting its records.

The five-volume *Times Literary Supplement Index* roughly covers the period of British modernism. Two volumes index materials from 1902 to 1939, and three volumes index materials from 1940 to 1980. Two supplements also expand indexing for the *TLS* for 1980 to 1985 and 1986 to 1990, which are useful for reviews of later secondary works concerning British modernist authors. The arrangement of the *Times Literary Supplement Index* is slightly more complicated than that of the *New York Times Book Review Index*. There are three categories of entries, all included in one alphabetical index. Different typefaces help to differentiate the categories, especially when the main entries are the same. These categories are personal names, title entries, and subject entries. For personal names of authors, the name can be located in the alphabetic index, where the main entry is followed by a listing of the titles of works by that author for which there are reviews, each designated by the page number and year the review appeared. Many British modernists are listed as subject entries as well as authors, so books reviewed that contain information about them or articles appearing in *TLS* that reference them can be located by page number and year as well. The Gale Group now offers a searchable electronic version of the *Times Literary Supplement Index* called the *Times Literary Supplement Centenary Archive*, which has *TLS* reviews from 1902 to 1990 and links to facsimile copies of the publication (http://www.tls.psmedia.com/default.htm).

For reviews of books published prior to the starting date ranges of the *New York Times Book Review Index* and the *Times Literary Supplement Index*, or for reviews printed in the newspapers themselves, researchers should consult the indexes to the *Times* (London) and the *New York Times* proper. The ***New York Times Index for the Published News*** goes back to 1851, providing full coverage of late nineteenth-century reviews of the British modernists. The ***Official Index to the Times*** begins with content from 1914, but prior to that, ***Palmer's Index to the Times Newspaper*** indexes material back to 1790. It should also be noted that electronic full-text collections of both the *New York Times* and the *Times* are now available. ProQuest offers full-text access to the *New York Times* back to 1851 through their ***ProQuest Historical Newspapers*** collection (http://www.proquest.com/products_pq/descriptions/pq-hist-news.shtml), and Gale is offering the ***Times Digital Archive***, which has full-text content back to 1785 (http://www.gale.cengage.com/DigitalCollections/products/Times/). These resources are all discussed in greater depth in chapter 7, concerning period journals and newspapers.

Marion Sader's ***Comprehensive Index to English-Language Little Magazines, 1890–1970*** is a massive eight-volume work that provides indexing to material, including book reviews, appearing in over one hundred English-language little magazines. These small magazines usually had limited circulation and were often overlooked by other indexing sources. Approximately half of the titles covered were published in the United States, with the remainder published in Britain or the Commonwealth nations. Some representative titles are the *Egoist*, *Little Review*, *Poetry*, and Yeats's short-lived *Arrow*, but not the *Dial*, which was one of the few little magazines indexed by *Book Review Digest*. The index is arranged alphabetically by authors' names. For a given modernist, a list of works written by that author follows the name. Book reviews are arranged as author, title, the designation "review," and a short citation. There is also a list of works about the author, where applicable, which will list reviews of these books as well, arranged in the same manner as described above.

Additional tools are available that index late nineteenth- and early twentieth-century periodicals and newspapers and that facilitate access to contemporary reviews of the works by British modernists. These can be found by visiting any large academic library and consulting a reference librarian. Starting with the resources listed above, covering general and scholarly periodicals, newspapers, book review digests, and little magazines, any researcher will get an excellent start on understanding the range of critical reception to a given work.

CONTEMPORARY REVIEWS OF INDIVIDUAL AUTHORS

Clarke, Graham, ed. *T. S. Eliot: Critical Assessments*. 4 vols. London: C. Helm, 1990.

Givens, Seon, ed. *James Joyce: Two Decades of Criticism by Eugene Jolas* [and others]. New York: Vanguard Press, 1963.

Majumdar, Robin, and Allen McLaurin, eds. *Virginia Woolf: The Critical Heritage*. London: Routledge, 1997.

Temple, Ruth Zabriskie, and Martin Tucker, eds. *A Library of Literary Criticism: Modern British Literature*. 3 vols. New York: F. Ungar, 1966.

Although it is fairly easy to track down the criticism and reviews of the works of British modernists in the various newspapers, periodicals, and books in which they appear, there is often such a plethora of materials that they can be difficult to manage. For this reason, it can be helpful to have a range of reviews and critical assessments for a single author pulled together in one easy-to-access package, particularly if the editors of such a work are knowledgeable and selective regarding what is included. Such collections of critical assessments are most likely to be available for major figures of the era, although some group or general assessments can be found. The works that follow are representative examples of critical assessment collections for three major modern British writers as well as a broader collection of criticism on a range of modern British writers.

Virginia Woolf: The Critical Heritage is an excellent example of this kind of critical resource. It is one volume of the Routledge *Critical Heritage* series, which reproduces significant contemporary responses to writers' works. The series also has volumes for other major modernists such as Eliot, Conrad, Forster, Auden, and Lawrence. The Woolf volume, edited by Woolf bibliographer Robin Majumdar and Allen McLaurin, contains reproductions in full of 135 contemporary critical reviews of Woolf's works. They are arranged chronologically, starting with an unsigned review of her first novel, *The Voyage Out*, which appeared in the *Times Literary Supplement* in 1915, and ending with a series of reviews of her final novel *Between the Acts*, appearing after Woolf's death in 1941. In between are reviews by E. M. Forster,

Desmond McCarty, Rebecca West, Edwin Muir, and other critics of note, concerning all of Woolf's major published works. The volume also provides a brief select bibliography and an index for journal and periodical titles and critics' names.

Another valuable series that reproduces contemporary reviews and criticism of selected British modernists along with much additional valuable information is the *Critical Assessments of Writers in English Series*, published by Christopher Helm. These works focus on canonical British and American authors from various time periods; the British modernists in the series in addition to Eliot are Conrad, Lawrcncc, Woolf, Forster, and Yeats. ***T. S. Eliot: Critical Assessments*** was the first of the series and can serve as a model for what each contribution contains. There are four volumes, each arranged chronologically. Volume 1 comprises memories, interviews, and contemporary responses, including reviews of collected editions of Eliot's work. Volume 2 focuses on Eliot's early poems and *The Waste Land*, reproducing early reviews and commentary as well as later critical essays and assessments. Volume 3 is similarly structured and considers *Ash Wednesday*, *The Four Quartets*, and Eliot's drama. Volume 4 has additional criticism as well as general assessments of Eliot's contribution to literature. The particular value of these collections lies in their breadth of coverage. While it is impossible to be fully comprehensive, an attempt has been made to bring together in one package a wide range of critical views and assessments of the writer's work.

Beyond series such as the two just mentioned, there are also individual monographs focusing on the contemporary critical assessment of individual writers. An example is ***James Joyce: Two Decades of Criticism . . .*** edited by Seon Givens, which brings together a selection of significant criticism and responses to Joyce's work that are roughly contemporary to the writer's life. Some of the essays reproduced here were written during Joyce's lifetime, such as T. S. Eliot's "*Ulysses*, Order and Myth," which first appeared in the *Dial* in 1923, and Edmund Wilson's "The Dream of H. C. Earwicker," which appeared in the *New Republic* in 1939. Others were written closely following the occasion of Joyce's death, such as Frank Budgen's "Joyce's Chapters of Going Forth by Day," which first appeared in *Horizon* in 1941, and Eugene Jolas's "My Friend James Joyce" from the *Partisan Review* in 1941. A number of the other essays reproduced here were written in the decade following Joyce's demise, as Joyce's critical reputation solidified and scholars had more time to wrestle with his often difficult works. These include James T. Farrell's "Joyce's *A Portrait of the Artist as a Young Man*," originally published in the December 1944 and January 1945 issues of the *New York Times Book Review*, and Joseph Campbell's 1946 piece from *Chimera*, "Finnegan the Wake." A few of the critical essays in the volume are published here for the first time, rounding out the critical response to Joyce's work. Givens's volume also contains a bibliography of both primary works and secondary works published since 1948, although both are necessarily inferior to the later, more complete bibliographies of Joyce mentioned in chapter 4.

Temple and Tucker's ***A Library of Literary Criticism: Modern British Literature*** is slightly different in that it provides excerpts of selected criticism, including contemporary reviews, for some four hundred modern British writers. The entries are arranged alphabetically by the author's last name; each has a short bibliography of major primary works along with excerpts from the reviews and criticism concerning those works. There are also detailed copyright acknowledgments concerning the excerpts, a cross-referencing index, and an index to critics' names. Thus it is easy to quickly ascertain Virginia Woolf's reaction to James Joyce or F. R. Leavis's take on D. H. Lawrence. Two supplemental volumes were published in 1975 and 1985. These update the work with additional authors and more recent criticism; the second supplement in particular also covers additional retrospective criticism. The value of this work lies in its presentation of criticism of a range of modernist authors, even those who may be considered more obscure. Seeing such an overview of critical response to a writer's work gives a picture of its general acceptance and how the criticism may have changed over time. It also makes for easy comparison to critical reaction to other authors of the same time period. Although full reviews are not reproduced in this work, the excerpts generally provide enough sense of the criticism's tone to judge whether it is worthwhile to pursue the full text.

It will be particularly easy to find collections of contemporary reviews and criticism for major modern British authors. However, it may be possible to find such works related to minor figures as well. Search the library catalog and *WorldCat* to discover these types of items owned by your institution or elsewhere. A good starting search strategy would be *cummings and critical*, which will also bring up critical biographies and more recent collections of critical essays but will usually be a small enough set of results to skim through easily.

CONCLUSION

When conducting literature research, it is important to remember that the body of knowledge on any particular topic is cumulative rather than successive. In other words, newer ideas and opinions do not necessarily supersede older ones. A more recent publication date on a work of literary criticism does not automatically translate into "better" or "more accurate," as it might in scientific fields. In fact, some seminal or classic older works of literary criticism remain timeless standards. Using the resources in this chapter will help scholars become acquainted with the first critical reactions to the works they are studying, providing a foundation upon which to compare and consider succeeding opinions. Luckily, scholars of modern British literature have comparatively easy means of finding the early review materials of their era. In the next chapter, we'll consider ways of accessing the period journals and newspapers in which these reviews were usually published.

Chapter Seven

Modern British Journals, Newspapers, and Literary Magazines

> If you want to know any fact about politics you must read at least three different papers, compare at least three different versions of the same fact, and come in the end to your own conclusion. Hence the three daily papers on my table.
>
> —Virginia Woolf's "daughter of an educated man" in *Three Guineas*, 1938[1]

The publishing industry in Britain in the late nineteenth and early to mid-twentieth century was extensive and diverse. In addition to the *Times* of London and other newspapers of national stature, there were a large number of regional and local newspapers published as dailies or weeklies. In contrast to our own age of media consolidation, the British modernists had access to an abundant number of daily and weekly newspapers, each expressing a unique editorial perspective and often a distinct political slant. Virginia Woolf, herself a daughter of an educated man, knew the importance of not relying on a single source of information for current events. She also knew the emotional impact of news photography and could make the judgment that "there is a very clear connection between culture and intellectual liberty and those photographs of dead bodies and ruined houses [from the Spanish Civil War]."[2] The British modernist writers were intelligent, educated men and women who followed the current events of their day, from the Dreyfus affair in the late nineteenth century and the Russian Revolution in 1917 to World War I, World War II, and the Spanish Civil War in between. To have access to the contemporary news reports of those times is to be immersed in the milieu in which the modernists lived and worked.

As mentioned in chapter 6, "Contemporary Reviews," newspapers and their associated literary supplements also were the sources of ample book reviews and critical commentary on the literature of the day. Specialty and popular periodicals also showed the influence of the modernists. The political and literary weekly *Athenaeum* published work by Katherine Mansfield, Virginia Woolf, Thomas Hardy, and T. S. Eliot. The British version of *Vogue* promoted popular knowledge of literary trends in addition to its fashion and lifestyle advice for the "new woman." Richard Aldington was the principal book reviewer for *Vogue* in the 1920s and also contributed essays on literary topics such as the work of T. S. Eliot and free verse; Aldous Huxley and Virginia Woolf were contributors as well.[3] Such journals reflected not just the political opinions or the popular feminine interests of the day but the incursion of literary and artistic modernism into each of those realms.

Another particularly important part of the publishing history of this time period is the phenomenon of the little magazines, which were generally small, limited-circulation journals focusing on literature and art. Although these journals were frequently in debt and often disappeared after only a few issues, their lasting impact on literary and artistic modernism stands in sharp contrast to their ephemeral nature. The roots of the little magazines of the early twentieth-century modernists can be found in publications of earlier cultural movements that placed themselves in an adversarial relationship to dominant literary and artistic trends. In the mid-nineteenth century, the Pre-Raphaelites felt themselves outside the main current of Victorian sensibilities around them and published four issues of *The Germ* in 1850. In the late nineteenth century, the decadent movement also found itself in a countercultural position to the dominant Victorian society. *The Yellow Book*, published from 1894 to 1897 and arising from the literary and artistic circles surrounding Oscar Wilde, is probably the best-known little magazine of that period. The proponents of aestheticism in the same time period felt themselves equally at odds with both the decadents and the literary establishment and produced another significant little magazine, *The Savoy*, from 1895 to 1896.

In the early twentieth century, there was a further explosion of literary schools and movements in Britain, each striving to create something "new" in reaction to the literature of the previous century. Among these were the Imagists, the Vorticists, and those movements rather awkwardly named for the reigns of post-Victorian royalty, the Edwardians (after Edward VII, 1901–1909) and the Georgians (after George V, 1910–1936). Feeling themselves cut out of the stuffy mainstream literary journals of the day, the up-and-coming British modernists created their own journals in rapid succession. A number of these little magazines were published and died, some lasting only a few issues. All seemed to contribute something to the energy and creative spirit of the times, and most involved a revolving door of now-famous writers, artists, and critics associated with modernism.

Probably the two most influential of the "littles" were the *English Review*, started by Ford Madox Hueffer (later Ford Madox Ford) in 1908, and the *Criterion* (later the *New Criterion* and the *Monthly Criterion*), started by T. S. Eliot in 1922. Hueffer maintained control over the *English Review* for only two years (although under changing editorships it turned out to be one of the most long-lived little magazines), but during that time period it had a profound influence on the literary scene. Hueffer not only published the best of the older generation of writers (Hardy, James, Wells) but is credited with discovering the "genius schoolteacher" D. H. Lawrence and promoting the increasingly influential American poet Ezra Pound. Eliot's post-World War I *Criterion* famously published Pound's *Cantos* and excerpts from Joyce's *Finnegans Wake* and exercised an international influence on not only literature but arts, criticism, and politics. An excellent overview of the British little magazines and their influence in general can be found in Malcolm Bradbury's essay on "Modernism and the Magazines."[4]

The resources that follow will provide insight into the coverage and content of the little magazines as well as the more mainstream newspapers and magazines of the modern British era.

FINDING ARTICLES

Bloomfield, B. C. *An Author Index to Selected British "Little Magazines" 1930–1939*. London: Mansell, 1976.

[*Guardian*] *Digital Archive*. http://archive.guardian.co.uk/.

Historical Newspapers. Chadwyck-Healy. http://historynews.chadwyck.com/moreinfo/htxview?template=basic.htx&content=about.htx.

Modernist Journals Project. www.modjourn.org.

Modernist Magazines Project. www.cts.dmu.ac.uk/exist/mod_mag/index.htm.

Official Index to the Times. London: Times Publishing Co., 1914–1957.

Palmer's Index to the Times Newspaper. London: Samuel Palmer, 1868–1943.

Periodicals Index Online. http://pio.chadwyck.co.uk/marketing.do.

ProQuest Historical Newspapers. Ann Arbor, MI: ProQuest. www.proquest.com/products_pq/descriptions/pq-hist-news.shtml.

Readers' Guide to Periodical Literature. H. W. Wilson. www.hwwilson.com/databases/Readersg.htm.

Sader, Marion, ed. *Comprehensive Index to English-Language Little Magazines, 1890–1970*. 8 vols. Millwood, NY: Kraus-Thomson, 1976.

Times Archive. http://archive.timesonline.co.uk/tol/archive/.

The Times Digital Archive, 1785–1985. Gale-Cengage Learning. www.gale.cengage.com/DigitalCollections/products/Times/.

Subject access to newspapers and periodicals for the modernist era can be found in a number of ways. In the previous chapter, guidelines were given for finding book reviews in the major newspapers of the time period. The same tools and similar techniques can be used for finding newspaper articles by subject. Once again, the *Times* of London is considered the British newspaper of record and thus has the longest-standing history of indexing. Between ***Palmer's Index to the Times Newspaper*** and the ***Official Index to the Times***, the entire run of the *Times* through the modern era (and beyond) can be traced. Both of these works may be found in many libraries in print, microfilm, or CD-ROM formats. In addition to being searchable by bylines for article writers, there is subject access of a general nature, including categories for stories involving "accidents," "deaths," or "books," and for specific news stories such as "crisis in China."

The ***Historical Newspapers*** collection from Chadwyck-Healy consists of searchable electronic editions of both *Palmer's Index* and the *Official Index*, combined with the *Historical Index to the New York Times* and full text of the *Times* from the late eighteenth and early nineteenth centuries. The searchable full text of the *Times* available from Gale-Cengage, ***The Times Digital Archive, 1785–1985***, will be of more interest to modernist scholars due to the full-text coverage of the modernist period. Simple keyword searching is available in this product for fast results based on key concepts. Advanced search options are also available, which allow the searcher to combine or exclude search terms and to narrow results. It is also searchable by author and by image as well as by type of article (news, editorial, obituary, etc.). All advertising is also searchable and accessible in the full text, which can be interesting in terms of booksellers' and publishers' ads from the period. You can also browse through the issues page by page, as if accessing a print version of the newspaper. Both of these resources are subscription-based products that may be available at some libraries but that may be inaccessible to outside researchers. The good news for independent researchers and scholars whose home institutions do not subscribe to any of these products is that the ***Times Archive*** online offers searchable, full-text access to two hundred years of the *Times*, from 1785 to 1985, to individuals at a reasonable price. This service features the same full-text access, with either full-page or article-specific results, as the commercial products. This online archive and the *Guardian/Observer* online archive mentioned below are described in further detail in chapter 10, "Web Resources."

Another major British newspaper, the *Guardian*, and its sister publication, the *Observer*, also have historical collections available that fully cover the modernist era. ***ProQuest Historical Newspapers***, which features searchable, full-text digital access to historical collections of a number of major newspapers printed in the United States (including the *New York Times* going back to 1851), offers the same digital access to these British publications. The content of the *Guardian* (formerly the *Manchester Guardian*) is from 1821 to 2003, and for the *Observer*, the world's oldest Sunday newspaper, content runs from 1791 to 2003. Both papers are fully indexed and searchable by author, title, and date, as well as by keyword and article type. As with the *Times*, the website for the *Guardian* also has a *Digital Archive*, which provides free searching of the archives for the *Guardian* from 1821 to 2000 (soon to move forward to 2003) and to the *Observer* from 1791 to 2000 (also to move forward to 2003). Access to the full text of articles from both papers and the ability to download them can be purchased by individuals on a timed basis from twenty-four hours to one month. The modernist era content is fully accessible through the newspapers' archival service, allowing for increased ease of access for researchers to these primary news source materials. More newspapers around the world will most likely take advantage of current technology and start to make similar high-quality reproductions of their back issues available for free or reasonable cost via the Internet.

Popular and specialty magazines, journals, and other serial publications were published by the thousands in Britain during the modern era. Probably the most useful and comprehensive tool for discovering content within these publications is the database available from Chadwyck-Healy called ***Periodicals Index Online*** (*PIO*), formerly *Periodicals Contents Index* (and before that, *Cumulative Contents Index*). It includes indexing to a variety of late nineteenth-century and twentieth-century journals and magazines. Geographic coverage is extensive; while the majority of the over five thousand periodicals originated in the United Kingdom or the United States, titles from Europe, Africa, Asia, and Latin America may also be found. Chadwyck-Healy also offers the option for add-on components to the database, consisting of various collections of full-text articles that link to the indexing in *PIO*. Marketed as *Periodicals Archives Onlin*e (*PAO*), this Chadwyck-Healy product offers options for various "general" and "liberal arts" collections, as well as "themed" collections focused on topics such as literature and literary studies, history and historical studies, or philosophy, religion, and theology. Two other add-on components, the *British Periodicals Collections I and II*, mainly consist of late nineteenth-century journals.

Another good index to general periodical literature is the ***Readers' Guide to Periodical Literature***, published by H. W. Wilson. Many public and academic libraries still hold print copies of this index. Wilson also makes the *Readers' Guide* available electronically; the retrospective portion of the online version has content from the years 1890 to 1982. This provides detailed indexing of some 375 magazines published in the United States, many of them within the modernist era. The focus on U.S. publications makes this tool somewhat less relevant to studies in British literature. As we have seen, however, there was considerable interest in modern British writers among the American reading public, and they are definitely covered within this literature.

Bloomfield's ***An Author Index to Selected British "Little Magazines" 1930–1939*** provides author indexing for more than seventy little magazines published in Britain during the decade of the 1930s. Most of these titles were relatively fleeting, appearing for only a handful of issues or less. Others, such as *Twentieth Century*, managed to publish for several years running. The index, which contains approximately eleven thousand entries, is arranged alphabetically by the authors' last names. Short citations are given for each author's contributions and identify the little magazine in which they appeared by means of a title abbreviation (listed at the front of the book). Where appropriate there is also a genre code indicating whether the work was poetry, fiction, or illustration. For book reviews, the author and title of the work reviewed are given in brackets if this is not obvious from the title. The emphasis of the work is definitely upon the authors whose work appeared in these particular little magazines. However, some limited subject access may be acquired by two means. First, there is a category listing for "Films reviewed," which gathers together all of the film criticism appearing in these 1930s little magazines. Each article is listed alphabetically by title, followed by the name of the author of the review. The author's name must then be referred to in order to obtain the complete citation. The second form of limited subject access appears when an author not only has work appearing in a little magazine, but has his or her published work reviewed by someone else in a little magazine. Due to the time frame of this reference tool, there are contributions both by and about the major "high" modernists such as Eliot, Joyce, Lawrence, Woolf, and Yeats, and also substantial contributions from and about the younger generation of modernists, most notably Auden, Isherwood, and Spender. Thus the entry for Stephen Spender, for example, has references to all of the works he published in various little magazines, followed by a listing of his own published works that are reviewed there. The review listings again require that the user refer to the listing of the name of the author of the review for a complete citation.

Two other indexes to materials published in little magazines may also be of interest to researchers in British modernism. The scope of Sader's ***Comprehensive Index to English-Language Little Magazines, 1890–1970*** is both a wider time period and a larger geographic area than Bloomfield's work. This massive work indexes one hundred little magazines published in English; a little over half of the titles were published in the United States, with the remainder mainly British or Commonwealth titles. Many contemporary, postmodern-era literary magazines are included in this index, but the broader time frame also means there are some significant modernist titles here not found in Bloomfield, such as *The Egoist* (1914–1919), *Little Review* (1914–1929), and *Arrow* (1906–1909). The *Comprehensive Index* does not have subject access to the magazines covered. It is arranged alphabetically by author's last name, with subsections listing "Works by" the particular authors and "Works about" them. The "Works by" subsections include the author's name, title of the work, genre of the work, and a complete citation. Genres identified are review, poem, letter, article, prose, fiction, and miscellaneous. "Works about" are arranged by name of the author of the article, title, the genre "review article," and a complete citation.

One aspect of the ***Modernist Magazines Project*** is an online index to thirty-eight significant little magazines from the modernist era. The larger project is directed by Professor Peter Brooker of the University of Sussex and Professor Andrew Thacker of De Montfort University, both in Britain. In addition to the index, the project will produce a three-volume scholarly work called *Critical and Cultural History of Modernist Magazines* and an anthology of reproductions of primary materials from the little magazines along with critical and contextual information. The *Modernist Magazines Project* has received major funding from the Arts and Humanities Research Council (AHRC) of Britain for the years 2006 to 2010. The online index has tables of contents for all issues of the little magazines covered, with the ability to sort the titles alphabetically or chronologically. No subject indexing is available, but the site does have an alphabetical author index and a search engine that allows keyword searching in either the author or the title field. Thus a search for *Yeats* in the author index turns up four variants of the author's name, with links to the works published under each one. A title search for *Yeats* returns one result, an elegy by Harry Brown published in *Twentieth Century* following Yeats's death. The *Modernist Magazines Project* has some overlap (six titles) with the ***Modernist Journals Project***, an online project related to little magazines, which provides tables of contents as well as full text of articles and creative works from thirteen modernist journals. This project, begun at Brown University in the United States, will be considered in more detail in chapter 8, concerning digital and microform collections.

IDENTIFYING NEWSPAPERS AND PERIODICALS

British Library, Newspaper Library. *Catalogue of the Newspaper Library, Colindale.* 8 vols. London: British Museum Publications Ltd. for the British Library Board, 1975.

British Library Newspapers Collection. www.bl.uk/reshelp/inrrooms/blnewspapers/newscat/newscat.html (accessed 4 February 2009).

Stanton, Michael N. *English Literary Journals, 1900–1950: A Guide to Information Sources.* Detroit: Gale, 1982.

Stewart, James D., Muriel E. Hammond, and Erwin Saenger, eds. *British Union-Catalogue of Periodicals: A Record of the Periodicals of the World, from the Seventeenth Century to the Present Day, in British Libraries.* 4 vols. London: Butterworths Scientific Publications, 1955–1958.

Sullivan, Alvin. *British Literary Magazines.* 4 vols. Westport, CT: Greenwood Press, 1983–1986.

Titus, Edna Brown, ed. *Union List of Serials in Libraries of the United States and Canada.* 3rd ed. 5 vols. New York: H. W. Wilson, 1965.

Toase, Charles A., gen. ed. *Bibliography of British Newspapers.* 6 vols. to date. London: Library Association; British Library, 1975–.

Watson, George, ed. *New Cambridge Bibliography of English Literature.* 5 vols. New York: Cambridge University Press, 1969–1977.

WorldCat. Dublin, OH: OCLC. www.oclc.org/firstsearch/.

While there is no single comprehensive list of newspapers and periodicals published in Britain during the modern era, a large number of tools can help a researcher get started on identifying and accessing serial publications that may be of interest. In addition to the electronic union catalogs mentioned in chapter 3, there are print bibliographies, checklists, and guides that give insight into the range of serial publications produced during this time period. "Serial publications" in this context are defined as printed works that are published over a period of time, usually at regular intervals. Thus a weekly or daily newspaper could be described as a "serial publication," as could a monthly or quarterly magazine. The definition excludes books (although some books are indeed parts of series of books published on related topics); another distinguishing characteristic of serials is their more ephemeral nature—newsprint and journals with paper covers have greater challenges in withstanding the ravages of time than do hardcover books or even some paperbacks. For practical purposes, the tools here are meant to address serial publications such as newspapers, journals, popular magazines, and special "literary" magazines that were intended to be published on an ongoing basis. There is considerable overlap in titles addressed in many of these tools, just as there are most likely omissions of some items as well. However, with the diligent use of a variety of the resources described here, a good picture of the most widely available periodical literature of the modernist era can be obtained.

Stanton's ***English Literary Journals, 1900–1950: A Guide to Information Sources*** focuses on a variety of periodical literature that Stanton defines as "literary journalism." This includes everything from the most self-consciously literary little magazines, to the *Times Literary Supplement*, to political magazines with significant literary content such as *Punch* and the *Nation*. As the name of the work indicates, titles selected for inclusion are limited to those published in England during the first half of the twentieth century. Stanton also excludes any titles that published fewer than six issues. The one exception to this rule is the little magazine *BLAST*, because of the significance of its two massive issues for presenting the theory and manifestos of the Vorticism movement and the work of Wyndham Lewis and Ezra Pound. *English Literary Journals, 1900–1950* is made up of two parts. Part 1 lists the journals themselves in alphabetical order by title. Each entry also provides the years the journal was published, any subtitles or other title information, the frequency of publication, and the names of the editor(s) associated with the work. There is also a brief overview of each work, noting its significance and contribution to the literary landscape of the time. Part 2 is a bibliography of secondary works concerning these resources in "literary journalism." It is divided into units consisting of general references to the journals, background readings related to the times and the genres, autobiographical and biographical writings as well as collections of letters relating to individuals associated with the journals, and critical and historical commentary on individual journals. There are two indexes: one for authors and titles of individual works and the other for journal titles and personal names associated with them. The strengths of this work are the breadth of its scope and its extensive bibliography of secondary sources.

Sullivan's ***British Literary Magazines*** covers similar territory but provides more depth by focusing specifically on literary magazines and containing more detailed information. It also has more breadth in looking at Britain as a whole and spanning a much longer time period, from 1698 to 1984. Sullivan's work consists of four volumes, the last two of which have information of interest to scholars of modern British literature: volume 3, *The Victorian and Edwardian Age, 1837–1913*, and volume 4, *The Modern Age, 1914–1984*. Each volume is arranged alphabetically by journal title and has a scholarly essay detailing the significance of the journal's contribution, its publishing history, major figures associated with it as writers or editors, and notes referring to sources of information drawn on for the essay. This is followed by a section called "Information sources" that consists of a bibliography of secondary works related to the journal or persons connected with it, the titles of indexes, which include the journal's content, citations of any reprint editions, and listings of locations where copies of original issues may be found. Next is a section called "Publication history," which presents the magazine title and any title changes, detailed volume and issue information, the frequency of publication, and names of publishers and editors along with their dates of tenure. Both volumes have a number of useful appendixes, such as chronologies of social and historical events along with landmarks related to these particular British literary magazines. Volume 4 also provides a list of magazines with short runs and an index to personal names and titles.

Volume 4 of the ***New Cambridge Bibliography of English Literature***, previously mentioned in chapter 4, has a section devoted specifically to "Newspapers and Magazines," including little magazines and those focused on particular genres. This section covers bibliographies of articles, books, and reports related to English newspapers and magazines and is broken up into five subsections. Subsection A focuses on "Historical and general studies" such as historical studies of the press, newspapers and their contents, general studies of magazines, little magazines and university magazines, and reminiscences and biographies. Subsection B relates to "Journalism" and is broken down into categories of bibliographies, general works, the profession of journalism, news agencies, advertising, and periodicals relating to newspaper and magazine publishing. "Accounts and studies of individual newspapers and magazines" are addressed in subsection C. These citations are grouped under an alphabetical listing of the titles of the newspapers and journals. Subsection D is particularly useful for locating English periodicals of the time period since it cites "Lists, indexes and directories" of these publications. Subsection E looks at "Individual newspapers and magazines" encompassing both literary and nonliterary newspapers and magazines, amateur journals, university and college magazines, and periodicals devoted to specific types of genre fiction such as romance, detective, thrillers, and so on. Each periodical is listed by title and subtitle, with volume numbers, dates of press runs, and editorial information given.

Once the existence of a particular journal is known, a researcher may want to find full-text copies. Some significant journals that have fallen out of copyright have been digitized and made available online; important examples are discussed in chapter 8. For items still under copyright and for those that are more obscure, looking for print copies may be the only option. Two major union lists of serial holdings have traditionally helped researchers locate these items. The ***Union List of Serials in Libraries of the United States and Canada*** identifies serial holdings for 956 libraries in the United States and Canada. It is arranged alphabetically by the publishing society or government entity producing it or, lacking that, by serial title. Years of publication are identified for each journal, and codes at the end of the listings identify which libraries hold copies. The ***British Union-Catalogue of Periodicals: A Record of the Periodicals of the World, from the Seventeenth Century to the Present Day, in British Libraries*** performs a similar function for serial holdings in 440 British libraries. Both works cover English-language and non-English-language materials and a wide range of publishing dates. There are no time lines or chronological indexes that would help identify which publications were specifically produced during the modern era. These tools are most useful for locating copies of known items in major libraries and research institutions. Although some of the information contained in these volumes may be out of date, both works retain enough value that they are a staple of most serious reference collections. For additional holdings information and more up-to-date listings for specific serial titles, researchers should also consult the ***WorldCat*** database, discussed in greater detail in chapter 3. The FirstSearch version of *WorldCat* provides the ability to limit records to "Serial Publications," and in the "Advanced Search" function of the online version of *WorldCat.org*, you may limit the format type to "Journal/Magazine/Newspaper."

The series of books that make up the ***Bibliography of British Newspapers*** is particularly useful for determining which newspapers were being published where and when, as well as where extant copies of them may be located. The first volume of the series covers the county of Wiltshire and was edited by R. K. Bluhm. This volume was published by the Library Association's Reference, Special and Information Section in 1975. This group no longer exists in this form, and subsequent volumes in the series have been published by the British Library. The format of each volume of this series, under the general editorship of Charles A. Toase, is highly consistent. At the beginning of the work is a bibliography of books and articles related to newspapers or publishing history of the area. Following that are the "Location of Files" of the extant copies of the newspapers. Then there are geographical listings of the newspapers themselves. First are the newspapers that had circulation areas ranging through all or most of the county. The newspapers are presented in alphabetical order by title, with dates given for both the span of the publication's run and the span of the available issues. Following this brief overview is an entry for each newspaper, providing the following information: title, any name changes, dates published, where found (relating to the locations listed at the beginning of the work), and date coverage for each location. If any histories or indexes to the publication are available, they are then cited. After this general section, there are other sections following the same format that are devoted to newspapers that have circulation focused within various cities in the county. These sections are arranged alphabetically by city name, with the newspapers arranged alphabetically by title within the category. Each volume within the series is devoted to one or two counties, and each has its own editor or editors. Currently, six volumes are available: Wiltshire; Kent; Durham and Northumberland; Derbyshire; Nottinghamshire; and Cornwall and Devon. The intention has been to produce volumes for all of Great Britain, county by county. The most recent volume was published in 1991, so it is unclear how active the publishing program still is and whether or not the series will be completed in this form.

Another publication of the British Library concerning newspapers published in Britain is the ***Catalogue of the Newspaper Library, Colindale***. This eight-volume work provides title and geographic location access to the half-million volumes of daily and weekly newspapers and periodicals held at the British Library's newspaper reading room at the Colindale location. The text consists of photoreproductions of the catalog cards from the library as of the early 1970s. The first four volumes are arranged geographically, and the last four volumes contain the same records arranged alphabetically by title. Of particular interest is volume 1, which covers national newspapers and journals published in London since 1801. Additionally, this volume provides access to information about local newspapers for the greater London area, subdivided into thirty-three borough locations. Volume 2 is devoted to the rest of England outside of London, as well as Wales, Scotland, and Ireland. Publications of the United Kingdom's armed forces and ships' newspapers are included in this volume as well. Volumes 3 and 4 focus on foreign newspapers held by the Library, arranged alphabetically by country and city. Volumes 5 through 8 consist of one alphabetical listing of the newspaper and periodical titles. Publications that have the same title are arranged by place of publication as well as chronologically. This tool is of particular interest to scholars of British modernism because it not only addresses the entire time period under consideration, but it also keys to actual full-text publications readily available at the British Library at Colindale. Note, however, that a limited number of the most popular titles have been transferred to the Humanities Collection at the British Library's St. Pancras location.

Scholars may also search the full current holdings of the ***British Library Newspapers Collection***, now containing over 693,000 volumes of newspapers and 370,000 reels of microfilm (representing over 52,000 newspapers and periodicals), by consulting the newspaper subsection of the British Library's online *Integrated Catalogue* (referred to in more detail in chapter 3), at http://catalogue.bl.uk. The *Newspapers Collection* has all United Kingdom national daily and Sunday newspapers from 1801 to the present, as well as most United Kingdom and Irish regional newspapers, many going back to the nineteenth century. The newspapers subset of the British Library collection can be accessed by selecting "Catalogue subset search" from the main search screen. Select the "Newspapers" option from the list provided, and the basic search screen for newspapers will appear. You may also opt to use the advanced search screen for the collection, which enables you to enter multiple search terms and to limit your search by language, date range, or format. The newspaper subset of the catalog can be challenging to use because of the large number of records and the common use of words such as "Times," "News," "Press," and "Chronicle" in newspaper titles. For this reason, the British Library also makes available a list of the most commonly sought major national newspapers and evening newspapers published in London and their shelfmarks (call numbers) on their website, which can be accessed at http://www.bl.uk/reshelp/findhelprestype/news/diffnews/index.html.

CONCLUSION

Although no single comprehensive source exists that provides bibliographic listings of all British newspapers and magazines of the modernist era, much less a single source indexing them, a wealth of information is still available concerning these publications. Using a combination of print reference tools, online proprietary resources, and Web-based indexes and archives, a good majority of British serial publications and their contents will come to light. Although some gaps in coverage certainly exist, with patience and persistence it should be possible for researchers to track down the most relevant serial publications for their research topics.

NOTES

1. Virginia Woolf, *Three Guineas* (New York: Harcourt, Brace, Jovanovich, 1938), 95.
2. Woolf, *Three Guineas*, 97.
3. Aurelea Mahood, "Fashioning Readers: The Avant Garde and British *Vogue*, 1920–9," *Women: A Cultural Review* 13, no. 1 (Spring 2002): 37–47.
4. Malcolm Bradbury, "Modernism and the Magazines," in *Transcultural Encounters—Studies in English Literatures*, Heinz Antor and Kevin L. Cope, eds. (Heidelberg: Winter, 1999), 187–313.

Chapter Eight

Microform and Digital Collections

Access to unique or hard-to-find primary materials was revolutionized by commercial microform technology in the 1950s and further revolutionized by the development of scanning technologies and widespread access to the Internet in the late twentieth century. Microfilm, microfiche, and other forms of microtechnology have been used both to collect and to preserve works of interest from various time periods. More recently, computer-based reproduction, including scanning and digitization of actual copies of primary materials and Web-based reproduction of texts, has been used to make both the text itself and reproductions of archival forms of the text widely available via the Internet. Basically, both technologies have made possible levels of preservation and access that continue to be of value to researchers. From a preservation perspective, some primary materials are fragile and should be handled as little as possible. Once initial scanning or photography takes place, the original can safely be stored without further wear and tear. Access via the Internet or through multiple copies of microforms available at various institutions also ensures that researchers will have an easier time making use of the materials. The potential need to travel a great distance to look at a unique item in an archive or special collection is eliminated or at least considerably mitigated.

Microforms have steadily fallen out of favor as a way of providing research copies of primary materials. Scanning and digitization technologies have conversely risen in popularity as a means of making such items available. There is also some middle ground with CD-ROMs, which require computers in order to view them but do not make the contents available on the Internet. In recent years, some standard resources previously found in many libraries in microform format have migrated to the digital environment. For example, copies of back issues of the *New York Times* and other major newspapers have been held by many academic and research libraries and special collections as rolls of microfilm organized by date. More and more, these titles are becoming available as searchable Internet-based collections (see more about newspaper collections in chapter 7). The movement from microforms to digitized collections has largely been spurred by ease of use. Microforms require bulky and expensive machines in order to read them, and these have been notoriously difficult for end users to navigate. Threading and focusing the machines are sometimes challenging and time consuming, and reading the materials in this context can be fatiguing and disorienting. Furthermore, a considerable amount of square footage of library space is required to make room for both the microform readers and the storage cabinets housing the microforms themselves. Many libraries have opted to save space and increase access by moving to Internet-based versions of long periodical runs previously held as microfilm.

In spite of the growing preference for online digitized materials, it seems unlikely that microform collections will disappear anytime soon. Many useful items available as microfilm have not been digitized and may never migrate to that format. Even for those collections that have migrated, not all libraries can afford to repurchase the item in the new format or pay annual access fees for online versions. Serious research libraries will continue to provide the means to view significant microform collections. The good news is that microform reader technology has improved considerably. In addition to being able to use the same machine to view multiple formats and magnification rates, most of the new style of readers allow the user to print copies from the microforms to a networked printer within the library or even to scan the materials wanted and download them to a jump drive or attach them to an e-mail for further research or educational use.

Another challenge associated with microforms is the lack of uniform titles for some collections. Various items may be gathered together but not have an official collective name. If the microform publisher did not clearly assign a title to the collection, it may exist in the same form in various libraries but be cataloged under different names assigned by the individual institutions. Related to this is the fact that many collections also lack any normal access points such as indexes, tables of contents, or other means of finding out what individual items might be included in them without paging through the entire collection. Some attempts have been made at indexing major collections held by many libraries (see Niles, below), but in many instances the researcher will need to develop the habits of the historian and spend time sifting through a great deal of dross to find nuggets of gold. This chapter offers some guidance on finding what materials are available in microform or digitized format as well as an overview of the most useful extant collections.

FINDING MICROFORMS AND DIGITAL COLLECTIONS

"Bibliographies and Guides." *Library of Congress Microform Reading Room.* www.loc.gov/rr/microform/bibguide.html (9 April 2009).

Dodson, Suzanne Cates, ed. *Microform Research Collections: A Guide.* 2nd ed. Westport, CT: Meckler, 1984.

Frazier, Patrick, ed. *A Guide to the Microform Collections in the Humanities and Social Sciences Division.* Washington, DC: Library of Congress, Humanities and Social Sciences Division, 1996. www.loc.gov/rr/microform/guide/ (9 April 2009).

Guide to Microforms in Print. Updated annually. Munich: Saur.

Niles, Ann, ed. *An Index to Microform Collections.* Westport, CT: Meckler, 1984.

———. *An Index to Microform Collections, Vol. 2.* Westport, CT: Meckler, 1988.

WorldCat. Dublin, OH: OCLC. www.oclc.org/firstsearch/.

The term *microform and digital collections* refers specifically to materials occurring in a particular format, most of which have been grouped together and reformatted into those media for the convenience of libraries and researchers. They are, normally speaking, items that originally occurred in some print or manuscript form. They may be collections of items appearing as periodicals, books, newspapers, pamphlets, images, or personal papers, manuscripts, or letters. Some of the materials reproduced as microform or digital collections may have had fairly wide distribution in their original lives, such as many newspapers or periodicals. Other microform and digital collections may reproduce unique archival materials that belonged only to the author and were never circulated. There are no hard-and-fast rules governing what is found in microform and digital collections. They may be irregular and haphazard collections representing the tastes of one individual; they may be limited by what is available in a particular institution or geographic location; or they may be limited or restricted by copyright law. One of the particular challenges of doing research in these collections is that it is sometimes difficult to locate the existence of individual items. Most library catalog records relating to microform and digital collections describe them only generally, and it is impossible to gain knowledge of individual items unless there is an index or finding aid available.

To begin research in microform collections, you should check to see whether your home institution has a special microform collection in the library. Larger academic and research libraries may have special collections and finding aids geared specifically to their microform collections. For example, the Library of Congress has a special Microform Reading Room, which is part of its Humanities and Social Sciences Division and houses approximately six million items in hundreds of collections. The library has been collecting microforms since the 1940s and has maintained a separate reading room for this collection since the early 1950s. Although none of the collections housed here deals specifically with British literary modernism, a number of collections are focused on topics at least peripherally related to the social, political, artistic, and cultural milieu of the British modernists. The main web page of the Microform Reading Room, http://www.loc.gov/rr/microform/, provides links to information about the collections and their contents and policies for using them. The webpage entitled ***Bibliographies and Guides*** features links to both "General Guides" and "Guides by Subject." Subject guides of potential interest to scholars of British modernism include those covering biographical collections, women's studies resources, and British government documents. In the general guides, ***A Guide to the Microform Collections in the Humanities and Social Sciences Division*** is also particularly useful. This guide was published in print in 1996 and is now available online in a version that was updated as of 2001. The *Guide* can be browsed alphabetically by title in the main body of the work or by subject in the subject index. The best place to start is probably the subject index (divided into two sections online: A–J and K–Z). Subject headings of potential interest are "Art—Great Britain"; "English Literature"; "Fabian Society, Great Britain—History"; "Great Britain—Politics and Government"; "Labor and Laboring Classes—Great Britain"; "Literature, Modern"; "Social Movements—Great Britain—20th Century"; and "Women—Great Britain—History." Under each subject heading is listed the title of the collection(s) pertaining to that subject. Once potential collections of interest are identified, brief descriptions can be located under the title listings, although there are sometimes gaps (such as missing records or missing information concerning date ranges of the original publications). In spite of any drawbacks in the descriptions, there is generally enough information to give a sense of whether the collection is worth pursuing or not. For example, the subject heading "Literature, Modern" sounds very promising. There are four collection titles under this heading, but only one of them clearly fits the time period for "modern" as we are defining it here—*Russian futurism, 1910–1916.* We can then look up this collection by title in the alphabetic listing and find the following description: "Monochrome and color microfiche containing manifestos, collections of poetry, journals, and illustrations concerned with Russian art and literature for the years 1910–1916. The originals have never been gathered into a single public collection, so it was necessary to film private collections in England, France, and America. Some of the originals were made of highly perishable materials and will not tolerate handling by researchers. This film collection is the only source for these valuable primary materials." We can also learn from the record that the collection consists of fifty-four microfiche and that a printed guide providing more detailed descriptions of the works is available. We can see that this collection, although not directly concerned with British literary modernism, contains materials that were of considerable influence on certain aspects of British arts and letters in the modern period and that may be difficult, if not impossible, to obtain access to elsewhere.

Even if your home institution does not have an extensive enough collection of microforms to warrant a special reading room or area of the library, chances are that at least some materials in this medium are held. The library website may give some insight into collections held in this format, and some library catalogs even allow you to limit your search by format to microforms. If you are looking for a known collection, try searching the library catalog by the collection title, which should allow you to quickly ascertain whether the collection is held by your institution or not. Reference librarians can also direct you to any relevant microform collections held by your library, along with any available indexes or finding aids describing the collections' contents in more detail.

In spite of not holding microform collections, many libraries still own standard reference tools that provide information about such collections. One of the most comprehensive is the ***Guide to Microforms in Print*** series, published annually by Saur. This guide is international in scope and covers microforms available for sale in a given year. Because researchers may be interested not just in what is currently available but also in what might be out of print, many research libraries retain back volumes of this publication. The subject series consists of two volumes, the bulk of which are the individual listings for the microform products, arranged in subject classes. Volume 1 begins with a foreword explaining the arrangement of the guide, the form and content of the entries, the codes for identifying different types of microforms, and other helpful information. There is also a listing of country-of-publication codes, mainly limited to North America, Europe, and Asia; a list of currency symbols; a key to abbreviated series; a list of abbreviations used, such as "r" for "reel;" a "Survey of Classes," which is a modified Dewey Decimal Classification system; and a brief "Survey of Subjects," consisting of a five-page listing of general subject areas, referring to particular class numbers that relate to that subject. Finally, the front matter includes a list of publishers and distributors, along with the identifying codes for each entity as reproduced in the main entries, and an index to publishers and distributors, cross-referencing them to alternative or previous names. Following the front matter, volume 1 also contains the entries for classes 000 through 390. Volume 2 follows with the entries for classes 400 through 990 and ends with an index of "Persons as Subject." This last index is particularly good for finding collections that have works by or about a particular author, even if this is not obvious from the title. Researchers in British modernism will also be interested in browsing the 420 and 941 classes, pertaining to "English Language and Literature" and "British/Scottish/Irish History," respectively. Individual entries have the same type of information found in catalog records, such as title information, names of authors and editors, and number of pages. Price information is also available, along with the code for the distributor. Another feature is the provision of place, publisher name, and publication date for both the original material and the microform edition. In addition to the subject series just described, Saur also publishes a two-volume author/title series. The same front matter is found in this series as in the subject series, but instead of being arranged by classification code, entries are arranged alphabetically by author and title. Volume 1 of the 2008 edition covers entries A through K, and volume 2, entries L through Z.

Microform Research Collections: A Guide, edited by Suzanne Cates Dodson, is more narrowly focused on significant research collections of microforms held by many larger academic libraries. The collections described in this guide are published by a specific set of institutions and companies, including the Library of Congress, Chadwyck-Healy, Library Microfilms, and a number of others. Some examples of the collections presented are the *British Labour History Ephemera, 1900–1926*, *British Birth Control Material at The British Library of Political and Economic Sciences, 1800–1947*, and *British Government Publications, 1801–1977*. Although none of these collections deals directly with the literary work of the British modernists, they may contain materials useful for understanding the modernists' social and political milieu. The *Guide* is arranged by title, and each entry has a price (which is most likely out of date at this point), a review of the work from *Microform Review*, information on arrangement of the collection and bibliographic control, bibliographies and indexes available for the collection, and a helpful scope and content note providing a more detailed description of the items found in the collection. At the end of the work, there is a single index combining entries for author, editor, and compiler names, as well as titles and subjects. Creative perusal of items listed under subject headings such as "Great Britain—History—20th Century," "English literature—19th Century," or "English Poetry" may reveal collections with items of relevance.

Ann Niles's ***An Index to Microform Collections*** and ***An Index to Microform Collections, Vol. 2*** have actual item-level indexing for selected microform collections, including many of the collections referred to by Dodson. The main index presents the collections alphabetically by title, and each collection entry has a listing of all items found within it, arranged alphabetically by author, along with title and date if available. If no author is available, the item can be found by title and date. In addition to the main index, there is a section that groups the collections by publisher name, a directory of publishers' addresses, and comprehensive indexes for all items by author and by title. In the first *Index*, for example, we learn that the *British Culture Series 1, 18th and 19th Centuries* contains items related to Oscar Wilde, W. B. Yeats, and Sidney Webb, which might be of interest to some researchers of British modernism. Unfortunately, the second *Index* does not seem to have had wide distribution and is available in only a small number of libraries, but luckily there is not as much of interest to the scholar of modern British literature in that volume. The one possible collection having some relevance to British modernism in the second *Index* is *Utopian Literature: Pre-1900 Imprints*, which has some British works from the late nineteenth century. Certainly this collection more broadly might be of interest to anyone specifically studying utopian literature or its more modern counterpart, dystopian literature. Both of these volumes, given their out-of-print status and potential continuing usefulness, would be good candidates for a publicly available digitization program such as *Google Books*.

The ***WorldCat*** database, discussed in greater depth in chapter 3, also includes catalog records for microform materials. You may limit a search within *WorldCat* to only microform materials by first selecting one or more material "types" from the list and then selecting "Microforms" from the drop-down menu under "Subtype limits." The term *microform* can also be used in a search as a keyword. Since there are no formal microform collections specifically focused on modern British literature, this is of limited use as a tool of discovery. However, when searching *WorldCat*, researchers should be aware of two important aspects of the database. One, if an item described by a particular record is a microform, that is indicated in the summary citation at the top of the record. The original format of the item is also provided, as in the case of a microfilmed book or archival materials. Farther down in the record is a field titled "Material type," and the specific type of microform is found there, such as microfilm or microfiche. The field immediately below "Material type" is "Document type," and that gives the original format of the item, such as book or archival materials. Also, if searching for a particular item by title, you may locate the item as part of a microform collection if it is listed in the content notes area. Figure 8.1 shows a *WorldCat* record for a microform version of a book.

There are currently no guides or finding aids available to digital collections. These items are too diffuse and too rare within the current subject area. The reasons for the scarcity of such materials in general is discussed in the next section.

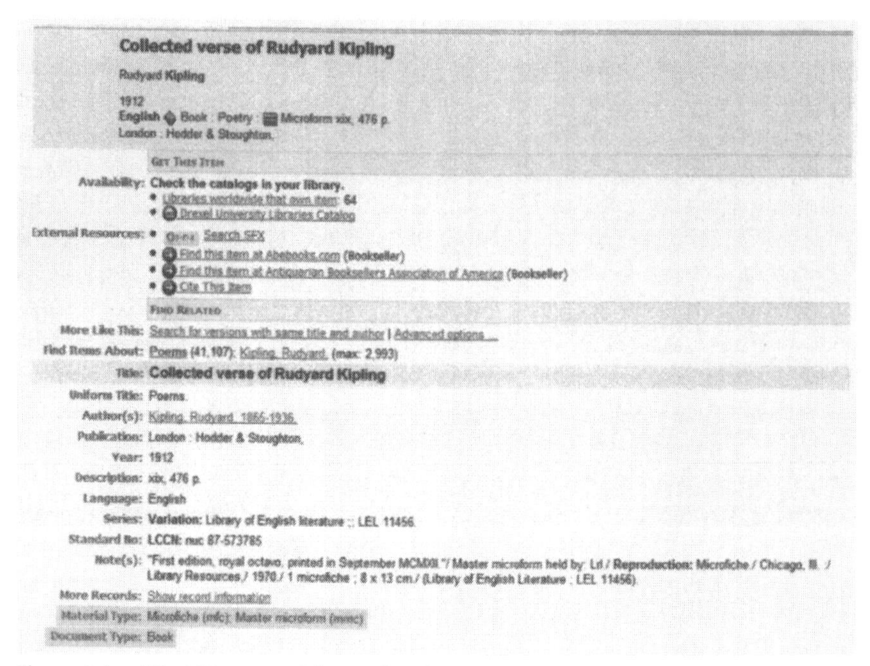

Figure 8.1. ***WorldCat*** **record for a microform version of a book.**

MICROFORM AND DIGITIZED COLLECTIONS

Google Book Search. http://books.google.com/books.

Modern English Collection. Electronic Text Center, University of Virginia Library. http://etext.lib.virginia.edu/modeng/modeng0.browse.html.

Modernist Journals Project. www.modjourn.org.

Open Library. http://openlibrary.org/.

Project Gutenberg. www.gutenberg.org/wiki/Main_Page.

Woolf, Virginia. *Major Authors on CD-ROM: Virginia Woolf*. Woodbridge, CT: Primary Source Media, 1997.

Collections of materials by and about groups of writers can certainly save researchers' time and energy by providing them with a convenient means of "one-stop shopping," especially for the primary materials they would like to use. Unfortunately, very few such collections exist for the works of modern British writers due to copyright laws and the concomitant difficulties of bringing together a body of work that may span a number of years and varying copyright coverage. In this volume, we are defining modernism as roughly spanning the years 1885 to 1945. Under current United States copyright law, works published prior to 1923 safely fall within the public domain, which allows greater access to and use of materials from the early (1885 through 1922) period of modernism. Works published in the United States from 1923 through 1963 with copyright protection renewed remain under copyright until ninety-five years after publication. Thus, 2018 will be the earliest date for works by British modernists published in the United States post-1922 to enter the public domain. In Great Britain, the European Union Directive on Term of Copyright was adopted in 1996; it extends the force of copyright protection to seventy years following the death of the author. Thus, works by Virginia Woolf and James Joyce, both of whom died in 1941, should enter the public domain in 2011. For further information about copyright law and public domain in the United States, Cornell University's website has a convenient guide at http://www.copyright.cornell.edu/public_domain/. For information on British copyright, the Harry Ransom Center of the University of Texas at Austin presents some useful insight at http://tyler.hrc.utexas.edu/uk.cfm.

If the restriction that copyright laws continue to place on materials by British modernists is the bad news, the good news is that their materials have been published near enough to our own time that they are generally accessible on some level to researchers. And unless copyright laws in both the United States and Great Britain continue in their pattern of ever-increasing extensions, the works of the British modernists will eventually enter the public domain at a time when they may be collected in more easily accessible and usable digital formats. A few collections covering materials by the British modernists exist already and can be quite useful. The previous section gave tips on finding materials related to the British modernists that may be buried in larger microfilm collections. This section gives an overview of digital collections that contain modern British literature materials. Many of these are currently in a state of development; it will be exciting to see what may become available in the coming years.

The one item that stands out as a model for what digital collections related to an author could be at their best is the CD-ROM product ***Major Authors on CD-ROM: Virginia Woolf.*** This product provides the full text of Woolf's complete fiction, her complete diaries, reproductions of letters and manuscripts from the Monks House Papers and the New York Public Library's Berg Collection, reproductions of U.S. and British first editions of her works, and even a sound recording of Woolf herself from a BBC broadcast. Also included is the full text of the reference work *Virginia Woolf from A to Z* by Mark Hussey, who edited the collection and wrote the introduction. The possibilities such a product presents for textual analysis and tracing themes across the body of Woolf's work is truly astonishing. One small example is the inclusion of an early draft and the galley proofs of Woolf's novel *The Years*, along with the published version. Being able to search through and compare these varying versions of the text would certainly yield considerable insight into Woolf's creative process. This specialized research tool is still held by a number of libraries, in spite of the fact that the CD-ROM format is rapidly falling out of use. The publisher of this product, Primary Source Media, was bought by the Gale Group, and Gale later marketed an Internet-based product called *Major Authors Online. Major Authors Online* was a collection of the digitized versions of the complete series of *Major Authors on CD-ROM*, consisting of works on Walt Whitman, the Brontë sisters, Virginia Woolf, Samuel Johnson and James Boswell, and Miguel de Cervantes. Unfortunately, neither the CD-ROMs nor the digital collections are currently marketed. Such products may have limited economic prospects from a business perspective, but their existence suggests the possibilities for future open-source versions to be developed by humanities computing experts.

An excellent example of an open-source project freely available online is the ***Modernist Journals Project***, which has been jointly developed by Brown University and the University of Tulsa. The centerpiece of this well-done resource is the journals collection, which provides reproductions of a number of modernist literary journals—some of the most important of the little magazines discussed in chapter 7. The time period covered is 1890 to 1922, which means all of the materials fall safely within the public domain under United States copyright law. In addition to the pre-1923 issues of *Blast*, *Coterie*, *The English Review*, *Poetry*, and others, the site contains the full text of several books (both contemporary and historical) and scholarly essays related to modernism. A search engine is also available to access the full contents of the site and additional features, such as examples of how the collection has been used in college-level courses. This site serves as a model of the type of project that could be undertaken by other institutions of higher education. The materials presented are of significant scholarly interest, but the potential audience for them as a commercial product would be small. Making them available freely on the Internet in high-quality formats increases their use in the research community and will potentially educate the broader public as well.

The Electronic Text Center at the University of Virginia Library in Charlottesville is another example of an online high-quality electronic text collection program with much publicly accessible content. Scholars of modern British literature will be most interested in the ***Modern English Collection***, which has over nine thousand titles. The time period covered by this collection is 1500 to the present, and while the emphasis is on American literature, international materials are available. A number of special collections reside within the *Modern English Collection*, such as "Bestsellers 1900–1930," which consists of English-language best sellers by American and British authors. Some materials are restricted to University of Virginia users only, but much is freely available, including a number of full-text works by British modernists.

For example, more than a dozen titles by Joseph Conrad are accessible, as well as works by other major modernists. This material is not necessarily in the public domain but may appear in the collection as a result of an agreement with the publishers and copyright holders. Researchers who use the collection may not download the text, reproduce or mount it elsewhere, or use the text for any commercial purposes. This collection represents what can be done when an institution takes responsibility for providing online access to useful scholarly materials in high-quality standardized formats.

Another high-quality archive of digital materials that contains public domain materials by modern British writers is ***Project Gutenberg***. The quick search on the homepage allows one to quickly locate materials by author name and/or title. The advanced search screen has additional options, including the ability to query by Library of Congress call number or subject, and to limit results by language or format of the work. Although not currently available, some enhanced search capabilities, such as being able to search by publication date or date range, would make the site even more useful to scholars. *Project Gutenberg* publishes materials in a wide variety of formats, such as HTML, PDF, TXT, and ASCII. The site producers have a stated preference for formats that are editable and that allow for open access (i.e., not restricted by patent or copyright protection). Some formats are also available for e-book readers, as well as MP3 or MIDI formats for audio files and music. Some works may be available in more than one format. In searching for work by British modernists, one can quickly ascertain that most pre-1923 works by the major modernists are currently available. For example, more than a dozen works by D. H. Lawrence are available, such as early editions of *Sons and Lovers* and *Women in Love*, plus collections of poems, essays, travel writing, and a play. Free and easy access to such full-text electronic books is a tremendous asset to scholars and casual readers alike. The scope and quality of *Project Gutenberg's* work is quite impressive, as is the level of use. On October 19, 2008, it was reported that 83,462 books were downloaded on that day alone. Currently there are more than one hundred thousand full-text electronic books available from *Project Gutenberg* and its partners and affiliates.

A related open-source project is the ***Open Library*** initiative, discussed in chapter 3, which has the goal of mounting "one web page for every book ever published." As such, *Open Library* provides records for both in-print and out-of-print books and seems to be vying for a position as a more populist version of OCLC and *WorldCat*. The initiative has been in negotiation regarding partnering with OCLC and *WorldCat*, but nothing has been settled as of this writing. *Open Library* records are considerably less detailed than those found in *WorldCat*, but they have added value such as pointing to *Project Gutenberg* and other freely available electronic texts, as well as to *Amazon.com* and library collections. *Open Library* currently exists in its beta version and contains records for almost 19,000,000 books, of which more than 340,000 are full text. Both *Open Library* and *Project Gutenberg* are affiliated with the *Internet Archive*, http://www.archive.org/index.php, which serves as a gateway for free digital collections of moving images, audio files, historical Internet pages, and more than 540,000 texts.

Another Web tool for finding free access to digitized materials is ***Google Book Search***, from the makers of the popular search engine. *Google Book Search* has taken a two-pronged approach to developing its digital collections and records: it has partnered with publishers that want greater exposure for their books, and it has partnered with libraries that want greater exposure for books in general. Currently available in its beta version, *Google Book Search* performs two important functions. First, it makes high-quality digital versions of the public domain works in its collection freely available. Second, it enables "inside the book" access to subject matter that might not be easily found based on typical bibliographic information such as title and subject headings. For example, take the book *No Man's Land: The Place of the Woman Writer in the Twentieth Century* by Sandra M. Gilbert and Susan Gubar. One might suppose that Virginia Woolf, as a pioneering woman modernist, might be discussed in this work. However, it would be impossible to determine this based on the records found either in *WorldCat* or in most library catalogs, which limit themselves to more general subject headings such as "English literature—20th century—History and criticism" and "English literature—Women authors—History and criticism." *Google Book Search*, however, directs a user to this book based on its "Key words and phrases" feature, which has the names of all authors discussed at length in the work, including Woolf. Once there, the reader can use the "Search in this book" feature to locate more than thirty times that Woolf is referred to in this work. Clicking on a particular cited passage brought up by this search takes you to that actual passage within the book, where it may be read in context. This book is an example of a work that is still under copyright protection but available in "preview" mode in *Google Book Search* because of an agreement with the publisher. This means that a limited number of pages may be accessed by a viewer, but not the full book. In addition to the limited preview and the full-text access to out-of-copyright works, there is also a "snippet" view, which has a few words or phrases from within the text that relate to your search, and a "no preview" view, which provides basically the same information as a catalog record. It is not known exactly how many books are currently available, to whatever degree of accessibility, in *Google Book Search*. What is known is that the number is constantly growing and that through partnerships with prestigious research libraries such as those at Columbia University, Harvard University, Oxford University, and Princeton University, many of the titles being digitized are of high quality and scholarly interest.

In October 2008, *Google Book Search* settled two lawsuits brought against it for copyright infringement by the Association of American Publishers and the Authors Guild. Under the terms of the settlement, a "Book Rights Registry" will be created as a mechanism to facilitate authors being compensated for the use of their copyrighted works. For in-print books, *Google Book Search* currently offers links to the publisher's website as well as to the websites of a number of popular online booksellers such as *Amazon.com*. Because of this legal settlement, in the future *Google Book Search* will be able to sell digital full-text copies of books that are out of print but still under the protection of copyright law, using the registry as a means to compensate the copyright holders. This means that scholars and consumers will have greater access to out-of-print books, even though a cost will be involved.

Large-scale digitization efforts exemplified by *Project Gutenberg* and *Google Book Search* may not focus specifically on the works most of interest to scholars of modern British literature. However, they can provide additional modes of discovery for materials that are available, access to some full-text items of relevance, and the ability to do preliminary research in some copyrighted items available in limited numbers. It is anticipated that the number of books available via such means will only increase over time and that their search capabilities and functionality will also increase and improve.

CONCLUSION

Because of copyright considerations, there are a limited number of available microform and digital collections that are directly related to the work of British modernist writers. However, there are some materials available that are relevant to the modernists' work or milieu that may be of interest to scholars. Tracking these down requires a certain amount of persistence and the creative use of existing union catalogs, finding aids, websites of libraries and scholarly projects, and expertise of reference librarians. Microfilm is in decline as a means of access and preservation, but digitization projects are on the increase. As more modernist writers' works enter the public domain, this bodes well for greater access to them via easily usable computer-based interfaces. Some materials related to the modernists and their works may be packaged by vendors with value-added materials and then sold either outright or by subscription to libraries. Although such proprietary uses of these materials may actually end up limiting access to them for certain classes of scholars, it is anticipated that increased digitization efforts will have an overall positive effect on scholarly use of modernist works and associated information.

Chapter Nine

Manuscripts and Archives

As discussed in chapter 8, many important collections of research materials have been available via microform for decades now, and with new computer and Internet technologies, more and more materials are becoming available in digital, electronic formats. In spite of these facts, millions of items of research value will not be available anytime soon through any technology simply because of the cost as well as the time and energy necessary to convert them. Often these items are of such specialized interest that their audience may consist only of a handful of people. Because of this, archives are and will remain important for many researchers.

This chapter provides some guidance in the use of archives as well as an introduction to some of the major print and Web-based tools for discovering manuscripts and archival materials of interest and locating the archives that house them.

GENERAL INFORMATION ABOUT ARCHIVES

Archives are the close cousins of libraries. The bulk of the materials collected by libraries are secondary materials—published books and journals, other serial publications, and a variety of reference tools and resources, both print and electronic. In archives, however, the bulk of the collection tends to be primary materials—manuscripts, letters, diaries, notebooks, and any and all other unpublished works. They may also include materials in other formats, such as photographs or slides, film or audio recordings, and personal items or other realia or ephemera. In whatever format, these are usually unique items, and they are sometimes of considerable monetary value. Manuscript holdings may range from a single letter to or from a person of interest to an entire collection of an author's personal papers spanning a lifetime and occupying yards of archival shelf space. Archivists catalog single items much as a book would be cataloged, making it accessible by author, correspondent, and often subject. For larger collections, archivists create special finding aids to describe the background and scope of the collection as well as give an outline of its contents. The most detailed finding aids give descriptions down to the "item level," while most are limited to more general descriptions at the "box level," such as "Correspondence, 1922–1924." Even though the full text of most manuscript collections may not appear online anytime soon, more and more finding aids are making their way to the Internet, giving researchers the opportunity to learn something about the contents of collections they may be interested in without having to travel or request photocopies ahead of time.

Most researchers in the field of literature tend to think of archival holdings in terms of collections of authors' personal papers, including their personal correspondence and draft copies of literary works. However, there are other forms of archival materials that may also be of interest to such researchers, even if they are less rarified on the surface. Records of government agencies, businesses, and charitable or nonprofit organizations are also retained in archives. Such records may contain information such as birth, death, and marriage records, military service records, minutes of board meetings or public hearings, and every item of correspondence entering or leaving an agency. Depending on one's research interest, these types of records may be of direct or peripheral interest. For agencies with retention policies in place, as with many governmental entities, these collections of records may be more complete and better organized than many personal collections. In any event, it is worth being aware of these types of archival materials. Finding and using them requires skills similar to those needed for using other types of archival materials.

"Special collections" is another term sometimes found in conjunction with archives and manuscripts. Special collections are normally specialized departments within larger research libraries, and they house items that will not be found in the general circulating collections because they have greater value and/or specialized uses. Many special collections house published secondary materials such as rare books or hard-to-find first editions. Their collections may be based on a particular theme or subject matter, such as the Openhym Collection at Alfred University, which is described in the nearly six-hundred-page volume *Bibliography of the Openhym Collection of Modern British Literature and Social History*.[1] This collection has over seven thousand printed books and pamphlets as well as correspondence from major and minor figures related to modern British literature. Another example of a potentially relevant special collection is the working library of Leonard and

Virginia Woolf held by Washington State University.[2] Although including few works by these authors themselves, the four thousand published works in this collection provide fascinating insight into what these two writers were reading and thinking. Special collections and archives may be housed together in a given research library, or they may be separate units. In most cases, they have similar policies governing access and use of their materials.

BEST PRACTICES FOR ARCHIVAL RESEARCH

Because of the specialized nature of manuscripts and other archival materials, archives operate very differently from libraries. Being aware of some of the traditions and cultural differences of archives will enable the novice researcher to approach the use of archives with more confidence and efficiency.

Archival research generally takes more time and planning than regular library research. Once you have located an archive that holds a collection you believe may be of interest to you, you should first visit the archive's website. Many archives are beginning to place digitized versions of finding aids online; if the finding aid for the collection you are interested in is available, you should be able to get a clearer idea of the contents of the collection and which particular sections are most relevant to your research. If an electronic finding aid is not available for your collection, you should at least find contact information for an archivist who answers reference questions. Calling, writing, or e-mailing an archivist familiar with the collection can help you gain insight into the collection's contents and which items would be of most interest to you.

Archives generally resist having too many strings attached to the materials in their collection, but be aware that you might encounter situations where donors have placed restrictions either on access to or use of items within a collection. Some donors may restrict access to certain types of researchers (such as those officially approved by the donors or their representatives). Some collections are given with the caveat that all or some of the records remain sealed until a certain number of years have passed following the death of the creator. Other collections may have restrictions on how information from the collection is used or have additional procedures for obtaining permission for use. If the collection you are interested in has any special restrictions placed on it, the archivists will be able to inform you of them, along with providing contact information for obtaining necessary permissions.

If a printed version of the collection's finding aid exists, you may be able to obtain a copy of it, either for a fixed price or for a per-page photocopy charge, directly from the archives. Once you've looked at the finding aid, you'll be in a better position to judge which items will be necessary to see. In some cases, it may be possible for you to order photocopies or digital images of manuscript items from the archives, thus saving the expense of traveling to the archives. In the case of particularly rare, valuable, or delicate items, however, reproduction may not be possible.

If it is necessary for you to physically visit the archives, you need to be aware of several things ahead of time. Unlike most libraries, which are generally open to the public (sometimes with restrictions), archives have more controlled access, and many require that you make an appointment prior to visiting. This is often due to limited seating and lack of staff to assist with the researchers' needs. Most archives also have more limited hours of operation. Research libraries are often open late-night and weekend hours to accommodate student study habits, but archives may be open only for standard business hours or even more abbreviated time periods. Once you have secured an appointment to visit the archive, you should arrive armed with as much knowledge as you can glean ahead of time about the collections you wish to use, drawing on information from the archive's website and various finding aids to which you may have prior access.

On the day of your visit, you will most likely be asked to go through a registration process prior to entering the reading rooms. Current photo IDs should be presented along with any proof of academic credentials or your research project, if required. You should also be aware that most archives do not allow researchers to bring in personal items such as briefcases, large purses, or backpacks. Some may also disallow coats and other outerwear. These personal items may be left in lockers or a secure location provided by the archives prior to entering the reading room. Most archives will allow laptop computers, and some will allow researchers' personal notebooks. Others may be more restrictive and allow researchers to use only plain white paper supplied by the archives. Most archives do not allow pens to be used in the reading rooms as manuscripts may be accidentally marked or marred by ink. Many will have pencils available for researchers' note taking.

Once you've gained entrance to the reading room, you may make use of the archive catalog, printed finding aids, or other resources for locating materials. Unlike libraries, most archives are "closed stacks," meaning that researchers cannot enter the areas where items are shelved, and they cannot browse or pull items off the shelves for their own use. Instead, a call slip must be filled out for all items you wish to look at, be it a single letter or a range of boxes. There are usually limits to the number of items that a single researcher can "call" for at any one time, and there may be daily limits as well. Archivists will take the call slips and return with the items requested. This may involve a wait, as the archivist may be pulling materials for a number of researchers from storage shelving on different floors or from a distance. Once your materials arrive, you will generally be free to read through them at your leisure. However, archivists may request that special techniques be used when handling certain items. Very old or fragile books may be placed on foam cradles to prevent damage by too much handling. Items with stiff binding may need an appropriately weighted cloth "snake" to hold the item open without applying too much pressure while the researcher takes notes. For handling some very fragile items, archivists may request that the researcher wear cotton gloves.

Historically, researchers doing archival research have had to take copious amounts of handwritten notes, and this is often still the case. The only way to record the contents of some items is to transcribe them by hand. For other materials that are less valuable and less fragile, it may be possible to request photocopies or digital images. Hand scanners are usually prohibited by most archives, but they may be able to scan certain items for you on a case-by-case basis. Some archives may allow the use of digital cameras or camera-phones to photograph materials for research use. Be aware of the restrictions upon copying imposed by the archives you're working in, and ask for permission if you are unsure.

If you use information from the archival materials you've looked at in your own writing, be sure to write proper citations. Most archives can provide you with a preferred format for citing their materials as well as the full and correct name of the collection used. Paying attention to their guidelines will help future researchers who may be following in your footsteps. Also carefully adhere to any restrictions regarding use of information from the archives. If you would like to reproduce any images, such as a photograph, illustration, or reproduction of a manuscript page, you must first secure permission from the archives. Most will have a permissions request form available, on which you will explain what you would like to use and how you would like to use it. To reproduce such images in published works, permission fees will normally be charged.

THE BRITISH LIBRARY

The British Library is the national library of the United Kingdom and one of the largest research libraries in the world. For historians and British literature researchers, it represents a place steeped in scholarship and literary tradition. Not only have many writers made use of the British Library collections, some of them have even written about it in their novels and essays. In *A Room of One's Own*, Virginia Woolf described the famous domed reading room, designed by Sydney Smirke, thus: "One stood under the vast dome, as if one were a thought in the huge bald forehead which is so splendidly encircled by a band of famous names."[3] This impressive architectural space, first opened in 1857, served as the main reading room of the British Library for over one hundred years. As with many libraries, it eventually outgrew its space. In 1997 the British Library collections were moved to a new and larger space nearby in the St. Pancras area of London. The reading room reverted to the British Museum with which it is physically connected. It has been architecturally restored and now serves as a temporary home for major exhibitions. A small research library specializing in world cultures is also on site, and the reading room and library may be accessed by British Museum visitors.

The new St. Pancras library building is a modern space with eleven reading rooms and is capable of accommodating far more researchers than the original Bloomsbury location. Newspaper collections are now housed in Colindale, North London, and an additional seven million items from the research collections are housed in Boston Spa, in North Yorkshire. In the past it was necessary to write ahead to obtain permission and an appointment to use the library collections. Now it is often possible to visit on a walk-in basis without an advance appointment. The only collections currently requiring advance permission for use are the Sound Archive, the Print Room of the Asia Pacific and Africa Collection, and the Philatelic Collection. Use of certain manuscripts, particularly the older illuminated manuscripts, also requires advance permission. For the researcher working on modern British literature, the Humanities Reading Rooms and the Manuscripts Reading Rooms will be of the most interest. The remainder of this section addresses best practices for making use of the manuscripts collection at the British Library's St. Pancras location in central London.

The first step in using the British Library's manuscripts collection is to do as much research prior to your visit as possible. Below are directions on how to use print indexes and Web-based catalogs to discover content in the manuscripts collection. Once you've determined which items or collections are of most interest to you, do some additional research to find out whether reproductions of the materials are available in microfilm or other format at a location more convenient to you. Once you've determined that the items you need would best be accessed at the British Library, you should contact the library using the e-mail address for manuscripts inquiries provided on the website. Let them know who you are, what your topic of study is, which manuscript items you are interested in seeing (including complete citations and manuscript numbers when possible), and your proposed dates of visiting the library. You may also ask whether they have additional suggestions for your research or whether there is anything you need to be aware of prior to your visit. Library hours and holiday closures are listed on the website, but library staff can inform you of any special circumstances affecting access to the library or use of the collections. While making your written inquiry, it may also be possible to request up to three manuscript items in advance, which will greatly speed the pace of your research visit.

On the day of your visit, you will first go to the reader registration office on the upper ground floor, where you will fill out a computer-based registration form. You must present two forms of identification, one showing your address and one showing your signature. Normally for U.S. visitors, a passport and driver's license with address is sufficient. Library staff will discuss your research needs with you and may suggest additional or alternative library collections for you to use. Readers' passes are valid for a period between one month and three years, depending on your needs. All visitors must read and agree to the conditions of use for the library, which is also posted on the website. No outerwear can be brought into the reading rooms, so outer coats and rain gear must be checked in the on-site cloakroom. For a one pound deposit, lockers are also available for securing any bags or personal items not allowed in the reading rooms. Clear plastic bags are provided for carrying personal papers or other items permitted in the reading rooms. Only pencils may be used in the reading rooms, no food or drink of any kind is permitted, and cell phones must be turned off or silenced. Laptop computers are permitted in designated areas.

Once in the Manuscripts reading room, you may consult the online *Manuscripts Catalogue* as well as handlists or specialized catalogs of items not yet available online. The *Manuscripts Catalogue* is not included in the British Library's *Integrated Catalogue* but can be searched online separately. More detailed information on searching the *Manuscripts Catalogue* can be found below. To order items you'd like to see, you must fill out a printed call slip or "ticket" with all identifying information, such as manuscript numbers. Library staff members are available to help if you have any questions. You may order up to ten items per day, four items at a time. Consult with the library staff if your research needs are likely to exceed these limits. In most cases you should be able to obtain copies of items you'd like to consult further for research purposes. The British Library posts helpful guidelines online for copying, quoting from, or publishing manuscripts from their collections at http://www.bl.uk/reshelp/bldept/manuscr/copyright/index.html. Also be aware that copies of both print and manuscript items from British Library collections may be requested online and mailed anywhere in the world. If you are able to pinpoint the exact items you need to use, this may be a cost-effective alternative to a physical visit. The online copy request form and current copying and mailing prices can also be found on the British Library website.

Whether your visit to the British Library is a real or virtual one, you are sure to be impressed with its resources and services.

This overview was intended to give some idea of the general procedures you would follow when making use of this fine library's collections. They may be similar to procedures used in other archives and special collections. In all cases, you should first begin by consulting the institution's website, as most now have information available online to answer researchers' questions. In addition to possibly finding online catalogs and finding aids, there is usually information regarding researcher visits, copying services, copyright and reproduction information, and contact information for librarians and archivists who can give further assistance.

LOCATING RELEVANT ARCHIVES AND MANUSCRIPTS

Ash, Lee, and William G. Miller, comps. *Subject Collections: A Guide to Special Book Collections and Subject Emphases as Reported by University, College, Public, and Special Libraries and Museums in the United States and Canada*. 2 vols. 7th ed., rev. and enl. New Providence, NJ: R. R. Bowker, 1993.

DeWitt, Donald L., comp. *Articles Describing Archives and Manuscript Collections in the United States: An Annotated Bibliography*. Westport, CT: Greenwood Press, 1997.

———, comp. *Guides to Archives and Manuscript Collections in the United States: An Annotated Bibliography*. Westport, CT: Greenwood Press, 1994.

Dictionary of Literary Biography. Detroit: Gale Research Co. www.gale.cengage.com/servlet/BrowseSeriesServlet?region=9&imprint=000&browseBy=series&titleCode=DLB.

Foster, Janet, and Julia Sheppard, eds. *British Archives: A Guide to Archive Resources in the United Kingdom*. 4th ed. New York: Palgrave, 2002.

Marcuse, Michael J. *A Reference Guide for English Studies*. Berkeley: University of California Press, 1990.

Matthew, H. C. G., and Brian Harrison, eds. *Oxford Dictionary of National Biography: From the Earliest Times to the Year 2000*. 61 vols. rev. ed. New York: Oxford University Press, 2004. www.oxforddnb.com/.

Sutton, David, ed. *Location Register of Twentieth Century English Literary Manuscripts and Letters: A Union List of Papers of Modern English, Irish, Scottish, and Welsh Authors in the British Isles*. 2 vols. Boston: G. K. Hall, 1988.

University of Reading Library, Research Projects Team. *Location Register of Twentieth Century English Literary Manuscripts and Letters*. 2003. www.reading.ac.uk/library/about-us/projects/lib-location-register.asp (10 April 2009).

As we have seen, the websites of archives and special collections are invaluable to researchers, potentially providing a number of services such as descriptions of collections, online finding aids, online catalogs, and even digitized copies of selected items from the collections. However, to take advantage of this information, you must first be aware of which collections are held where. A well-planned Internet search may easily turn up some of the most significant collections related to your research interests, but it will not be possible to do a comprehensive search for manuscripts using an Internet search engine. For this, you will need to turn to the tools discussed here, which will help you to track down everything from major collections of an author's personal papers to a single handwritten letter from the same author, which might very well be held on separate continents.

A good place to start is with the ***Oxford Dictionary of National Biography*** (*ODNB*, covered in greater detail in chapter 2), long considered the gold standard of quality biographical information for British citizens of note (along with other significant figures with important ties to Britain). The latest edition has been updated to the year 2000 and contains all major figures and most minor figures related to British literary modernism. In addition to the excellent biographical essay on the author of your choice, there is, where appropriate, a section called "Archives" at the end of the entry. This section lists archives and libraries where the author's papers may be found, along with a very brief description of the holdings. For example, in the entry for T. S. Eliot, the "Archives" section lists dozens of institutions holding papers related to this important author and critic, two of which read: "Boston PL, MSS and letters" and "NL Wales, corresp. with David Jones." Libraries may subscribe to the electronic version of the *ODNB* in addition to or instead of the print volumes; some limited full text is also available on its website at http://www.oxforddnb.com. The ***Dictionary of Literary Biography*** (also discussed in chapter 2) provides a section called "Papers" at the end of the biographical essays, which has a brief overview of some of the locations of the author's papers, with minimal if any description of the holdings. Standard or recent biographies of the figure in question are also important tools for locating personal papers. Most biographers cite the materials used in their research, or at least acknowledge the use of significant collections in the introduction or acknowledgments section of their book. All of these resources are good starting points for finding manuscript materials, but none of them is comprehensive. Additional research will be required to find all of the available materials related to your topic of interest.

There is no single finding aid for all manuscript repositories holding materials related to British modernists. There is a very evident continental divide in that reference tools related to manuscripts will tend to be geographically limited to either Britain or the United States. Since manuscripts related to British writers can be found on both continents, it will thus be necessary to consult resources related to both areas. Ash and Miller's ***Subject Collections: A Guide to Special Book Collections and Subject Emphases as Reported by University, College, Public, and Special Libraries and Museums in the United States and Canada***, has the advantage of including Canadian collections as well as those found in the United States. The emphasis here is on special collections as opposed to manuscripts, although oftentimes manuscripts are found in special collections even if the bulk of the materials are printed books. This tool is particularly helpful in uncovering some of the manuscripts that may be "hidden" in special collections. *Subject Collections* does not have an index; rather, both volumes act as a giant subject index to the collections. The subject headings are arranged alphabetically and are based, with some modifications, on standard Library of Congress subject headings. Headings of author names as subjects are particularly good for homing in on persons of interest. For example, the first subject entry in the work is for the Irish modernist poet AE. Under each subject heading, entries are arranged alphabetically by state name, followed by U.S. territories such as Puerto Rico, then by Canadian province. Each geographic category is further broken down alphabetically by city name and then by institution name. Entries contain the following information: institution name and name of collection, if applicable; address, telephone number, and e-mail address (which may be out of date at this point); holdings information, such as number of volumes, where applicable, whether the collection is cataloged, and whether it has manuscript items; and a notes field that gives helpful descriptive information regarding the collection. In addition to author names as subject headings, researchers in British modernism will also do well to browse the entries under "Literature, Modern" and "Literature, Modern—Twentieth Century" as well as any other particular subjects related to their research interests.

Donald DeWitt's two companion annotated bibliographies, *Guides to Archives and Manuscript Collections in the United States* and *Articles Describing Archives and Manuscript Collections in the United States*, are useful tools for finding further information regarding manuscript holdings in the United States. ***Guides to Archives and Manuscript Collections in the United States*** is a bibliography of published finding aids for unpublished materials. It covers manuscript materials on a variety of topics and is organized by broad subject categories. The section concerning "Literary Collections" will be of most interest here. Within this category, finding aids are arranged alphabetically by the author's last name. Complete citations are given, along with brief annotations detailing further information about the collection. ***Articles Describing Archives and Manuscript Collections in the United States*** is a bibliography of published articles concerning manuscript collections, archives, or special collections. As with *Guides*, this volume is organized topically by broad subject headings, and the one entitled "Literature," which includes over two hundred articles, will be most pertinent. Within the "Literature" category, citations are arranged alphabetically by the author's last name, along with annotations that clarify and expand upon information provided in the titles. The annotations also identify people and events documented in the collections described as well as the types of materials held in the collections. Both volumes have helpful subject and name indexes that may help identify less-obvious connections to materials of interest. A quick perusal of the indexes in these volumes reveals items relevant to several of the major British modernists, such as D. H. Lawrence and James Joyce.

On the other side of the Atlantic, Foster and Sheppard's ***British Archives: A Guide to Archive Resources in the United Kingdom*** provides a directory of the numerous archival repositories throughout the United Kingdom. The front matter of the book contains much helpful information, such as advice on how to use the book, an explanation of the arrangement of entries, and lists of useful organizations, websites, and publications. The main body of the work consists of the entries for the individual archives, which are arranged in alphabetical order by name of the town in which they are located. Each entry has the name of the archives and its parent organization, as well as full contact information, as available (including address, telephone and fax numbers, e-mail address, website URL, and who to contact for inquiries). Hours and days of normal operation are also given, along with rules for access and a statement of the archives' acquisitions policy. Brief descriptions of the archives are presented, detailing date range of holdings, and any major collections are noted, as well as the existence of nonmanuscript materials. Each entry also notes the availability of any finding aids (defined as catalogs, lists, indexes, etc.) that can be found either on-site or online. The facilities and services are also described (such as photocopying equipment and microform readers available). There is also a note on the archives' conservation practices. Finally, any published guides or other relevant works about the archives or its collections are listed, whether or not they are still in print. Following the main body of entries, there are three appendixes, covering institutions reporting transferred collections, those reporting no collections, and those not responding to the editors' inquiries. There are also two indexes. The main index is for repository titles, parent organizations, significant predecessor organizations, organizations listed in the appendixes, and titles of collections mentioned in entries. Numbers associated with entries in the index are the individual repository numbers rather than page numbers. There is also a "Guide to Key Subjects" with some subject indexing, although this is very brief and general. The "Literature" category, for example, is divided into sections for general, plays, poetry, popular, and writers but lists no specific author names or time periods.

British Archives is not comprehensive, but it does represent one of the most thorough listing of archives in the British Isles; it will serve as a good tool of discovery for archives in particular geographic regions as well as a centralized source for archival collection policies and terms of use. However, to really get a sense of where modern British literary manuscripts may be found in Britain, it will be necessary to consult David Sutton's excellent two-volume set entitled ***Location Register of Twentieth Century English Literary Manuscripts and Letters: A Union List of Papers of Modern English, Irish, Scottish, and Welsh Authors in the British Isles***. The funding to produce this work came from the Strachey Trust after British poet Philip Larkin made his impassioned plea for British libraries to collect more of the personal papers and manuscripts of living British writers.[4] The focus of the work is the papers of modern British literary authors. This work defines "British" as those authors from England, Ireland, Scotland, and Wales who write in English, as well as immigrants (such as Tagore) who have spent a significant period of time in the British Isles. The definition of "modern" is anyone who lived beyond the year 1899, which means a significant number of Victorian authors are included as well. The register lists letters and manuscripts held by publicly accessible archives and library collections in the British Isles.

The work is arranged alphabetically by the authors' last names; volume 1 covers authors from A to J, and volume 2, authors from K to Z. Each entry provides a description of the item, the date(s) associated with the item or collection, the format, and the location and collection in which the material is found. Notes following the main entry for each author also mention overseas collections, particularly those in North America, holding materials by the writer. For example, in the entry for Vera Brittain (1893–1970), we learn that there is a major collection of original materials held by the McMaster University Library in Hamilton, Ontario, as well as a large file of correspondence in the Macmillan Collection held at New York Public Library. This is followed by forty-four entries listing letters and other materials held in Britain. The appendix following the main listings lists addresses for all institutions cited; there is no index.

Since the set was completed in the late 1980s it does not reflect the current holdings of these institutions. Luckily, the Research Projects Team at the University of Reading Library completed a supplement to Sutton's work in 2003. Currently, all records related to twentieth-century manuscripts from both works are online and searchable via the University of Reading website, titled ***Location Register of Twentieth Century English Literary Manuscripts and Letters***, including updated records for the 1988 work and the 2003 supplement materials. The site offers two search interfaces: one a keyword search for author, title, and/or word or phrase; the other a browse search by author or title. In either case, once records of interest are found, they need to be marked for saving. At the completion of your search, you may return to all marked records by going to the "Kept" link, where you can sort the records, remove ones you are no longer interested in, and either print out or e-mail brief or full records for each listing.

Additional manuscripts information can be found in Marcuse's section H on "Archives and Manuscripts" in his ***Reference Guide for English Studies***, which was addressed at greater length in chapter 2. Of greatest interest to the researcher in modern British literature will be the following subsections: "II. British Repositories"; "III. American Repositories"; "V. English Studies—Manuscripts"; "VII. British Archives"; and "VIII. American Archives." The items covered in Marcuse's work consist of printed catalogs and guides to the collections of individual repositories published prior to 1990. Marcuse provides useful annotations for the published works as well as helpful descriptions of the collections in question.

WEBSITES FOR LOCATING ARCHIVES AND MANUSCRIPT COLLECTIONS

Abraham, Terry, comp. *Repositories of Primary Sources*. www.uiWeb.uidaho.edu/special-collections/Other.Repositories.html (10 April 2009).

Archive Finder. http://archives.chadwyck.com/marketing/index.jsp (10 April 2009).

The ARCHON Directory. www.nationalarchives.gov.uk/archon/ (10 April 2009).

British Library *Manuscripts Catalogue*. www.bl.uk/catalogues/manuscripts/INDEX.asp (10 April 2009).

DocumentsOnline. www.nationalarchives.gov.uk/documentsonline/ (10 April 2009).

Guide to the Contents of the Public Record Office. 3 vols. London: H. M. Stationery Office, 1963–1968.

Index of Manuscripts in the British Library. 10 vols. Teaneck, NJ: Chadwyck-Healey, 1984–1986.
Index to Personal Names in the National Union Catalog of Manuscript Collections, 1959–1984. 2 vols. Alexandria, VA: Chadwyck-Healey, 1988.
Index to Subjects and Corporate Names in the National Union Catalog of Manuscript Collections, 1959–1984. 3 vols. Alexandria, VA: Chadwyck-Healey, 1994.
National Archives. www.nationalarchives.gov.uk/ (10 April 2009).
National Archives Catalogue. www.nationalarchives.gov.uk/catalogue/ (10 April 2009).
National Register of Archives. www.nationalarchives.gov.uk/nra/default.asp (10 April 2009).
National Union Catalog of Manuscript Collections (NUCMC). www.loc.gov/coll/nucmc/ (10 April 2009).
Nickson, M. A. E. *The British Library: Guide to the Catalogues and Indexes of the Department of Manuscripts*. 3rd rev. ed. London: British Library, 1998.
WorldCat. Dublin, OH: OCLC. www.oclc.org/firstsearch/.

As mentioned previously, websites for special collections and archives are becoming increasingly indispensable for locating specific manuscript materials. Once you've used some of the tools mentioned in the previous section to locate collections of possible interest, you should visit the website of the organization holding the collection for further information. The trend has been to make more and more manuscript information available online, through the catalog and/or by way of finding aids for larger manuscript collections. The institution's website should present information regarding where to search for what, including information about materials that may not yet have an online presence. This section covers some of the major online manuscript catalogs as well as some of their earlier print counterparts, many of which are still held by research libraries.

Once again, the British Library may be the most logical place to start. Researchers may wish to start by consulting Nickson's print volume ***The British Library: Guide to the Catalogues and Indexes of the Department of Manuscripts***, which provides an overview of the catalogs and indexes for the library's various manuscript collections. The ***Manuscripts Catalogue*** for the British Library's primary manuscript collection is available online (along with separate catalogs for more specialized manuscripts collections, such as the *Catalogue of Illuminated Manuscripts*, which will be of less interest to the researcher in modern British literature). The primary manuscripts collection has records for items ranging from pre-Christian times to the present day.

There are two ways of searching within the manuscripts catalog. Searching by descriptions is basically a form of keyword searching; the terms entered are searched across all fields in the records. Index searching searches one or more of the alphabetical indexes for names or other descriptors. The first field is the "name" field, but it can be searched by surname only. This is not intuitive and can cause problems finding materials related to authors with common surnames such as "Joyce" or "Lawrence." Given names can be added to the "Additional name" field to help narrow the search, and title keywords can be added to the "Index entry" field to find manuscripts related to a particular work. For example, placing "Woolf" in the name field and "Dalloway" in the index entry field returns a record for three notebooks containing drafts of Woolf's novel, *Mrs. Dalloway*. An extensive "Search Tips" section is included on the website, giving practical advice and examples of how to best approach each type of search and providing insight into why some searches may fail entirely. There is also a thirty-two page online "User's Guide," which gives information about the collections and how best to search them. It is important to consult both of these resources before attempting to search the catalog in order to learn best practices and avoid wasting time. The online catalog is the result of the electronic scanning of the available print indexes, so inconsistencies and errors may have crept into the records over time. Efforts are being made to find and correct errors and impose consistency within the catalog, but be aware that names of writers you are searching for may appear in more than one form. For example, while the majority of records related to Virginia Woolf state her name as "Woolf née Stephen (Adeline Virginia)," records can also be found for "Woolf (Virginia)" and "Woolf (Adeline Virginia)."

Many research libraries own copies of the ten-volume set entitled ***Index of Manuscripts in the British Library***. This is essentially a microphotographic reproduction of the main entry catalog cards from the now-obsolete card catalog for the manuscripts collection. Because it includes only items and collections that were acquired up to the year 1950, there is not in-depth coverage of materials related to modernist writers. There are listings for only one letter apiece for both Virginia Woolf and D. H. Lawrence, for instance, although the older W. B. Yeats has entries for nine separate items. For almost all purposes, researchers in modern British literature will be best served by consulting the British Library's online *Manuscripts Catalogue* since the majority of modern materials were collected in the last half of the twentieth century or more recently.

The other major repository of manuscripts in the United Kingdom is the government archive currently called the ***National Archives***. Administratively, it is an executive agency of the Secretary of State for Justice and brings together the Public Record Office, the Historical Manuscripts Commission, the Office of Public Sector Information, and Her Majesty's Stationery Office. Since the emphasis of the *Archives* is on governmental records, there are significantly fewer materials here directly related to authors and literature than is found in the British Library. However, there is much that might interest a researcher from the perspective of gaining greater historical insight into the political and social milieu of the modernist time period as represented in these records. There are also gems of information that might be encountered along the way which are related to modernist writers, such as the reports of T. S. Eliot's 1947 tour to Italy, lecturing on poetry in the theater and the influence of Poe on European literature, his 1949 tour to Germany, lecturing on the aims of poetic drama, and his planned tour to Austria, found in the British Council's files of "Tours by Specialists." Researchers may also wish to consult the three-volume print set entitled ***Guide to the Contents of the Public Record Office*** in order to familiarize themselves with the overall organization and numbering system employed by the National Archives. This *Guide* covers collections up until the 1960s, and you will find that the Eliot tour reports are part of the BW series for the British Council, which concentrates on British relations with other countries.

As with the British Library, the website of the National Archives contains considerable information regarding both its holdings and their policies and procedures for visiting and using materials onsite. The web page entitled "Plan Your Visit to the National Archives" gives a brief overview of the materials collected, explains how to register for a reader's ticket, and details procedures for ordering documents in advance of your visit. It explains policies regarding what is and isn't allowed in the reading rooms, the number of documents that can be requested at any one time, and the wait period for receiving them. There is also a "virtual tour" of the archives available on the website, providing pictures and descriptions of different areas of the archives and how to use them; everything from parking your car to reading, copying, and returning documents is covered. An interactive map is provided to orient you to the overall physical layout of the archives.

Prior to visiting, a great deal of research can be conducted online to help prepare for an on-site visit. The archives recommends starting with the "Research Guides: A–Z" section of the website, which lists guides on a variety of topics of interest. These guides give an overview of the collections and their particular foci; several of these, such as the guides relating to World War II or the one concerned with the 1916 Easter Uprising in Ireland, may be of interest to scholars of modern British literature. There are also a number of online catalogs and finding aids available. Unless you are specifically interested in hospital records, migration records, or other specialized record groups with separate search engines, it is most likely that the main ***National Archives Catalogue*** (formerly called *PROCAT*) will serve your needs. This catalog contains records for almost eleven million manuscripts from the central government, courts of law, and other national organizations within the United Kingdom. The catalog search is essentially a keyword search for a word or phrase, with the option to limit your search to a particular date range or a particular department or series code, if known. The catalog also offers the option to search specifically for the name of "places, prominent people & subjects," although this search homes in on the most important records related to the search term as opposed to each occurrence in the catalog. For example, "places, prominent people & subjects" can be used to search for "Edward VIII" and returns a record giving his birth and death dates and the most relevant details of his life. Clicking on "Search" from this record leads to descriptions of two documents, one from the miscellaneous records of the Foreign Office and one from the Privy Council concerning his abdication. In contrast, doing a phrase search in the regular catalog on "Edward VIII" returns a two-page list of government bodies that have records related to him, from 158 items in the records of the Home Office to one record from the British Council. An "Advanced Search" option is also available in the catalog, but this is most useful for persons who are intimately familiar with the collections of the National Archives. It allows for professional-level searching on such parameters as closure status, custodial history, and physical condition.

The National Archives also has a separate search interface called ***DocumentsOnline***, which provides access to digitized versions of some of the most popular items held by the archives. These include such things as the collection of wills, World War I diaries, and Cabinet Papers from 1915 to 1977. Some items are available online for free, and copies of the images of others may be ordered (for a fee) directly through the *DocumentsOnline* search interface. Since many of these items fall within the modern time period, this is an interesting area to browse for full-text materials. It can save considerable time and effort if researchers can purchase copies of relevant documents without making a trip abroad to obtain them. In addition to those materials available through *DocumentsOnline*, almost any nonrestricted record held by the *National Archives* can be ordered in a variety of formats (print, digital, or microform) and obtained by post or electronic download. Information on requesting a cost estimate and other ordering information can be found on the archives website.

Two other resources are available on the *National Archives* website that may prove useful to researchers in modern British literature. The first is the ***National Register of Archives***, which contains location and coverage information concerning tens of thousands of historical records created by individuals, families, businesses, and organizations. Previously administered by the Historical Manuscripts Commission (HMC), one of the National Archives' parent organizations, this register is now a project falling under the larger umbrella of the Archives. The *Register* does not provide thematic or subject-level access but is searchable by personal name of an individual or family or by business or organization name. Five indexes are available for online searching: the business index, the organizations index, the personal index, the families and estates index, and the diaries and papers index. The personal index is reserved for those individuals who are "known" on some level and can be traced through standard sources such as the *Dictionary of National Biography* or *Who Was Who*. The diaries and personal papers index focuses on materials produced by "average" citizens who would not be located in standard biography resources. These diaries and papers do have the advantage of limited keyword searching for topics such as travel and local history. Simple searches are available for each index, as well as additional advanced search functions such as the ability to limit results by date or other parameters. Records returned describe the scope of the collection (date ranges and types of materials), the name of the repository holding the records (along with a hotlink to the repository's website, if available), a record reference (call number of materials in their home repository, including a link to their records, finding aids, or catalog, if available), an NRA catalogue reference (if a hard copy of the catalog describing the collection is held by the National Archives), and other references (to standard reference sources, such as the *Location Register of Twentieth Century English Literary Manuscripts and Letters*, which may further describe the collection). Sample searches for personal names "David Herbert Lawrence" and "Virginia Woolf" returned thirty-one and twenty records, respectively, for items held in repositories in Britain and the United States.

The other resource of interest that is available on the *National Archives* website is the ***ARCHON Directory***. This searchable online directory has both an A to Z list for browsing and a search engine for finding contact information for business, local, national, special, and university repositories of records within the British Isles. A typical entry has the name of the institution and its *ARCHON* code, mailing address, telephone and fax numbers, e-mail address, and website URL. If available, there may also be access information, such as hours of operation, and NRA information, such as which NRA indexes include entries for this repository. Links to specific online finding aids may be provided as well. *ARCHON* additionally contains information concerning overseas repositories that hold collections noted in the *National Register of Archives*. These collections may be located via the online search engine or through an alphabetical list spanning Australia to

Zimbabwe. The same information is presented as for domestic institutions. The *ARCHON Directory* is linked to the *National Register of Archives*, described above, so that any collections or materials in that resource have links to the *ARCHON* entry for complete contact information and any additional details. In turn, *ARCHON* links to the repositories themselves and to any available online resources.

Another ambitious online directory of archival and manuscripts resources is the website called ***Repositories of Primary Sources*** hosted by the University of Idaho and compiled by Terry Abraham, emeritus professor and former head of special collections and archives at the university library. The list is primarily arranged geographically, with separate sections covering the various regions of the United States and Canada, Latin America and the Caribbean, Europe, Asia and the Pacific, and Africa and the Near East. Each category is further broken down geographically by country or by state/province. Institutions are arranged alphabetically by name within each category. The listing consists merely of the name of the institution with a hotlink taking the researcher to the institution's webpage that best describes its collections. Entries are limited to those institutions housing original primary materials, as opposed to virtual collections or exhibitions. The "Additional Lists" link goes to a page recommending useful websites that also list institutions housing primary research materials. Most of these deal with archival holdings within individual countries or with materials focused on specific subject matter, such as history of science, Judaica, or gay and lesbian materials. Although the *Repositories of Primary Sources* site does not provide any topical or subject indexing, it is a fascinating resource serving as an easy-access gateway to the top archives and special collections from around the world.

For archival materials held in the United States, where many modern British literature materials are found, the ***National Union Catalog of Manuscript Collections*** (*NUCMC*) is the main resource available. *NUCMC* is a cooperative cataloging project administered by the Library of Congress and is intended to aid smaller organizations that may not belong individually to the OCLC cataloging system (the resource also includes materials from the Research Libraries Group, or RLG, which merged with OCLC in 2006). The records in *NUCMC* are supplied by libraries, archives, and other cultural institutions across the nation and around the world. The online database contains only those records that have been submitted since 1986 (note that the materials may originate from a much earlier time period; the cutoff date relates to the actual inputting of the records only). These records supplement those found in the freely-available *WorldCat.org* database; their combined holdings are similar in coverage to the paid version of *WorldCat*. The *NUCMC* records are comparable to those that can be located in the proprietary version of ***WorldCat*** by limiting the search to "Archival Materials." *NUCMC* offers four search forms: a simple search form (basically a keyword search) for titles, notes, and subject fields; a simple search form (keywords again) for all names fields; another simple search form for all names fields but focusing on left-anchored phrases, such as a standard Library of Congress name listing, with the most important elements (normally author's last name) anchored to the left; and an advanced search form. For manuscripts materials input from *NUCMC*'s 1959 starting date to the 1986 cutoff date, it is necessary to consult the print versions of the work. Currently, the Library of Congress has no plans for retrospective conversion to electronic format for these earlier records, although ***Archive Finder***, a commercial product from Chadwyck-Healey/ProQuest, provides access to them. *Archive Finder* has *NUCMC* records from 1959 through 2006, a number of useful directory listings and links to online finding aids, and the *National Inventory of Documentary Sources in the United Kingdom and Ireland*, previously available on microform or CD-ROM. For those researchers lacking access to these proprietary databases, it will be necessary to consult the cumulative two-volume ***Index to Personal Names in the National Union Catalog of Manuscript Collections, 1959–1984*** and the three-volume ***Index to Subjects and Corporate Names in the National Union Catalog of Manuscript Collections, 1959–1984***. There are also volumes for 1985 and 1986 that were not included in the cumulations and must be searched separately.

CONCLUSION

Using manuscripts and other archival materials can be one of the most exciting and rewarding aspects of pursuing an in-depth research project. At this point in time, we are definitely in a "hybrid" period for conducting archival research. Guides, location registers, and other printed resources are still necessary components in the research process, especially for locating relevant collections and the institutions housing them. On the other hand, this area has been dramatically affected by computerization, with more and more information becoming easily available online. Most special collections, archives, and other cultural institutions holding manuscript materials have websites available, and many of them provide resources like online catalogs, reproductions of finding aids, and even digitized copies of selected archival materials. It's faster and easier than ever to find out what is held in a particular collection and to at least make preliminary judgments about which items may be most relevant to one's research. In the past, a researcher might be required to travel a long distance to visit an archives and spend a number of days on-site painstakingly taking handwritten notes or making transcripts of the items found there. In today's online environment, a researcher can virtually "visit" an archives, peruse a relevant finding aid, perhaps view certain items online, and quickly order copies of items of interest without leaving the home or office. Old standbys such as the *National Union Catalog of Manuscript Collections* and the *National Register of Archives* are now completely or partially available online, while more and more digitization efforts such as *DocumentsOnline* are rapidly becoming available. This area of research will continue to change and develop as additional resources move to the electronic environment. In spite of this, it will be impossible to have digital copies of all archival materials available online in the foreseeable future, and for that reason these items will remain somewhat elusive to the researcher. Following the practices outlined here and having the patience to ensure a thorough search for materials will continue to produce the best results whether using print or electronic finding aids or, more likely, some combination of the two.

NOTES

1. See Evelyn Tennyson Openhym and Alan Littell, comp., *Bibliography of the Openhym Collection of Modern British Literature and Social History, Herrick Memorial Library, Alfred University* (Alfred, NY: Alfred University Press, 1980).
2. See *The Library of Leonard and Virginia Woolf: A Short Title Catalog* at www.wsulibs.wsu.edu/Holland/masc/woolflibrary.htm.
3. Virginia Woolf, *A Room of One's Own* (New York: Harcourt, 2005), 26.
4. See Larkin's speech, "A Neglected Responsibility: Contemporary Literary Manuscripts," presented to the Manuscripts Group of the Standing Conference of National and University Libraries (SCONUL) at King's College, London in 1979. It is reproduced in Philip Larkin, *Required Writing* (Ann Arbor: University of Michigan Press, 1999), 98–108.

Chapter Ten

Web Resources

As we've seen throughout this book, an increasing number of resources are becoming available electronically. Some of the most important tools are proprietary databases that are Web-based and require payment in order to access. Most of these resources are beyond the budget of individuals; check with the reference staff at your institution to find out what's available through the library. The current chapter instead focuses on publicly available websites, those resources that are free (or available at nominal cost in the case of some newspaper archives) and available for anyone to access.

Researchers in modern British literature will find both a plethora of resources and some frustrating gaps when it comes to Web resources. On the one hand, a number of useful sites explore modernism as a concept, often broadly, in terms of art, architecture, and other concerns in addition to literature. On the other hand, there are fewer full-text websites for literature from this time period, in contrast to literature from earlier eras, due to copyright restrictions still in place on much of this material in both Britain and the United States. In spite of these drawbacks, a number of Web-based resources will still be of interest, including union catalogs, bibliographies, scholarly gateways, online journal sites, and individual author sites. The resources considered here represent a sampling of some of the most high-quality materials available on the Web relevant to British modernism.

Before considering individual resources, it's important to be aware that searching the Web is very different from searching an abstracting and indexing database or an online library catalog. Databases and catalogs have specific rules and conventions that govern their construction and facilitate the end user's ability to search them. The Web, on the other hand, does not have rules that govern its construction in the same way. Thus the Web is more open and unpredictable, which make it more dynamic but also harder to search at times. Materials referenced in databases and catalogs are also vetted to a certain degree for quality and appropriateness; no such vetting occurs on the Web, so it is up to the individual searcher to determine what constitutes a quality resource and what does not. What follows are some evaluation criteria that professional librarians have agreed will enable end users to make such determinations regarding website quality. These criteria can also be used for evaluating other types of print and electronic resources as well.

When looking at a particular website (as well as other Internet resources such as blogs or wikis), here are some things to look for and questions to keep in mind:

Authority. Who is responsible for the content of the website? What qualifications does the author or responsible agency have, and how relevant are they to the content of the web page? Is there an "About" or "Contact" link that might shed light on where a web page originates? Check out the extension of the main web page's URL. If the site has a .edu or .gov extension, that means it's coming from an approved institution of higher learning or a governmental agency. These sources can usually be relied upon to contain quality information. Be aware, however, that many colleges and universities provide server space to students, and student web pages can vary considerably in terms of quality and accuracy.

Accuracy. How reliable and free of factual error is the website? Can the information be verified in other resources? Some things to look for include citations to outside reliable sources, descriptions of research methods, and good quality of presentation within the website such as working links and absence of spelling and grammatical errors. Although this is less likely to happen in the world of literary scholarship, be aware that there are intentional hoaxes on the Web. Most of these are relatively benign, but some are more insidious, for example, the white supremacist site that attempted to mimic the website of the Martin Luther King, Jr. Center.

Objectivity. Is the material biased in any way? Are the viewpoints expressed intended to promote a particular agenda or school of thought? Every writer or producer of a website has a particular viewpoint, so objectivity in its purest sense is probably impossible to achieve. However, it's important to be aware of viewpoint and any secondary agendas that might be behind material found on the Web. For example, resources posted by a family member or literary heir of a significant writer might have an agenda of showing the writer in the best possible light and thus may not be as objective as material coming from a source less directly connected to the writer.

Coverage or scope. What is the depth and breadth of the subject presented? Who is the intended audience for this website? Sites may be geared toward the general public, enthusiasts, scholars, or some other audience. Even popular sites targeted at the general public may have useful information, but being aware of the level at which the information is focused may influence your use of it.

Currency. When was the information written or last updated? No firm standards exist, but many websites post the date of the most recent update at the bottom of the page. Wiki entries and blog posts are normally dated. Currency is less of an issue for most literary subjects since ideas do not go out of date as quickly as in other fields of knowledge. However, knowing when something was written (placing it as contemporary with the author, for instance) can influence one's interpretation of its meaning.

Following are selected Web-based resources that may interest the scholar of modern British literature. Some of these sites are mentioned here for the first time, while others have been discussed in previous chapters. They are drawn together here as a matter of convenience for those seeking guidance in finding quality information freely available on the Internet. Many worthwhile websites exist beyond the few referenced here, and Internet resources are continuously changing, so conducting your own search based on the criteria outlined above will also be an important step in the ongoing research process. For example, you might want to regularly conduct an Internet search in either *Google* or *GoogleScholar* for various keywords related to your research interests; use the "Advanced Search" options, which will allow you to seek out new or recently modified websites or electronic resources based on date ranges. When using Web portals or gateway sites, which are web pages that collect and link to other web pages relevant to particular topics, you may encounter broken links that do not lead to the desired page. In that case, try doing a *Google* search for the title of the Web resource mentioned, as it is possible that the URL has changed.

SCHOLARLY GATEWAYS

Internet Public Library. British: 20th Century. www.ipl.org/div/litcrit/bin/litcrit.out.pl?pd=British:+20th+Century (10 April 2009).

Liu, Alan. *Voice of the Shuttle: Modern (Brit. & Amer.).* http://vos.ucsb.edu/browse.asp?id=2747 (10 April 2009).

Lynch, Jack. *Literary Resources—Twentieth-Century British, Irish, and Commonwealth.* http://andromeda.rutgers.edu/~jlynch/Lit/20th.html (19 January 2009).

Instead of trying to wade through the results of a search of the entire Internet, sometimes it's easier and more efficient to consult a gateway or portal site—a website that provides links to other websites based on subject matter. A number of gateways are devoted to modern or twentieth-century literature. Some of them are specifically focused on British writers, while others may include American or other international writers. Most of these sites are produced by scholars in the field and contain a wide range of interesting and useful links.

The ***Voice of the Shuttle*** website from Alan Liu (University of California, Santa Barbara) has long been acknowledged as one of the most comprehensive gateway sites for the humanities. Sections within the main website cover a variety of humanities topics as well as some that are more relevant to the social sciences or technology. Scholars of modern British literature will be most interested in the ***Modern (Brit. & Amer.)*** page within the literature area. The *Modern* page consists of a number of subsections: "General Resources in Modern Lit."; "Modern British Authors, Works, Projects"; "Modern American Authors, Works, Projects"; "Criticism"; "Course Syllabi"; "Journals"; "Listservs & Newsgroups"; and "Conferences." The largest subsections are the ones related to major British and American authors. These have everything from scholarly or popular websites devoted to the author to sites with full text of some of the author's work. Parties responsible for producing the linked websites are listed, along with the name of the website as a hotlink. In some cases, entries may also have a brief explanatory annotation. Although broken links are not always promptly corrected on this site, it remains one of the most extensive listings for websites focused on modern literature. The *Voice of the Shuttle* page on *General English Lit. Resources* may also be of interest.

Jack Lynch (Rutgers) maintains a large collection of gateway web pages related to literature and criticism from a number of time periods and perspectives. The page devoted to ***Literary Resources—Twentieth-Century British, Irish, and Commonwealth*** is most relevant here. The bulk of its links are also devoted to individual author sites, although unlike the *Voice of the Shuttle*, it focuses primarily on British authors and includes a number of minor writers (such as Wyndham Lewis, Seamus Heaney, and George Orwell) in addition to the usual canonical figures. Links to general resources as well as those related to "The Great War" are also presented. Each entry consists of a hyperlinked title of the web page, the name of the individual or institution responsible for it, and a brief annotation. While there are some problems with broken links here as well, it is worth consulting this page in addition to the *Voice of the Shuttle* website as each site supplies unique and valuable content.

The *Internet Public Library* (*IPL*) is a far-ranging website maintained by a consortium of graduate schools in the field of library and information science and currently hosted at Drexel University. As the name implies, the site is intended to operate as a "virtual" public library, and toward that goal it organizes and facilitates access to freely available information on the Internet. One resource of particular interest from its Online Literary Criticism Collection is the ***British: 20th Century*** page. This consists of a listing of "Sites about British: 20th Century literature" and a set of links to author pages also maintained by the *IPL*. The site listings have the title of the web page referred to (with an embedded hyperlink), the URL of the website written out, and a fairly substantial description, often in the form of a quotation taken directly from the source itself. Additional information is also provided, if available, concerning the contents, the author, the parent web page, and any applicable keywords. The author pages contain information for both modern and contemporary authors and for lesser-known writers as well as those who are more canonical. Critical, biographical, and other sites are linked here as well. For many authors, there are links to *IPL* pages supplying information regarding sites focused on specific works. As with the other gateway sites, the *IPL* sometimes has a problem with broken links. However, it also provides access to some interesting and unusual materials not cited elsewhere.

ELECTRONIC TEXT ARCHIVES

Electronic Text Center, University of Virginia Library. *Modern English Collection*. http://etext.lib.virginia.edu/modeng/modeng0.browse.html (10 April 2009).

Oxford Text Archive. http://ota.oucs.ox.ac.uk/ (10 April 2009).

Project Gutenberg. www.gutenberg.org/wiki/Main_Page (10 April 2009).

As mentioned in chapter 8, there are no comprehensive collections of modern British literature texts in electronic format available either commercially or free on the Internet. This is due to the fact that many modernist works still remain under copyright in both the United States and the United Kingdom. As time passes and more works enter the public domain, it is anticipated that these materials will be added to the electronic text sites already available on the Web. Perhaps new websites will also emerge that are focused more discreetly on modernist literature. In the meantime, some earlier modern works can be found in the more general text sites currently available.

Probably the oldest and the largest digital library on the Internet is ***Project Gutenberg***. It began in 1971 as a project of graduate student Michael Hart at the University of Illinois. From humble beginnings at the dawn of the electronic age, the archive has grown to over 28,000 free, public domain e-books available on the parent site, with over 100,000 full-text electronic books available through the combined efforts of *Project Gutenberg* and its partners and affiliates. Most pre-1923 works by the major British modernists, which are safely in the public domain in both the United States and Great Britain, are available. Every e-book can be found in plain text format, and most have additional formats available as well, such as PDF, HTML, or ASCII. Many materials are also available in formats for e-book readers and audio files. The home page has search boxes for quickly finding resources by author and/or title keywords. The advanced search screen provides additional options, including the ability to search by Library of Congress call number or subject and to limit results by language or format of the work. Although not currently available, enhanced search capabilities, such as being able to search by publication date or date range or by place of publication, would make the site even more useful to scholars. In addition to most of the major works of James Joyce, several early works by Virginia Woolf, and more than a dozen works by D. H. Lawrence, there is also a good representation of other works by major and minor British writers of the modernist era, such as Forster's *A Room with a View* and Conrad's *Heart of Darkness*.

The ***Modern English Collection***, from the University of Virginia Library's Electronic Text Center, is a much smaller collection that also contains high-quality reproductions of texts of scholarly interest. Here the term *modern* is defined much more broadly than we define it here, encompassing writing going back to the 1500s. The collection is international in scope, with an emphasis on American writing. Some materials are restricted to University of Virginia users only, but much is freely available, such as some full-text materials by British modernist writers Joyce, Conrad, and Woolf. The special collection of "Bestsellers 1900–1930" has English-language best-selling novels by American and British authors, including many who are now considered "minor" or are entirely overlooked. As mentioned in chapter 8, this material is not necessarily in the public domain but may appear in the collection as a result of an agreement with the publishers and copyright holders. Researchers who make use of the collection may not download the text, reproduce or mount it elsewhere, or use the text for any commercial purposes, but it is available for scholarly use.

The ***Oxford Text Archive*** (***OTA***) is a similar, university-based scholarly electronic text initiative. Thousands of primary documents in twenty-five languages have been collected, cataloged, and preserved through this archive, with the focus on materials of value for teaching and research in higher education. Works collected range from the ancient Greeks through the present. The full text of a number of works by British modernists are preserved here, although most of them have restricted, rather than free, access. To obtain access to restricted materials, it is necessary to apply for approval. This is a relatively simple process, involving filling out an online form with contact information and agreeing to comply with all copyright restrictions. The entire list of over 2,500 texts can be browsed, or the holdings may be searched by using a customized *Google* search interface associated with the site. This search function allows for either a single-box simple keyword search or an advanced search that enables further fine-tuning of results. Documents are available in a number of formats, depending upon what has been provided to the archive. Some titles can be found in more than one format, such as plain text, SGML, and COCOA. The *OTA* is actively seeking to increase its holdings, so it is assumed that the collection of modern British literature titles found here, as well as in the other repositories listed above, will continue to grow.

AUTHOR SITES

International Virginia Woolf Society. www.utoronto.ca/IVWS/ (10 April 2009).

International James Joyce Foundation. http://english.osu.edu/research/organizations/ijjf/default.cfm (10 April 2009).

University of Nottingham. *DH Lawrence: Celebrating a Literary Life*. www.dh-lawrence.org.uk/ (10 April 2009).

Websites focused on particular British modernist authors or movements can be found in abundance on the Internet. Many of these are sites maintained by scholarly societies devoted to the author or movement in question; others may be maintained by libraries holding significant collections of papers related to the topic, or they may be projects of individual scholars or aficionados. Quality and content vary greatly from site to site, as does the timeliness of updating. The websites listed here are meant to be representative of some of the specific author sites available. More resources of this type on a wide range of authors may be located through some of the gateway sites listed above or by doing a focused Internet search.

The website for the ***International Virginia Woolf Society (IVWS)*** is typical of many produced by scholarly societies. The site provides information about the society's activities, such as its participation in the Annual International Virginia Woolf Conference and its sponsored programs at the annual meeting of the Modern Language Association (MLA). The society's bylaws and list of officers are posted, as are instructions for joining the *IVWS* and requests for conference paper proposals. The society produces an annual bibliography of works (including books, articles, dissertations, and theses) related to Virginia Woolf; the bibliographies for 1996 forward are available electronically on this website. The site has a page for news items, although this appears to be updated infrequently. The *IVWS* also sponsors a listserv that anyone can join; a page on the website describes the list and gives instructions for signing up. Two additional pages containing useful information are the page for "Other Societies," which directs the reader to other Virginia Woolf societies and related academic societies, and the "Links" page, which lists Virginia Woolf resource materials such as out-of-print books, publishers, electronic texts, research materials, and related sites covering such topics as travel and film.

The ***International James Joyce Foundation***'s website is hosted by the Ohio State University's Department of English. It is set in frames within the department's website, which sometimes makes navigation confusing. The foundation is a membership society similar to the *IVWS*, and its website has many comparable materials. There are links to information about the board of trustees of the foundation and its bylaws as well as an online membership form. A "News and Events" page provides details about upcoming conferences, available scholarships, educational opportunities related to Joyce, and news regarding the foundation. A special page on the website is devoted to "Joyce & Copyright," explaining when various works will enter the public domain in the United States, the European Union, and other nations, as well as information about copyright lawsuits related to Joyce's work. Another extremely useful feature of this website is the "James Joyce Research Center." This area has a number of resources such as a "Joycean Timeline," a list of works by Joyce, including editions with major revisions, an extensive bibliography of books on Joyce, a small image gallery, citations to criticism on Joyce from various theoretical standpoints, a list of links, addresses, and mailing lists, and an online bookstore that links citations for books about Joyce to *Amazon.com* for immediate purchase.

The website produced by the University of Nottingham titled ***DH Lawrence: Celebrating a Literary Life***, has a slightly different focus from the previous two author websites run by scholarly societies. The university has direct ties to Lawrence; he studied there for his teaching certificate in 1906 and used that experience as the model for the character Ursula's college life in his novel *The Rainbow*. The university now boasts not only an impressive collection of materials related to the author and his circle in the D. H. Lawrence Collection maintained by the library's Manuscripts and Special Collections section, but has a Research Centre devoted to Lawrence. This website is copiously illustrated with photographs from the Lawrence Collection and has a number of interactive elements. The "Biography" section, which briefly covers Lawrence's life from birth to death, was written by University of Nottingham professor and Lawrence scholar John Worthen. There is also an interactive time line of Lawrence's life and career and a virtual tour of sites and institutions related to Lawrence in the East Midlands region of England. Descriptions of the facilities at the university that have some connection to Lawrence are also provided, including links to the D. H. Lawrence Collection pages. The library pages have further links to the catalog for print materials, the finding aids for manuscript materials, and additional information about Lawrence, such as a bibliography of his works and the full text of John Worthen's extensive biography. Both the main web page and the "Collection" web page have links to other resources concerning Lawrence, such as scholarly societies, criticism, and reviews.

CONTEMPORARY NEWSPAPERS AND JOURNALS

British Library Newspapers Collection. www.bl.uk/reshelp/inrrooms/blnewspapers/newscat/newscat.html (10 April 2009).
Guardian and Observer Digital Archive. http://archive.guardian.co.uk/ (10 April 2009).
Modernist Journals Project. www.modjourn.org (10 April 2009).
Modernist Magazines Project. www.cts.dmu.ac.uk/exist/mod_mag/index.htm (10 April 2009).
New York Times Article Archive. www.nytimes.com/ref/membercenter/nytarchive.html (10 April 2009).
Times Archive. http://archive.timesonline.co.uk/tol/archive/ (10 April 2009).

Due to ongoing copyright considerations, a good portion of modern-era newspapers and periodicals have not yet entered the public domain. This situation certainly limits the access to research materials that the World Wide Web could potentially facilitate, as evidenced by journal and newspaper collections currently available for earlier eras. In spite of this drawback, there are still a number of Web-based resources available for free or minimal cost that will be of interest to researchers in modern British literature.

The ***Modernist Journals Project***, referenced in chapter 8, is a joint project of Brown University and the University of Tulsa. Of particular interest is its journals collection, which provides high-quality scanned PDF reproductions of twelve of the most important modernist literary journals published between 1896 and 1922. The journals are *Blast*, *The Blue Review*, *Coterie*, *Dana*, *The English Review*, *The New Age*, *The Owl*, *Le Petit Journal des Réfusées*, *Poetry*, *Rhythm*, *The Tyro*, and *Wheels*. The site has a search engine that can access the full contents of these journals as well as the parent website. Searching can be conducted by field (author, title, or subject) or across the entire full text. Another useful feature is the section called "On or About December 1910"—a reference to a quote from Virginia Woolf that "on or about December 1910 human character changed" and modernism officially gained ascendancy. This section features two dozen reproductions of representative popular journals from the 1910–1911 time period, including individual issues of *Cosmopolitan*, *Good Housekeeping*, *The Ladies' Home Journal*, *National Geographic*, and *The Saturday Evening Post*. These issues present a snapshot of the cultural milieu of this important time period in both Britain and the United States. These periodicals cannot be accessed through the site's main search engine but can be searched individually. A number of books, book chapters, and essays relating to modernism are also available in full text; these are either public domain works from the modernist period or more recent works for which copyright permissions have been obtained. The website also has a "List of modern magazines of literary or artistic significance operating during the period 1890–1922," a searchable biographical database of modernist artists and writers, and a list of resources for teaching with the *Modernist Journals Project*.

The ***Modernist Magazines Project***, the brainchild of a team of United Kingdom researchers, currently indexes thirty-eight "little magazines" ranging in publication date from 1850 to 1942. Titles may be sorted alphabetically or chronologically, and contents for each issue are listed in page order. An alphabetical author index is also available, as well as a search engine that allows you to search by author or title words. Magazines indexed include *The Blue Review* (1913), *Contemporary Poetry and Prose* (1936–1937), *Twentieth Century Verse* (1937–1939), and the *Yellow Book* (1894–1897). Although only a very limited amount of full text is provided at this time, the resource is quite useful for easily searching both the contents of various little magazines and the publication trends of various authors. There is some overlap between the journals indexed here and those found in full text at the *Modernist Journals Project* website. Unique content is covered in each website, however, so both will prove of interest to researchers concerned with the periodical literature of the modernist time period.

Three major newspapers from Great Britain now have searchable Web-based interfaces for deep back files of their reporting. The ***Times Archive*** offers two hundred years of the *Times*, from 1785 to 1985, and the ***Guardian and Observer Digital Archive*** provides access to the *Guardian* (formerly the *Manchester Guardian*) from 1821 to 1990 and to the *Observer* (the world's oldest Sunday newspaper) from 1791 to 1990. The *Times Archive* offers free access to a smattering of historical articles of popular and topical interest directly on its home page. A search box allows for keyword searching of the entire archive with the ability to limit the date range. A search box is available to select a particular date for a "single-day" search, which essentially allows you to browse the contents of that issue. Both of these searches are free and return thumbnail pictures of a given article's placement within the page as well as the first few lines of text. To access the PDF version of the full article, however, you must register and pay a fee. Rates are fairly reasonable and may be purchased for a day, a month, or a year, in U.S. dollars or British pounds sterling. The *Guardian and Observer Digital Archive* does not supply any free content on its web page, and its fee schedule is considerably higher than that of the *Times Archive* (a three-day pass for the *Guardian* is the same price as a month-long pass at the *Times*, as of February 2009). The *Guardian and Observer* site offers a quick keyword search box on the home page, or you can freely use the advanced search, which allows the ability to limit your results by date range, type of article, and publication. Citations returned include the name of the publication, the date, and the page number and section number, if applicable. A PDF of the headline for the article where search terms are found is also presented, but you will need to be a paid registered user in order to access the full-text PDF.

Researchers in British modernism may be most interested in British newspapers; however, given the cultural ties and exchange between Britain and the United States during the modern period, a major American newspaper such as the *New York Times* may also prove useful. The ***New York Times Article Archive*** allows the ability to search the complete back file of the newspaper from 1851 to the current day. The *Archive* is divided into two parts, one covering 1981 to the present and the other, 1851 to 1980. In the more contemporary section, articles from 1987 forward are freely accessible to users who register. The second part, for the deeper back file, will be of more interest to researchers of modernism. The good news here is that articles from 1851 to 1922 are considered in the public domain and are also freely available to registered users. Articles from 1923 through 1986 can be purchased at a per-article price or at a discounted rate for a ten-article package. The search interface for the *New York Times Article Archive* is clumsier than those of its British counterparts. A simple search in the 1851–1980 section of the *Archive* is likely to return literally millions of results. The advanced search interface does allow the ability to narrow the date range and also to search the headline or for a specific author. Search results return the headline, first words of the lead paragraph, date of issue, and byline. Clicking on the headline brings you to a preview of the article, which has essentially the information from the search results and a link to either a PDF of the article or a means to purchase it. For researchers who do not have access to commercial databases for historical newspapers, such as those discussed in chapter 7, these online newspaper archives are a valuable service. The ability they provide to search these newspaper back files and to obtain full-text articles for free or reasonable cost will certainly prove to be a time-saver over searching microfilm collections.

Additional access to a wide variety of British newspapers and periodicals dating from the modern time period can be found by searching the catalog of the British Library ***Newspapers Collection***, discussed in chapter 7. This extensive collection contains all United Kingdom national daily and Sunday newspapers from 1801 to the present as well as most United Kingdom and Irish regional newspapers, many going back to the nineteenth century. The holdings include a number of United Kingdom and Irish popular periodicals. To access the information concerning the *Newspapers Collection*, it is necessary to search the "Newspapers" subset of the British Library's *Integrated Catalogue*. The catalog gives holdings and publication information only, but no article-level indexing. This is a good tool for finding out which newspapers were being published in a given time period and which were active in certain areas of the country, but it will require further research to locate particular articles of interest.

LIBRARY AND ARCHIVAL RESOURCES

The ARCHON Directory. www.nationalarchives.gov.uk/archon/ (10 April 2009).

British Library. *Integrated Catalogue*. http://catalogue.bl.uk (10 April 2009).

Copac. www.*Copac*.ac.uk (10 April 2009).

Library of Congress. *Online Catalog*. http://catalog.loc.gov/ (10 April 2009).

National Archives. www.nationalarchives.gov.uk/ (10 April 2009).

National Archives Catalogue. www.nationalarchives.gov.uk/searchthearchives/catalogue.htm (10 April 2009).

National Register of Archives. www.nationalarchives.gov.uk/nra/default.asp (10 April 2009).

National Union Catalog of Manuscript Collections (NUCMC). www.loc.gov/coll/nucmc/ (10 April 2009).

WorldCat. www.worldcat.org (10 April 2009).

The resources in this category represent the freely accessible Web resources related to major national and international institutions providing library and archival services and materials. Most of these have been discussed more in depth in chapters 3 and 9, but they are listed again here as a convenience because of their Web-based medium and their importance to researchers. The majority of these websites are the products of government institutions in the United Kingdom and the United States. For more information on locating and exploring the resources of the many excellent academic and private libraries and archives on both sides of the Atlantic, please consult the additional print resources presented in chapters 3 and 9.

The two major "national" library catalogs, which offer access to citations for an almost comprehensive listing of English-language books and other resources, are the British Library ***Integrated Catalogue*** and the Library of Congress ***Online Catalog***. The Library of Congress *Online Catalog* contains about fourteen million records for books, serials, manuscripts, maps, sound recordings, visual materials, and other items. The British Library *Integrated Catalogue* has thirteen million records of its holdings, and the interface provides links for searching other collections held by the Library but not found in the *Integrated Catalogue*, such as the *Manuscripts Catalogues*, the *Sound Catalogue*, and *Images Online*. The parent websites for both the *British Library* and the *Library of Congress* have dazzling arrays of additional information, such as image galleries, educational resources, news, and helpful aids for navigating the websites and collections.

Another important library catalog of interest to researchers is ***Copac***, a union catalog of approximately thirty-two million records representing the combined holdings of dozens of major research collections and national libraries across the United Kingdom and Ireland. Some contributing members of *Copac* are the British Library, the National Library of Scotland, the National Library of Wales, the libraries at Oxford and Cambridge as well as other major universities, and special research institutions such as the Royal Academy of Music and the Victoria and Albert Museum. More academic and research libraries continue to join the *Copac* consortium each year, and thus the catalog continues to expand.

The open-access version of ***WorldCat***, available at http://www.worldcat.org/, takes the idea of a union catalog a step further by including millions of records from more than 69,000 libraries around the world. Both basic and advanced search options are available, along with the ability to find out where items are held. You can input your zip code or city and state location, and *WorldCat* will list the nearest libraries owning a copy of the item. This is useful for locating items you want to use quickly, but given the large dataset of *WorldCat*, it will also help identify more obscure items that may not be located nearby. In addition to books and journals, you may also search for audio and visual materials as well as computer files, music, maps, and archival collections.

Britain's ***National Archives*** is the official archive for England, Wales, and the central government of the United Kingdom. Administered by the Secretary of State for Justice, the Archives brings together records from the Public Record Office, the Historical Manuscripts Commission, the Office of

Public Sector Information, and Her Majesty's Stationery Office. Holdings include records from over nine hundred years of history, from parchment to electronic files. The ***National Archives Catalogue***, formerly called *PROCAT*, provides the ability to search for the majority of the records held in the archives. The National Archives has a number of additional services online that may also prove useful to researchers. One is the ***National Register of Archives***, which features location and coverage information concerning tens of thousands of historical records created by individuals, families, businesses, and organizations. Another is the ***ARCHON Directory***, which has both an A-to-Z list for browsing and a search engine for finding contact information for business, local, national, special, and university repositories of records within the British Isles.

In the United States, the ***National Union Catalog of Manuscript Collections (NUCMC)*** is the major online gateway to archival records. *NUCMC* is administered by the Library of Congress and operates as a cooperative cataloging project. It contains records representing historical and literary documents, public records, and other primary source materials. This free online database includes only those records that have been submitted since 1986, but these records may concern materials dating from much earlier. Participants contributing to *NUCMC* are libraries, archives, and other cultural institutions from the United States, Great Britain, and additional international locations.

CULTURAL AND HISTORICAL WEB RESOURCES

EuroDocs: Online Sources for European History. http://eudocs.lib.byu.edu/index.php/Main_Page (10 April 2009).

Halsall, Paul, ed. *Internet Modern History Sourcebook*. www.fordham.edu/halsall/mod/modsbook.html (10 April 2009).

Harry Ransom Center. www.hrc.utexas.edu/ (10 April 2009).

Intute: Arts and Humanities. www.intute.ac.uk/artsandhumanities/ (10 April 2009).

Library of Congress. *Portals to the World: United Kingdom*. www.loc.gov/rr/international/main/uk/unitedkingdom.html (10 April 2009).

Modernist Studies Association (MSA). http://msa.press.jhu.edu/ (10 April 2009).

Museum of London. *Exploring 20th Century London*. www.museumoflondon.org.uk/English/Collections/OnlineResources/X20L/default.htm (26 May 2009).

Museum of Modern Art (MOMA). www.moma.org/ (10 April 2009).

Tate Online. www.tate.org.uk/ (10 April 2009).

In addition to the websites presented in the categories above, there are many more that may be of interest to the researcher focused on modern British literature. The websites in the current category are selected examples of quality resources that focus on history, culture, and/or literature and include information relevant to British modernism.

Intute: Arts and Humanities is a subject group of the larger *Intute* website, which also covers the "Social Sciences," "Science and Technology," and "Health and Life Sciences." *Intute* is run by a consortium of higher education and further education institutions within the United Kingdom. The *Intute: Arts and Humanities* site is a gateway providing access to over 2,100 quality Web resources, selected by consortium members and partners. More than just a static listing of websites, the home page features links for searching the resources by categories such as "Cultural Studies," "Visual Arts," "History," "Religion and Theology," and more. A search box on the home page allows for quick keyword searching. A search for *modernism* produced over one hundred results, from online art gallery exhibits, to electronic journals, to archives and historical sites. The term *modernism* is interpreted broadly here, so not every website returned relates to the modern time period as it is defined in this book. An advanced search function is also available that enables you to refine your search by specifying a field to search (title, description, or keywords) or to limit results by subject or resource type.

The Library of Congress's ***Portals to the World: United Kingdom*** web page is another gateway linking to quality websites. Focusing specifically on websites related to the United Kingdom, it is broad in both subject and time period coverage. The home page has a list of categories that lead to secondary and tertiary pages of hotlinks. Categories of potential interest to researchers in modern British literature include "History," "Language and Literature," "Libraries and Archives," "Religion and Philosophy," and others. A simple map of the United Kingdom is also found on the home page, along with a link to the Central Intelligence Agency's *World Factbook*, which contains up-to-date statistical information on countries around the world.

EuroDocs: Online Sources for European History is a wiki created by Richard Hacken, the European Studies bibliographer at the Harold B. Lee Library of Brigham Young University. *EuroDocs* links to full-text historical documents related to Western Europe that are available over the World Wide Web in some format, whether transcribed, reproduced in facsimile, or translated. The documents pertain to important historical events within the countries covered and bear some political, economic, social, or cultural significance. The main page consists of a list of the Western European countries included and links to related sites of interest. Modern British literature researchers will be most concerned with the United Kingdom page, but there are separate pages for Ireland and Scotland as well. The links on the secondary page for the United Kingdom are mainly divided by time period; of most relevance here are "Britain 1816–1918" and "Britain 1919 to the present." There are also categories for "British Legal and Governmental Documents"; "British Regional, Local and Family History Sources"; "Other Collections Relevant to British History"; and a "See also" reference to the "History of Scotland." Example links to primary texts are the "Selected Speeches of Winston Churchill," "British War Posters," and documents related to World War I and World War II.

The ***Internet Modern History Sourcebook*** is part of the larger *Internet History Sourcebooks Project* from Paul Halsall of Fordham University. A number of other sourcebooks or subsidiary sourcebooks are available for different time periods or specific subjects. The focus of the *Internet Modern History Sourcebook* is on materials related to European, American, and Latin American history, and to a lesser degree on materials related to other world cultures. In this context, "modern" means from the Renaissance forward. The site contains links to full-text primary sources available on other web pages as well as information specially mounted on this website. Categories of potential interest to the researcher in modern British literature are "19th Century Britain," "Socialism" (such as materials related to the modern British Fabian socialists), "World War I," "An Age of Anxiety" (the interwar period), and "World War II." Primary source material linked to the site include Sidney Webb's "The Historic Basis of Socialism" from 1889; World War I poetry by Siegfried Sasson, Wilfred Owen, Herbert Read, and others; and Winston Churchill's "Their Finest Hour" speech to the House of Commons in 1940.

On a more local level, the Museum of London's ***Exploring 20th Century London*** website gives insight into the time period through the lens of life in Britain's political and social capital. More than seven thousand images and artifacts from the museum's collections are displayed, focusing on themes such as art and design, transport, London at war, power and politics, and work. There are a number of interactive elements, including a time line and games. This fascinating site provides explanatory text and immerses the viewer in visual images covering everything from art inspired by the Blitz to an art deco tea service.

Since modernism was much broader than a literary movement, some researchers may be interested in exploring the manifestations of modernism in related arts, particularly the visual arts. Although most modern art resources are not specifically British, it should be recognized that modernism was an international movement and British writers of the time tended to be highly aware of what was happening in both the literary and artistic worlds at home and abroad. The ***Museum of Modern Art (MOMA)*** in New York City holds impressive collections of modern and contemporary art from around the world, including not only painting, drawing, and sculpture but also photography, architecture and design, film, prints, and illustrated books. Its website allows users to browse high-quality images of highlights, recent acquisitions, and selected works from each category of materials. In addition to information about visiting the museum, upcoming exhibitions, and educational opportunities, the website provides links to research resources. These resources feature a library, the museum archives, study centers devoted to different subsets of the collections, and a searchable online catalog called *Dadabase*. *Dadabase* contains records for reference materials, auction catalogs, artists' books, and archives and manuscript materials from MOMA, the Brooklyn Museum Libraries & Archives, the Frick Art Reference Library, and the libraries that are a part of the New York Art Resources Consortium.

In Great Britain, the Tate Collection is the national collection of British art from 1500 to the present and of international modern art. The Tate has four galleries: one in Liverpool, one in St. Ives, Tate Britain in London, and Tate Modern, which is also in London. Tate Modern houses the international collection of modern art, which it defines as post-1900. Works of major modern British artists, such as Francis Bacon, Henry Moore, and Ben Nicholson, can be found at both Tate Britain and Tate Modern. ***Tate Online*** is the Web presence for all the museum's locations. It provides interfaces for each of the four galleries and contains information about the collections as well as current and past exhibitions. The "Collection" link from the *Tate Online* home page allows searchable access to images of the artwork held in the collection. Users may search by artist's name or title of work; they may also browse by artists' names or by subject matter. Searches return a high-quality image of the work and a description and history if available. The Tate also has a research center, library, archives, and searchable catalogs for both the library and archives collections. An interesting online feature made available by the Tate Archives is its "Archives Journeys," which presents subject-focused content from its collections. One of these is the *Archives Journey Bloomsbury* (http://www.tate.org.uk/archivejourneys/bloomsbury.html/), which has biographical information, images, and audio related to the best-known artists within the Bloomsbury Group (Vanessa Bell, Duncan Grant, and Roger Fry). There is some additional content relevant to other members of the group, including writers Virginia Woolf and Lytton Strachey.

The ***Harry Ransom Center***, located at the University of Texas at Austin, is a major research center for the study of modern American and English literature. Everything from incunabula to contemporary works may be found in the center's collections, but books and manuscripts related to modernism are among its major strengths. The focus on modern works dates to the acquisition in the 1950s of T. Edward Hanley's library, which contained a wealth of twentieth-century manuscripts, particularly those of G. B. Shaw and D. H. Lawrence. The center has continued to build on this strength and has amassed what is probably the world's largest and most impressive collection of modern literary works and manuscripts. The book collection has "Author Collections" devoted to Samuel Beckett, James Joyce, D. H. Lawrence, T. E. Lawrence, Ezra Pound, and George Bernard Shaw. The manuscripts collection has extensive holdings related to D. H. Lawrence, James Joyce, W. B. Yeats, Virginia Woolf, and a number of other major British modernist writers. Minor British modernists are also well represented, with holdings related to W. Somerset Maugham, A. A. Milne, J. B. Priestley, and Evelyn Waugh, among others. Online finding aids are available for manuscript collections that have been cataloged or recataloged since 1990. Significant manuscript collections and materials cataloged in 1990 or earlier may not be found online, and interested researchers should contact the center's librarians for further information. In addition to the available online finding aids, the center's website provides searchable databases for periodicals holdings and the photography collections. Books and microform holdings in the center may be searched through the University of Texas library catalog, which allows the ability to limit the search to the *Harry Ransom Center* in most cases. The website also features online exhibitions of materials from the collections and information helpful to researchers wanting to use the collections, such as policies, fees, and forms, copyright information, and contact information for curators and librarians.

A number of scholarly societies are devoted to individual authors and literary movements; information about these can be obtained via the "Scholarly Gateways" websites listed above or through a resource such as Gale's *Encyclopedia of Associations*. Whatever their specific topics of interest, researchers in modern British literature should be aware of the ***Modernist Studies Association (MSA)***. The *MSA* is the only scholarly society concerned with modernism within a broad international and interdisciplinary context, encompassing all of the arts, including literature. The *MSA*'s definition of the time period covering modernism is late nineteenth to mid-twentieth centuries, roughly the same as espoused here. An official affiliate organization of the Modern Language Association (MLA), the *MSA* holds meetings in conjunction with the MLA's annual conference in December. It also sponsors its own annual conference, generally held in the fall. The journal *Modernism/modernity* is the *MSA*'s official publication. It also sponsors an annual book prize, awarded to a publication making a significant contribution to modernist studies. Other benefits of association with the *MSA* are two listservs, one for announcements and one for discussion, access to the membership directory, and the ability to read *Modernism/modernity* online. The *MSA* website offers useful information even to nonmembers, such as a link to the *Modernism/modernity* tables of contents at *Project Muse* and a database of "Calls for Papers" from conferences and periodicals that may be of interest to modernist scholars of various stripes.

CONCLUSION

The resources available on the World Wide Web are constantly in flux. New websites become available every day, older ones are updated or left to go stale, and some disappear from active use or change Web addresses with little notice. For these reasons, along with the fact that an estimated approximately 156 million websites are currently available, it's difficult to have the "big picture" of what's available on the Web at any given time. The resources in this chapter are meant to serve as a representative sample of some of the websites that may be of interest to researchers in modern British literature. When checking out these or any other Web-based resources, be sure to proceed with caution and to take the time to determine the reliability of the information presented. While many excellent information sources are available "free and on the Internet," websites should be seen as complementary to your research rather than the dominant mode of it. This is especially true for research concerning the modern time period because of the many copyright restrictions still in place. At this point in time, and for much of the foreseeable future, websites will not readily replace the print materials or proprietary electronic resources provided by your library.

Chapter Eleven

Researching a Thorny Problem

Throughout this book, a number of reference tools and research resources relevant to the study of modern British literature have been discussed, along with some guidelines and best practices for making use of them. In pursuing any research problem, it will be necessary to consult a range of these resources in order to gain a firm knowledge base on which to build your scholarly argument. This chapter provides an example of how a researcher might work through a particular research question, consulting a number of the tools discussed in this book along the way. Although each research question has its own unique path of information gathering, the general ideas and principles presented here can form the basis for approaching almost any scholarly problem.

As with other disciplines in the humanities, research questions in literature tend to be somewhat open to interpretation. Seldom is there one "correct" answer to a problem, as would be more typical in the hard sciences. Rather, a range of answers to the same question can be suggested by different researchers; the test of what is a "better" answer to a particular question rests in qualities such as the ability to give convincing evidence and make a strong argument as well as the reader's own experiences and subjective disposition toward the case made. Questions of "influence," both personal and literary, upon a writer continue to bear fruit and are never definitively answered. To illustrate the steps one might take in pursuing a line of inquiry regarding influence, we will look here at the question, "How did her father's role as a biographer influence Virginia Woolf's writing?" Woolf's father was Leslie Stephen (1832–1904), the first editor of the *Dictionary of National Biography*, the definitive source of biographical information concerning prominent citizens of the United Kingdom. He was knighted for his efforts on this work in 1903. It is reasonable to believe that Stephen's concentrated efforts over a ten-year period (1882 to 1891, roughly from the time of Virginia's birth to when she was ten years old) on a massive writing project involving telling the stories of people's lives must have had significant influence on both his daughter's childhood and her subsequent writing career. Teasing out the nature of this influence and the ways it was manifested in Woolf's own writing should prove to be an interesting and challenging pursuit.

As with any other research topic, if you are approaching it "cold," that is, with little prior knowledge of the persons or circumstances involved, it would be best to begin by consulting some general reference sources in order to gain the background for a more detailed search. Consulting general works such as the *Oxford Companion to English Literature* and the *Cambridge Guide to Literature in English* will present the opportunity to get a capsule overview of both Woolf's and Stephen's lives and careers. Cross-references and additional entries will lead to further information and background on such topics as biography as a genre, modernism as a movement, the *Dictionary of National Biography* and its importance in Stephen's life, and other subjects relevant to Woolf and her writing (such as the Bloomsbury Group and stream of consciousness). The *Oxford Dictionary of National Biography* (as it is now known) itself will give even more detailed information about both Woolf and Stephen and should be consulted as well.

After having obtained a baseline of information on both figures from the general reference resources, the next step might be to consult more detailed primary and secondary sources of information about their lives, such as book-length biographies and published diaries and letters. Consult the catalogs of libraries you have access to in order to ascertain which materials might be immediately available to you. Additionally, consult the *WorldCat* database and/or the *WorldCat.org* website to find other works that may be obtained via interlibrary loan services. Searching for *Stephen, Leslie* as a subject in any catalog will turn up a number of books containing information about him. The earliest and most enduring biography of Stephen is Frederic W. Maitland's *The Life and Letters of Leslie Stephen*, first published in 1906 and subsequently republished on a number of occasions up to the 1990s. This work was written by a contemporary and personal friend of Stephen and focuses more on his professional life and scholarly interests than on his family life. It is an excellent source of primary information in the form of letters and for its coverage of Stephen's biographical work. Since Stephen remains a figure of interest in his own right, a number of subsequent biographies concerning him have emerged over the years, including one by Woolf's contemporary, Desmond MacCarthy (*Leslie Stephen*, Cambridge, 1937) and a more recent offering from Noel Gilroy Annan (*Leslie Stephen: The Godless Victorian*, Random House, 1984). Additional *Selected Letters of Leslie Stephen* were published by Ohio State University Press in 1996. Because of Woolf's prominence as a literary figure, searching for her as a subject will return an almost overwhelming number of materials; more refined search techniques are called for. Searching for *Woolf, Virginia* as a subject combined with *biography* as a keyword will narrow the results somewhat. Additional consultation of the review literature will help narrow the field further, revealing a couple of lengthy and critically well-received scholarly biographies of Woolf that were recently published—James King's *Virginia Woolf* (Norton, 1995) and Hermione Lee's *Virginia Woolf* (Random House, 1997). Exchanging *diaries* or *letters* for *biography* in the keyword field will also show that Woolf's complete diaries and letters have been published in multiple volumes and that shorter "selections" from each have been separately published as well. Consulting the indexes to these works will help pinpoint observations Woolf may have made about her father or the genre of biography, as well as other topics of interest.

After gaining some background knowledge of Woolf's and her father's works, as well as more in-depth biographical knowledge of each, some interesting facts begin to emerge related to Woolf, her relationship to her father, and the experience they had with both the genre of biography and writing in general. For example, although Stephen is best remembered as a biographer, he also had a career as a literary journalist, editing the *Cornhill Magazine* and writing about Swift, Pope, and Fielding. While his work on the *Dictionary of National Biography* was focused on the lives of great men, Stephen created *The Mausoleum Book*, containing biographies of deceased family members, for his children in 1895. This work is still extant and was published by Clarendon Press in 1977. As for Woolf, one of her earliest pursuits related to writing was aiding Maitland in preparing his biography of Leslie Stephen. Late in her life, Woolf was involved in the "Memoir Club," a group of family members and friends who shared reminiscences of their early lives; Woolf's contributions have been published in *Moments of Being* (Hogarth, 1978). Woolf's well-known and often-read novel *To the Lighthouse* is heavily autobiographical, and the character of Mr. Ramsey is clearly based upon her father. Woolf wrote one book-length biography herself, *Roger Fry: A Biography* (Hogarth, 1940). She also wrote two pseudobiographies that may be seen as paying homage to the genre and/or subverting it; these are *Orlando: A Biography* (Hogarth, 1928), a time-traveling fantasy loosely based on the life of Vita Sackville-West, and *Flush: A Biography* (Hogarth, 1933), detailing the life of Elizabeth Barrett Browning's cocker spaniel. Any one or more of these details may suggest a means of focusing one's research in a particular direction while still attempting to answer in some part the question of how her father's role as a biographer influenced Woolf's writing.

At this point, consulting a printed bibliography detailing the publishing history of Woolf's works may be helpful. Kirkpatrick and Clarke's *A Bibliography of Virginia Woolf* (4th ed., Clarendon, 1997), discussed in more detail in chapter 4, is useful for identifying first editions of Woolf's novels as well as subsequent scholarly editions. Additionally, this bibliography may also help identify more ephemeral materials such as pamphlets or contributions to newspapers, which may have some bearing on the subject at hand. An important factor in any literary research is a close reading of the author's texts with a critical eye focused on passages, style, or writing techniques that will shed light on the question asked or further the argument you are trying to make.

Another important step in the research process is searching for relevant materials in the secondary literature. Consulting your local library catalog and *WorldCat* may have already brought to your attention a number of books or other items with relevant content. Using electronic abstracting and indexing tools such as the *Modern Language Association International Bibliography* (*MLAIB*) and the *Annual Bibliography of English Language and Literature* (*ABELL*) will enable you to find journal articles, dissertations, books, conference papers, edited volumes, and other forms of information. As in the library catalogs, you may want to start your exploration by looking for both Stephen and Woolf by name. In the case of material related to Woolf, you will want to add additional search terms in order to focus your results, such as the titles of particular works you are interested in pursuing or specific keyword concepts such as *biography*, *father*, or *daughter*. You may also want to consult a print bibliography such as Majumdar's *Virginia Woolf: An Annotated Bibliography of Criticism, 1915–1974*, as it will provide both a deeper back file of citations and the ability to browse a large number of resources concerning Woolf in a single volume. The index will allow you to locate materials dealing with specific works by Woolf as well. To bring your quest for secondary materials more up to date, you may want to browse recent issues of scholarly journals known to publish on your topic, such as the *Journal of Modern Literature*, *MFS: Modern Fiction Studies*, and the *Virginia Woolf Quarterly*, among others.

At this point, it is probably worth mentioning that many research topics have interdisciplinary aspects to them, and it may prove useful to consult a broader range of research tools. For example, in terms of the particular research question at hand, resources in women's studies and psychology may be helpful for finding information related to father-daughter relationships and the influence of the father on a woman's career. Because biography has ties to both literature and history, research tools related to history should be consulted for information concerning the use of the genre, particularly during the Victorian and modern eras. Historical resources are also useful in finding additional perspectives on the modernist era and the general social milieu of that time period in Britain. And since Leslie Stephen was also known as a philosopher of some repute, particularly in the context of his defense of agnosticism, consulting resources in philosophy and religion may also be called for. See the appendix in this volume for suggested reference resources in other disciplines that could help further flesh out research related to modern British literature.

Once a number of primary and secondary resources have been located via catalogs, bibliographies, and related tools, the next step may be to do a little deeper historical research into such resources as contemporary reviews and period journals and newspapers. In Great Britain particularly, Leslie Stephen would be a known figure, and it is possible that some contemporary reviews of Woolf's work may have made a connection to her father and his work. An easy way to start your search would be to consult *Virginia Woolf: The Critical Heritage*, edited by Robin Majumdar and Allen McLaurin, which reproduces the full text of 135 contemporary critical reviews of Woolf's works. Arranged chronologically, this work makes it easy to locate reviews of particular works with potential ties to biography and thus to Leslie Stephen. Unfortunately, there is not a general index available in this volume that would enable a reader to locate all occurrences of Stephen's name. To find additional reviews of Woolf's work, consult some of the general review sources listed in chapter 6, such as the *Book Review Digest*, the *Combined Retrospective Index to Book Reviews in Humanities Journals, 1802–1974*, and the *Times Literary Supplement Index*. For reviews appearing in little magazines of the era, Marion Sader's *Comprehensive Index to English-Language Little Magazines, 1890–1970* should prove useful.

Searching indexes for major newspapers such as *Palmer's Index to the Times Newspaper*, the *Official Index to the Times*, and the *New York Times Index for the Published News* may reveal additional information about familial relationships and influences in news reports, reviews, and obituaries. If your library provides access to searchable full-text versions of major newspapers through *The Times Digital Archive* or *ProQuest Historical Newspapers*, you will be able to search for, view, and print out any materials located. Websites for both the *Times* and the *New York Times* allow free use of their search engines to locate articles in deep back issues, but you will have to pay to access full text or purchase copies of articles. Knowing the dates of particular events, such as Leslie Stephen's death on February 22, 1904, will enable you to more efficiently perform a manual search through other newspapers that are not indexed but that may be available to you in microform or other format.

If you are lucky enough to have access to a library owning *Major Authors on CD-ROM: Virginia Woolf*, this product will offer a unique opportunity for easily performing textual analysis on Woolf's work. This CD-ROM contains searchable, electronic versions of Woolf's complete fiction, her complete diaries, reproductions of letters and manuscripts from the Monks House Papers and the New York Public Library's Berg Collection, and reproductions of U.S. and British first editions of her works. Searching for terms such as *father* or *biography* will find every instance of Woolf's use of the words within her published and unpublished works. Most libraries don't own the *Major Authors* CD-ROM, however. It may be easier to locate a copy of Haule and Smith's impressive three-volume *Concordance to the Novels of Virginia Woolf*. Although more limited in scope than its electronic counterpart, the concordance provides useful, focused information for those conducting literary research. Here you can find that the term *father* or some variation of it was used more than four hundred times in Woolf's novels, while the term *daughter* or some variation of it was used slightly fewer than two hundred times. The word *biography* or *biographer* or another variation was used only forty-four times, but even from the scant context available, you can see that the *Dictionary of National Biography* was specifically referred to at least twice. Seeing the number of times a term of interest is used, as well as the context in which it occurs, may lead to additional insights concerning the research question. Full-text electronic versions of selected early works by Woolf may also be found in *Project Gutenberg* and the *Modern English Collection* of the University of Virginia's Electronic Text Center. These searchable electronic texts can be used for more focused attempts at textual analysis as well.

While *Major Authors on CD-ROM: Virginia Woolf* provides access to two important manuscript collections related to Woolf, you may not have access to this tool or may still feel the need to explore more deeply in nonpublished manuscript materials. The scholarly biographies consulted earlier may very well give clues to the locations of significant collections of primary materials in their notes, prefaces, introductions, or acknowledgments. The *Oxford Dictionary of National Biography* also states that significant manuscript collections for Woolf exist at the British Library, the University of Sussex, and other locations, and that collections of Stephen's correspondence and personal papers are held at the British Library, Cambridge University Library, the Bodleian Library, Oxford, and elsewhere. Consulting additional finding aids such as the *Dictionary of Literary Biography*, the *Location Register of Twentieth Century English Literary Manuscripts and Letters*, and the *National Register of Archives* may give additional insight into holdings of primary source materials for both figures. Search the website of any institution found to hold materials of potential interest to see whether more information, such as catalog records or online finding aids, are available. Follow the guidelines laid out in chapter 9 concerning contacting librarians or archivists in charge of archival and special collection materials. Between the institutional websites and any personal contacts made, you should quickly be able to ascertain either how to obtain copies of items you are interested in or how to arrange an on-site visit.

You may want to perform some Internet searching in order to see what information may be available online. As befitting a major literary figure, many websites are devoted to or contain information about Woolf; there is also a surprising amount of Internet materials available regarding Stephen. As mentioned in chapter 10, Web resources can be of widely varying quality and accuracy. Carefully review each website to determine its origin and the qualifications of the author, and make a sound judgment of reliability before citing or using Web-based materials in research. You may also wish to visit the websites of scholarly societies, such as the *International Virginia Woolf Society* (*IVWS*) or the *Virginia Woolf Society of Great Britain*, in order to find out more about current activities and publications related to Woolf. Joining such scholarly societies may also give you access to listservs populated by Woolf scholars and enthusiasts, who may welcome the opportunity to share their own insight into your research question.

CONCLUSION

Although beginning your research by seeking background information is a good choice, particularly if you have little familiarity with your subject to begin with, the steps outlined above are not necessarily meant to be indicative of a rigid path to follow in the research process. Various types of reference tools may be consulted in any order, simultaneously, and repeatedly. Research is most often a recursive process; information discovered in one resource may lead you back to other resources previously consulted in order to approach the question in a slightly different way. This loop may happen multiple times before you are satisfied with all the information gathered.

The tools mentioned above and throughout this volume are currently recommended as some of the most useful, complete, and/or up-to-date resources available. Reference tools are in a state of flux, however. Many tools are updated periodically, some may be superseded by other works that cover the topic more completely, and the migration from print to digital resources continues apace. Use these recommendations with a grain of salt and be open to finding newer, more cutting-edge research materials. Developing an understanding of the basic types of reference tools and of the research process itself will enable you to start your exploration of any topic in a myriad of settings and with a wide range of tools.

Most questions in the humanities are never definitively answered but can always be reopened and subjected to further analysis or a different mode of interpretation. By following the steps outlined above, you are sure to gather a critical mass of information on which to start building an argument in support of your own contribution to the scholarly dialogue.

Appendix

Resources in Related Disciplines

Almost every research project in literature has interdisciplinary aspects since it is difficult to divorce literature from the cultural context in which it is written. Knowledge of the historical time period along with its distinctive political and social concerns is bound to impact the way many scholars read and interpret a given piece of creative writing. Modernism is no exception to this rule; as mentioned earlier, it was, in fact, an international movement in all the arts, and modernist writers tended to be aware of what was taking place in sister art forms, from painting, to music, to film. The modern era was also marked by greater international awareness and significant social upheaval brought on by two world wars, rapid technological change, and increased scientific advancement. Therefore, most researchers will find themselves in need of information resources in one, if not several, fields outside the realm of literature. What follows is a highly selective list of reference resources in a number of disciplines, which is intended as a starting point for continuing your research in compelling new directions.

Most of the resources included here are general reference tools providing overviews and background information about the particular field in question. They may be international in scope and cover a broad time frame. Other works, such as the *Routledge Dictionary of Modern British History* and the *Columbia Encyclopedia of Modern Drama*, are more narrowly focused on modernism or the twentieth century; some confine their content to Britain. In each of the subject categories listed below, you will find the same types of tools found in this book, such as encyclopedias, dictionaries, handbooks, guides, indexes, chronologies, and so on. The same research principles suggested here also hold true for pursuing information in other fields. You will most likely be able to find books related to your topic by conducting a search in your library catalog or in *WorldCat*. Additional reference tools may be located through print or electronic research guides or subject guides produced by your library, or by consulting a reference librarian. The works by Marcuse and Harner, discussed in chapter 2, give suggestions for readings and background materials in related fields, and many of the guides, handbooks, and companions listed here also refer the reader to some of the most useful and highly regarded tools in their respective disciplines.

GENERAL

Guides

Balay, Robert, ed. *Guide to Reference Books*. 11th ed. Chicago: American Library Association, 1996.

This is one of the two standard guides for general and specialized reference tools that have been most often consulted by reference librarians throughout the past decades. *Guide to Reference Books* is the American equivalent to the Walford guides from Britain, which are referenced below. Times change, however, and it has been over ten years since the American Library Association has published a new edition of this classic guide. It has been replaced by the electronic database *Guide to Reference*, now available as an online subscription. As the more general name suggests, the publishers recognize that many reference materials are no longer published as books or in print format. Bob Kieft is the general editor for this new product; more information can be found at http://www.guidetoreference.org/HomePage.aspx.

Blazek, Ron, and Elizabeth Aversa. *The Humanities: A Selective Guide to Information Resources*. 5th ed. Englewood, CO: Libraries Unlimited, 2000.

This textbook introduces library and information science students to general and subject-specific reference materials in the humanities. Chapters cover general resources, philosophy, religion, visual arts, performing arts, and language and literature. A new edition of this work is rumored to be in the planning stages.

Lester, Ray, gen ed. *The New Walford: Guide to Reference Resources*. 3 vols. London: Facet, 2005–.

For many years, *Walford's Guide to Reference Material*, published by the Library Association (London), has been considered one of the two standard guides for general and specialized reference tools. The other is the American Library Association's *Guide to Reference Books*, listed above. *Walford's* last published volumes in its eighth edition in 1999 and 2000. The present work, now produced by a new publisher, is seen by many as essentially the ninth edition of *Walford's*. The *New Walford* comprises three volumes: volume 1, science, technology and medicine; volume 2, the social sciences; and volume 3 (not yet published), the arts, humanities, and general reference.

Indexes and Bibliographies

Academic Search Premier. EBSCO. www.ebscohost.com/.

Academic Search Premier is considered the world's largest article database for scholarly information in multiple disciplines. It indexes more than 8,300 journals in the humanities, social sciences, science and technology, and general-interest magazines. Full-text articles are provided for more than 4,500 of those titles.

Expanded Academic ASAP. Gale/Cenage Learning. www.gale.cengage.com/ExpandedAcademic/.

Expanded Academic ASAP indexes more than four thousand journals in the humanities, social sciences, science and technology, and general interest. Full-text articles are also available for almost 2,500 of the titles indexed. While there is some overlap in content with *Academic Search Premier*, there are also unique materials. Researchers should take advantage of as many multidisciplinary databases as they have access to when completing a broad literature search.

ProQuest Dissertations and Theses. ProQuest. http://www.proquest.com/en-US/catalogs/databases/detail/pqdt.shtml.

Some libraries may still hold print or microfilm editions of *Dissertation Abstracts* from UMI. For a long time, this was the standard tool for finding information about dissertations written in the United States and abroad. As with many other resources, the company has been purchased by another vendor, and the tool has migrated to the electronic environment. Known as *Digital Dissertations* for a brief period, the product now called *ProQuest Dissertations and Theses* includes citations to 2.4 million dissertations and theses from institutions of higher learning around the world. Coverage ranges from 1861 to the present. Some versions of the product include full-text access to at least some of the materials cited; dissertations may also be purchased in a variety of formats.

Web of Science. New York: Thomson Reuters. http://thomsonreuters.com/products_services/scientific/Web_of_Science.

The *Web of Science* is the interface for access to the three ISI Citation databases: *Arts & Humanities Citation Index*, *Social Science Citation Index*, and *Science Citation Index Expanded*. The *Arts & Humanities Citation Index* indexes over 1,200 arts and humanities journals as well as selected items from more than six thousand scientific and social sciences journals. Date range coverage depends on your library's subscription.

ART

Dictionaries, Encyclopedias, and Handbooks

Chilvers, Ian. *A Dictionary of Twentieth-Century Art*. Oxford: Oxford University Press, 1998.

This work provides more than 1,500 articles on modern and contemporary artists, critics, collectors, movements, styles, and genres. It is also available in electronic format through *Oxford Reference Online*. A second edition, retitled *A Dictionary of Modern and Contemporary Art*, is due to be published in August 2009.

Oxford Art Online. Oxford: Oxford University Press. www.oxfordartonline.com/public/.

Oxford University Press now makes available the electronic version of Grove's classic *Dictionary of Art* (also known as *Grove Art Online* in a previous online version) listed below. In addition to this classic work, *Oxford Art Online* also includes searchable electronic versions of *The Encyclopedia of Aesthetics*, edited by Michael Kelly, *The Oxford Companion to Western Art*, edited by Hugh Brigstocke, and *The Concise Oxford Dictionary of Art Terms*, by Michael Clarke and Deborah Clarke.

Turner, Jane, ed. *The Dictionary of Art*. 34 vols. New York: Grove, 1996.

Long considered the standard scholarly reference resource for art and art history, this dictionary acts more like an encyclopedia, with lengthy, illustrated articles written by top experts in the field. Many academic libraries retain the print editions of this classic even though they also subscribe to the searchable electronic version, which is part of *Oxford Art Online* listed above.

Guides and Handbooks

Arntzen, Etta, and Robert Rainwater. *Guide to the Literature of Art History*. Chicago: American Library Association, 1980.

Marmor, Max, and Alex Ross. *Guide to the Literature of Art History 2*. Chicago: American Library Association, 2005.

These two works remain essential tools for locating reference resources for art history research. The 1980 *Guide* is divided into four sections covering "General Reference Sources," "General Primary and Secondary Resources," "Particular Arts," and "Serials." The first three sections have geographic subdivisions with entries for Great Britain and Ireland. There are also two indexes, one for author-title entries and one for subject entries. The 2005 *Guide* follows more or less the same organizational scheme but provides additional sections on "Patronage and Collecting" and "Cultural Heritage" (which includes preservation, law, and policy related to the arts). It also contains one general index.

Pollard, Elizabeth B. *Visual Arts Research: A Handbook*. New York: Greenwood Press, 1986.

Although some aspects of this book, particularly the section on computerized reference sources, are now out of date, the basic research process presented here remains valid. The strength of the work is its focus on visual arts through many lenses. It begins with an overview of research strategy and how to make use of the library. Also provided are sections on different types of information such as art history sources, art education information sources, and biographical sources. Also covered are special research techniques involved with using a work of art as a starting point or for studies focused on techniques and materials. The work also contains two useful appendixes, one comparing Dewey Decimal classification numbers and Library of Congress classification numbers for visual arts materials, and the other listing printed equivalents of online databases.

Sacca, Elizabeth J., and Loren R. Singer. *Visual Arts Reference and Research Guide, for Artists, Educators, Curators, Historians, and Therapists*. Montréal, Québec: Perspecto Press, 1983.

While its content is now somewhat dated, this guide remains helpful for its coverage of classic reference sources related to a wide range of visual arts. A topic index begins the work, providing a table of various art forms and linking them to the sections of the book and the resources listed that contain relevant information for their study. The bulk of the work is made up of descriptions of various reference tools concerning everything from use of library catalogs to theses and dissertations, government publications, children's literature, events, photos and reproductions, style manuals, periodicals, and bibliographies. There are two indexes for authors/editors and titles of works.

Images

AP Images. New York: Associated Press. www.apimages.com.

This subscription database allows searchable access to over one million photographs and graphics from the Associated Press and its partner agencies. Historical photographs date back to 1826 and are international in scope. Included are images of major historical events such as both world wars and important political and historical figures, as well as images of common life.

ARTstor. New York: ARTstor. www.artstor.org/index.shtml.

ARTstor is a subscription-based searchable repository of hundreds of thousands of digital images and related data from museums, special collections at libraries, photo archives, and individual photographers and scholars. It includes examples of photography from its inception as well as many representative works of art and architecture from the modernist era. Search for images by keyword, title, or creator's name; the site also allows for searching by geographic location, medium, collections, and date range.

Indexes and Bibliographies

ARTbibliographies Modern. Bethesda, MD: CSA. www.csa.com/factsheets/artbm-set-c.php.

ARTbibliographies Modern contains citations and abstracts for some 375,000 individual journal articles, books, dissertations, exhibition catalogs, and other material concerning modern and contemporary artists, movements, and trends from the late nineteenth century to the present. Coverage includes photography since its invention, painting, sculpture, drawing, illustration, theater arts, crafts, contemporary computer art and performance art, and more.

Art Index. New York: H. W. Wilson. www.hwwilson.com/databases/artindex.htm.

Art Index, currently available in print or online, indexes over five hundred periodicals published from 1984 to the present related to fine, decorative, and commercial art. It is international in scope and includes publications in

French, Italian, German, Spanish, Dutch, and English. For deeper back files, *Art Index Retrospective* is available, which covers publications from 1929 to 1984. A related electronic product from Wilson is *Art Full Text*, which provides the same indexing as *Art Index* but also contains full-text articles from almost two hundred of the journals, going back to 1997.

Bibliography of the History of Art (*BHA*). Los Angeles: J. Paul Getty Trust. www.getty.edu/research/conducting_research/bha/.

The *Bibliography of the History of Art* indexes and abstracts art-related books, conference proceedings, dissertations, exhibition and dealer's catalogs, and articles from more than 1,200 periodicals. The scope is European and American art from late antiquity to the present. The bibliography includes and extends the coverage of two predecessor art indexes: *Répertoire d'Art et d'Archéologie* (*RAA*) from 1973 to 1989 and *International Repertory of the Literature of Art* (*RILA*) from 1975 to 1989. *BHA* is available on a variety of platforms from a number of vendors.

Historical Atlases

Cunliffe, Barry, Robert Bartlett, John Morrill, Asa Briggs, and Joanna Bourke, eds. *The Penguin Atlas of British and Irish History: From Earliest Times to the Present Day*. New York: Penguin, 2002.

This work provides visual overviews of important historical events and trends in Britain and Ireland, from Neolithic times to the twentieth century. Maps, photographs, and graphic information illustrate political, social, economic, and other trends. Of most interest to scholars of modern British literature will be part 4 on nineteenth-century Britain and Ireland and part 5 on modern Britain and Ireland. Topics covered include working-class housing to the aftermath of empire.

Overy, Richard. *Collins Atlas of 20th Century History*. New York: Collins, 2006.

Similar to the *Penguin Atlas* referenced above, the *Collins Atlas of 20th Century History* provides maps, photographs, graphs, and other illustrative material to bring to life important events from the historical record. It is broader in geographic scope (covering the entire world, although with more emphasis on the West) but narrower in time period (limited to the twentieth century only). The first half of the book, ranging from the empires of 1900 to the end of World War II, will be of most interest to the scholar of modern British literature.

HISTORY

Dictionaries and Encyclopedias

Davies, John, Nigel Jenkins, Menna Baines, and Peredur Lynch, eds. *The Welsh Academy Encyclopaedia of Wales*. Cardiff: University of Wales Press, 2008.

This one-volume national encyclopedia attempts to cover all material, natural, cultural, and historical aspects of Wales. Brief entries are provided concerning the most important people, places, and concepts related to literature, arts, politics, history, and society. There are also occasional longer entries, such as the one on "Government and Administration," which is further subdivided by time period. A comprehensive index is included.

Panton, Kenneth J. *Historical Dictionary of London*. Lanham, MD: Scarecrow Press, 2001.

The bulk of this dictionary consists of short explanatory entries for people, places, events, and objects related to the political and cultural capital of Britain. Although the literary references exhibit a dearth of content related to modernism, there is still much of interest here, from coverage of the Blitz to Wimbledon. A brief but useful introduction by the author includes a section on "London since 1900." Additional features are a chronology of historical events, maps, charts of population growth from 1801 to 1996, and an extensive bibliography.

Plowright, John. *Routledge Dictionary of Modern British History*. New York: Routledge, 2006.

This work provides brief descriptive overviews of important political and social events as well as major figures associated with modern British history. Both the nineteenth and twentieth centuries are covered, as is all of Britain geographically.

Stearns, Peter N., ed. *Oxford Encyclopedia of the Modern World*. 8 vols. Oxford: Oxford University Press, 2008.

This impressive set contains over two thousand signed articles by leading scholars covering specific countries, regions, ethnic groups, social history, politics, economics, religion, education, science, technology, and culture. It is international in scope and covers the time period of 1750 to the present. This work also includes bibliographies of useful secondary sources.

Guides, Handbooks, and Companions

Butler, L. J., and Anthony Gorst, eds. *Modern British History: A Guide to Study and Research*. London: I. B. Tauris, 1997.

This guide provides informative chapters covering techniques for researching modern British history, including use of public records, archives, libraries, and the Internet. There are also chapters detailing research techniques for various subfields, including political history, diplomatic history, military history, and social history.

Cook, Chris, and John Stevenson. *Longman Handbook of Modern British History, 1714–2001*. 4th ed. New York: Pearson/Longman, 2001.

Concisely written and accessible, this handbook contains brief articles, statistics, lists, time lines, and bibliographies related to political history, social and religious history, economic history, and foreign affairs and defense. The geographic and chronological focus of this work makes it particularly useful for scholars of modern British literature.

Flemming, N. C., and Alan O'Day. *Longman Handbook of Modern Irish History since 1800*. New York: Pearson/Longman, 2005.

Similar in scope to the Cook and Stevenson volume listed above, this work provides in-depth coverage of modernism in Ireland as well as the time periods immediately preceding and following it. More than one hundred pages are devoted to a detailed chronology of the years 1801 to 2001. The bulk of the work contains articles related to Ireland's political, social, religious, and economic history. A glossary and index are included.

Loades, David, ed. *Reader's Guide to British History*. 2 vols. New York: Fitzroy Dearborn, 2003.

According to the editor, this work is not intended to serve as an encyclopedia but rather as a bibliographic reference source that provides brief articles on various topics and then guides the reader to the most useful secondary sources. Coverage includes all of Britain for all time periods.

Lynch, Michael. *Oxford Companion to Scottish History*. New York: Oxford University Press, 2001.

This work consists of fairly substantial articles arranged alphabetically, covering topics such as emigration, geography and landscape, regional identities, libraries, the Scots language, and more. Other useful features include a chronology covering the years 81 to 2000, maps, genealogies, an extensive "Guide to Further Reading," and an index.

Chronologies

Williams, Neville, and Philip Waller. *Chronology of the Modern World, 1763 to 1992*. 2nd ed. New York: Simon & Schuster, 1994.

This useful tool allows the reader to view a chronological time line of significant events in world history and places any event within the context of contemporary events in other fields or geographic areas. The left-hand pages reproduce significant headlines from the world press arranged in chronological order. The right-hand pages list significant achievements and events in literature, music, art, scholarship, politics, philosophy, religion, and science and technology.

Indexes and Bibliographies

Historical Abstracts. EBSCO. www.ebscohost.com.

The print version of the *Historical Abstracts* bibliography began in 1955 and covers the history of the world, excluding Canada and the United States, from 1450 to the present. More than 1,700 academic historical journals in over forty languages are indexed, covering world history, military history, women's history, history of education, and additional historical and related social science topics. *Historical Abstracts* is also available in searchable electronic versions through ABC-CLIO and EBSCO. A version including full text of many of the articles is anticipated for release in the fall of 2009.

Historical Sources

Baxter, Stephen B., ed. *Basic Documents of English History*. Boston: Houghton Mifflin, 1968.

This compilation provides easy access to the full text of important primary documents of English law, from seventh-century Anglo-Saxon Dooms to Parliamentary laws passed in the twentieth century. It is arranged in chronological parts. Of most interest to the researcher in modern British literature will be part 7, covering the first part of the twentieth century from 1902 to 1967, as well as the later documents included in part 6, covering the nineteenth century from 1815 to 1901. Representative modern documents are the Abdication of 1936 and the Education Act of 1944.

MUSIC

Audio Resources

Classical Music Library. Alexandria, VA: Alexander Street Press. www.alexanderstreet.com.ezproxy2.library.drexel.edu/products/clmu.htm.

Classical Music Library is the largest collection of classical music (including symphonies, operas, choral work, and more) available as a database for educational purposes. It currently contains almost six thousand albums with almost 56,000 tracks. The database is searchable by genre, instruments, people's names, and both recording date and time period. Almost six thousand works from the twentieth century may be found here.

Naxos Music Library. Naxos. www.naxosmusiclibrary.com/home.asp.

Naxos Music Library provides access to over 130,000 music tracks, including classical, jazz and blues, rock and pop, world, folk, and Chinese music. In addition to the ability to search for music by genre, instruments, names of composers and performers, and time period, it also provides the ability to search by country of origin and "moods and scenarios." More than six thousand works are available dating from the twentieth century.

Dictionaries, Encyclopedias, and Handbooks

Latham, Alison, ed. *Oxford Companion to Music*. Oxford: Oxford University Press, 2002.

The *Oxford Companion to Music* contains more than eight thousand articles on composers, performers, conductors, individual works, instruments, notation, forms, and genres. While some entries consist of a brief definition, the longest and most substantial articles are written and signed by scholars in the field. This work contains some illustrations.

Oxford Music Online. Oxford. www.oxfordmusiconline.com/public/.

Formerly known as *Grove Music Online*, this electronic resource includes searchable full texts of *The New Grove Dictionary of Music and Musicians* (2nd ed., 2001; see entry below), *The New Grove Dictionary of Opera* (1992), and *The New Grove Dictionary of Jazz* (2nd ed., 2001). Since moving to Oxford, the resource now also includes the full text of *The Oxford Companion to Music* (2002) and *The Oxford Dictionary of Music* (2nd ed., rev., 2006). Updated articles and additional materials are uploaded quarterly.

Randel, Don Michael, ed. *Harvard Dictionary of Music*. 4th ed. Cambridge, MA: Harvard University Press, 2003.

This work is similar in scope to the *Oxford Companion to Music*, described above. It is international in scope and covers a range of musical genres, although it has a strong classical bias. It contains a range of entries from brief definitions to lengthier signed articles. Some illustrations are also included, particularly examples of instruments and musical notation.

Sadie, Stanley, ed. *New Grove Dictionary of Music and Musicians*. 2nd ed. 29 vols. New York: Grove, 2001.

This extensive work has long been considered the standard for a comprehensive music reference tool. It contains scholarly articles on musical forms and musicians from across the world (albeit with a Western bias) and across time periods. Entries include a list of "Works" for composers, theorists, and other producers of written works. Bibliographies of secondary materials are also provided. The *New Grove Dictionary of Music and Musicians*, 2nd ed., is now available electronically as part of *Oxford Music Online* (see the entry above). Some libraries may retain print copies of this dictionary while also subscribing to the electronic edition.

Handbooks

Gottlieb, Jane. *Music Library and Research Skills*. Upper Saddle River, NJ: Pearson Prentice Hall, 2009.

In addition to covering the usual research tools such as bibliographies, dictionaries, periodical indexes, and encyclopedias, this work has special chapters devoted to music topics, including discographies, music publishing, composer thematic catalogs, text translation, and resources for careers in music. It also has two glossaries, one on select German terms and the other on bibliographic terms and abbreviations, plus a comprehensive index.

Sampsel, Laurie J. *Music Research: A Handbook*. Oxford: Oxford University Press, 2009.

This research handbook is divided into two parts. The first focuses on "Research Process and Research Tools" and includes general and specialized music encyclopedias, dictionaries, periodical indexes, catalogs, discographies, iconographies, and Internet sources. The second part is devoted to "Writing, Style Manuals, and Citation." The strength of this tool lies in the fact that not only does each chapter contain introductory materials about the types and uses of the materials discussed, but the work provides individual annotations for most of the resources. It also contains a number of useful appendixes, covering the Library of Congress "M" classification for music, search terms, and information on major citation style systems, such as Chicago, APA, and MLA.

Indexes and Bibliographies

Music Index. Warren, MI: Harmonie Park Press. www.harmonieparkpress.com/MusicIndex.asp.

The *Music Index* provides subject access and indexing for material in more than 875 international music periodicals. It includes both classical and popular music, and materials range from articles about music and musicians to news items and reviews. The coverage of the print version is from 1949 to the present; the scope of the electronic *Music Index Online* is from 1972 to the present.

RILM Abstracts of Music Literature. New York: RILM. www.rilm.org/.

RILM Abstracts addresses all types of publications concerning music, such as books, journals, online resources, sound recordings and films, dissertations, and conference proceedings. It is international in scope, indexing publications from over 150 countries and providing title translations and abstracts in English for items appearing in other languages. Subjects include musicology, ethnomusicology, instruments and voice, dance, and music therapy, as well as works in other fields relevant to music such as literature, performing and visual arts, anthropology, sociology, and physics. Coverage goes back to 1967; the print publication ceased with the edition for 1999 materials. The *RILM Abstracts* are now being produced in searchable electronic format only, which is updated monthly.

Sources and History

Burkholder, J. Peter, and Claude V. Palisca, eds. *Norton Anthology of Western Music*. 5th ed. 2 vols. New York: W. W. Norton, 2006.

Almost two hundred historically significant scores are reproduced in this work, along with professional recordings of each on the accompanying CDs. Arranged chronologically, the latter part of volume 2, covering the "Classic to Modern" time periods, will be of most interest to modernist scholars. Significant modern works of jazz and blues are represented. Also provided are commentaries that explicate the importance of each work and its historical context.

Taruskin, Richard. *Oxford History of Western Music*. 6 vols. Oxford: Oxford University Press, 2005.

This massive five-volume scholarly work covers the entire history of Western music. Of most interest to scholars of the modern time period will be volume 4, focusing on the early twentieth century. Parts of volume 3, on the nineteenth century, and volume 5, on the late twentieth century, may also be useful. Volume 6 serves as a master index for all five volumes. It includes five hundred halftone illustrations and 1,800 musical examples.

PERFORMING ARTS

Encyclopedias and Companions

Chambers, Colin, ed. *Continuum Companion to Twentieth Century Theatre*. New York: Continuum, 2002.

The *Continuum Companion to Twentieth Century Theatre* provides brief overviews of major figures (actors, directors, playwrights, etc.), plays, and concepts related to modern theater. There are occasional longer pieces on more general topics of interest, such as "Directing" and "Playwriting."

Cody, Gabrielle H., and Evert Sprinchorn, eds. *Columbia Encyclopedia of Modern Drama*. 2 vols. New York: Columbia University Press, 2007.

International in scope, this work focuses on the time period of 1860 to the early twenty-first century. Most entries are related to major figures and individual plays, but there is also some coverage of drama in particular countries or regions, as well as major concepts such as "Melodrama." Each entry is fairly substantial and includes a list of suggestions for "Further Reading." A synoptic outline and general index are also provided.

Grant, Barry Keith. *Schirmer Encyclopedia of Film*. 4 vols. Detroit: Schirmer Reference, 2007.

This comprehensive encyclopedia covers international film history of all eras. Its two hundred entries provide in-depth consideration of film genres, studios, national cinemas, cultural approaches to film, and technology and industrial topics. Essays are 1,500 to 9,000 words in length, and there are also 230 briefer sidebars focused on major actors and directors. Most entries include a color or black-and-white photo, "see also" references to other relevant essays, and a brief list of materials for further reading. Each volume contains the entire index for the set, and volume 4 also features a glossary of film terms.

McFarlane, Brian, ed. *Encyclopedia of British Film*. 2nd ed. London: Methuen, 2005.

Covering over one hundred years of the British film industry, this encyclopedia has entries for major figures (such as actors, directors, producers, and screenwriters), genres, motifs, and companies. Copiously illustrated with black-and-white photos, its 3,800 brief essays address everything from film noir to Alfred Hitchcock. There is also a useful list of title changes for British films released under a different name in the United States and a select bibliography, subdivided by topic.

Guides

Simons, Linda Keir. *The Performing Arts: A Guide to the Reference Literature*. Englewood, CO: Libraries Unlimited, 1994.

This guide provides citations and annotations for selected resources in the performing arts, specifically theater and dance. Coverage includes bibliographies, catalogs, biographies, dictionaries, encyclopedias, review sources, chronologies and histories, core periodicals, professional organizations and societies, and even electronic discussion groups. Two indexes are also included, one for authors and titles, the other devoted to subjects.

Indexes and Bibliographies

Film & Television Literature Index with Full Text. Ebsco. www.ebscohost.com/.

Although the "television" side of this database is beyond the scope of modernism as we've defined it here, there is no doubt that the medium of film was a hallmark of modernism in its blend of technology and creativity. This database provides indexing and abstracting for three hundred publications along with selected content from three hundred more. Full text for more than ninety journals is also included. Topics covered are film theory, cinematography, preservation and restoration, reviews, and more.

International Bibliography of Theatre and Dance. Ebsco. www.ebscohost.com/.

The premier research tool for the study of theater and the performing arts, this bibliography provides indexing for over 60,000 journal articles, books, book chapters, and dissertations from 126 countries. Indexing is handled by the Theatre Research Data Center (TRDC) at Brooklyn College.

International Index to the Performing Arts (*IIPA*). Chadwyck-Healey. http://iipa.chadwyck.com/marketing.do.

Broader in scope than the *International Bibliography of Theatre and Dance*, described above, the *IIPA* covers theater, dance, film, stagecraft, musical theater, television, performance art, storytelling, opera, pantomime, puppetry, magic, and other performing arts. It provides indexing and abstracts for some 400,000 citations from over 240 journals published in seventeen countries.

Sources and History

Trussler, Simon. *Cambridge Illustrated History of British Theatre*. Cambridge: Cambridge University Press, 1994.

Trussler's history covers British theater from first-century Roman times to 1990. It is arranged in twenty-two chapters, each covering a specific time period. Each chapter's narrative focuses on the history and development of the British theater as well as significant plays and figures. Included are illustrations of theater layouts and drawings or photographs of performances. Of particular interest to the researcher of British modernism are chapter 17, "Romance and Realism 1891–1914," chapter 18, "The War and the Long Weekend 1914–1939," and chapter 19, "The Utility Theatre 1939–1956." The work also provides a chronology of significant events, a glossary of theater terms, a "who's who" of important figures, a select bibliography, and an index.

PHILOSOPHY

Dictionaries, Encyclopedias, and Handbooks

Blackburn, Simon. *Oxford Dictionary of Philosophy*. 2nd ed. rev. Oxford: Oxford University Press, 2008.

This comprehensive work has thousands of entries covering all areas of philosophy as well as related concepts from religion, science, and logic. It is international in scope; in addition to coverage of traditional Western philosophy, it also includes concepts from Chinese, Indian, Islamic, and Jewish philosophy. Biographies of almost five hundred individuals are provided. This work is available both in print format and electronically through *Oxford Reference Online*.

Bullock, Alan, and Stephen Trombley, eds. *Norton Dictionary of Modern Thought*. 2nd rev. ed. New York: W. W. Norton & Company, 1999.

The *Norton Dictionary of Modern Thought* provides brief overviews of important twentieth-century intellectual ideas, from the political, to the artistic, to the scientific. It is international in scope, but its focus on the twentieth century makes it particularly valuable for the researcher of modern British literature.

Craig, Edward, gen. ed. *Routledge Encyclopedia of Philosophy*. 10 vols. New York: Routledge, 1998.

This extensive work covers a wide range of topics in philosophy and related fields, such as religion, science, history, and language. In-depth treatments of topics such as ethics, aesthetics, political philosophy, metaphysics, and logic are provided, as well as biographical information concerning significant thinkers in the field. Each article is authored by an expert in the field. The *Routledge Encyclopedia of Philosophy* is also available in electronic format. It currently contains more than two thousand entries and is continuously updated and revised.

Horowitz, Maryanne Cline, ed. *New Dictionary of the History of Ideas*. 6 vols. New York: Charles Scribner's Sons, 2005.

The *New Dictionary of the History of Ideas* was selected as an "Outstanding Reference Work" for 2005 by the Reference and User Services Association of the American Library Association; it updates the *Dictionary of the History of Ideas*, discussed below. The chronological coverage ranges from antiquity to the twenty-first century and is international in scope. Essays written by academics and other knowledgeable experts address diverse intellectual concepts such as "Nationalism," "Monarchy," "Humanism," and "Genre." It also includes an extensive essay on "Modernism."

Stanford Encyclopedia of Philosophy. http://plato.stanford.edu.

This full-text Internet resource is sponsored by Stanford University and supported by grants from the National Endowment for the Humanities and other sources. It is continuously added to and updated by a team of experts. The emphasis of the work is on Western philosophy, although Eastern and comparative philosophies are considered as well. The *Stanford Encyclopedia of Philosophy* is a model for publicly accessible Web-based scholarly works.

Wiener, Philip P., ed. *Dictionary of the History of Ideas: Studies of Selected Pivotal Ideas*. New York: Charles Scribner's Sons, 1973–1974. http://etext.lib.virginia.edu/DicHist/dict.html.

Considered a classic, this compendium of Western thought contains essays by a number of highly regarded scholars, including George Boas, Mircea Eliade, and Rene Wellek. The work is broken up into seven parts covering "Nature," "Humanity," "Art," "History," "Politics," "Religion and Philosophy," and "Math and Logic." The published version of this work is now out of print, but the full text has been made available online by the University of Virginia Library's Electronic Text Center. It contains much useful information and is freely available on the Internet, although the work is considered to have been updated and superseded by the *New Dictionary of the History of Ideas*, considered in the entry above.

Guides and Companions

Bynagle, Hans E. *Philosophy: A Guide to the Reference Literature*. 3rd ed. Westport, CT: Libraries Unlimited, 2006.

Recent reference sources for the field of philosophy, such as bibliographies, dictionaries, encyclopedias, and indexes, are the emphasis of this guide. It covers general resources as well as those focused on more specific subfields and ranges in time period from the ancient world to the twenty-first century. Non-Western and Western philosophy are both included, along with special topics such as African American philosophy, Jewish philosophy, feminist philosophy, free thought, and others. Complete citations and in-depth annotations are provided for each resource.

Moran, Dermot, ed. *Routledge Companion to Twentieth-Century Philosophy*. London: Routledge, 2008.

This companion provides an excellent overview of the field of philosophy, from the rise of analytical philosophy and the influence of Wittgenstein and Hegel at the beginning of the twentieth century to the ascension of French critical theory at the end. The five parts of the resource consist of "Major Themes and Movements"; "Logic, Language, Knowledge, and Metaphysics"; "Philosophy of Mind, Psychology, and Science"; "Phenomenology, Hermeneutics, Existentialism, and Critical Theory"; and "Politics, Ethics, and Aesthetics." Each section contains a number of scholarly essays by experts in the field. Also included are annotated bibliographies for further reading at the end of each section and a comprehensive glossary.

Papineau, David, gen. ed. *Western Philosophy: An Illustrated Guide*. New York: Oxford University Press, 2004.

Written with the layperson in mind, this accessible guide provides a good overview of the tradition of Western philosophy from its ancient roots to the modern day. Written by specialists in the field, it includes essays on concepts such as "conscience" and "relativism" and on major figures from Plato to Foucault. It is arranged in six topic chapters covering "Mind and Body," "Faith," "Society," and more.

Indexes and Bibliographies

Noesis: Philosophical Research On-line. http://noesis.evansville.edu/index.htm.

The highlight of this publicly accessible website is its *Google*-based search engine, which is designed to retrieve "academic scholarship in philosophy that is freely available online." It provides some sample searches for concepts like "causation" and representative major figures such as Kant and Heidegger, which quickly illustrate the quality of results returned. The site also contains links to philosophy associations, philosophy departments at colleges and universities, faculty web pages, and online philosophy journals and reference works.

Philosopher's Index. Bowling Green, OH: Philosopher's Information Center. www.philinfo.org/.

Available in print or electronically through a number of vendors, the *Philosopher's Index* provides indexing and abstracts for articles from more than six hundred journals, as well as books and anthologies. Topics covered include ethics, aesthetics, social philosophy, political philosophy, epistemology, metaphysics, logic, and the philosophy of law, religion, science, history, language, and education.

RELIGION

Dictionaries, Encyclopedias, and Handbooks

Eliade, Mircea, ed. *Encyclopedia of Religion*. 16 vols. New York: Macmillan, 1987.

This encyclopedia has long been considered the standard reference work for religious studies, and many libraries still retain their copies despite also owning the 2005 second edition (covered below). Many of the entries, written by esteemed scholars in the field, are considered classics and have been heavily cited elsewhere. The first fifteen volumes contain scholarly essays arranged alphabetically by topic. The final volume includes a directory of contributors, an alphabetical listing of entry topics, a synoptic outline of the contents, and a combined index covering names, titles, and subjects.

Jones, Lindsay, ed. *Encyclopedia of Religion*. 2nd ed. 15 vols. Detroit: Macmillan, 2005.

This second edition of the classic work edited by Mircea Eliade (see above) has been updated and revised to reflect expansions to the field of religious studies. Many of the original essays are retained from the first edition, while others have been revised and updated. Approximately six hundred of the essays are new to this edition. Hundreds of color and black-and-white illustrations add to the value of this set, along with the synoptic outline of the contents and an exhaustive index. It is also available in electronic format from Thomson-Gale.

von Stuckrad, Kocku, ed. *Brill Dictionary of Religion*. rev. ed. 4 vols. Boston: Brill, 2007.

This four-volume work is the revised edition of the *Metzler Lexikon Religion*, translated from the German. It is far more detailed, ecumenical, and international in scope than the *Introductory Dictionary of Theology and Religious Studies* covered above. A number of useful chronologies are provided for various themes related to world religions, and the final volume contains a general index.

Guides

Johnston, William M. *Recent Reference Books in Religion: A Guide for Students, Scholars, Researchers, Buyers & Readers*. rev. ed. Chicago: Fitzroy Dearborn, 1998.

While not entirely up to date at this point, this guide nonetheless includes useful, detailed evaluations of more than three hundred reference works related to religion that were published between 1970 and 1997. The majority of the works relate to Christianity, but Judaism, Islam, Buddhism, mythology, philosophy, and the social sciences of religion are covered as well. Each entry has a complete citation and brief summary and scope of the tool. Where appropriate, information is also provided on competitors, strengths, weaknesses, and a critique.

Kennedy, James R., Jr. *Library Research Guide to Religion and Theology: Illustrated Search Strategy and Sources*. 2nd ed. rev. Ann Arbor, MI: Pierian Press, 1984.

Kennedy's guide provides a step-by-step overview of the research process, from choosing and narrowing your topic to using and evaluating books, collecting current information, and using literature guides and other information resources. It also includes an overview of basic reference sources.

Indexes and Bibliographies

ATLA Religion Database. Chicago: American Theological Library Association. www.atla.com/products/catalogs/catalogs_rdb.html.

This database, produced by the American Theological Library Association (ATLA), provides indexing for more than five hundred journals as well as individual essays in multiauthor works, book reviews, and conference proceedings. Subject coverage includes the Bible, archaeology, and antiquities; human culture and society; church history, missions, and ecumenism; pastoral ministry; world religions and religious studies; and theology, philosophy, and ethics. It is international in scope; about half of the materials included are in English, and the other half are in German, French, Italian, and Spanish.

Religious & Theological Abstracts. Myerstown, PA. http://rtabstracts.org/.

Similar in scope to the *ATLA Religion Database*, *Religious & Theological Abstracts* provides indexing to several hundred scholarly journals in the fields of religion and theology. It is also strongest in the Judeo-Christian tradition but does include materials from other world religions. In addition to indexing, its main selling point is its helpful English-language abstracts of all articles in English, Hebrew, Afrikaans, and major European languages.

SCIENCES AND MEDICINE

Dictionaries, Encyclopedias, and Handbooks

Daintith, John, and Elizabeth Martin, eds. *A Dictionary of Science*. 5th ed. Oxford: Oxford University Press, 2005.

A comprehensive specialized dictionary, this work contains over nine thousand brief entries covering all aspects of scientific knowledge. It also provides ten "features," one to two pages in length, focused on topics of particular interest such as "genetically modified organisms." Other useful aspects of this work include ten separate chronologies, 160 biographical entries, and eight appendixes covering such topics as units of measurement, the periodic table, and useful websites.

Hamblin, Jacob Darwin. *Science in the Early Twentieth Century: An Encyclopedia.* Santa Barbara, CA: ABC-CLIO, 2005.

Part of ABC-CLIO's *History of Science* series, this work contains over two hundred entries on important scientific developments that took place between 1900 and 1950. Accessibly written, the volume begins with an introductory essay by the author, giving an overview of the scientific importance of the time period. The main body consists of alphabetical entries. A useful "Topic Finder" at the beginning of the book breaks up the entries into categories for easy browsing. Covered are "Concepts," such as the age of the earth or mutation; "Invention/Innovations," including the atomic bomb and computers; and "People" of significance such as Albert Einstein, Marie Curie, and Edwin Hubble. Each entry has a brief list of references, and many are illustrated. The work also provides a chronology, a longer selected bibliography, and a general index.

Krige, John, and Dominique Pestre, eds. *Companion to Science in the Twentieth Century.* New York: Routledge, 2003.

This work consists of lengthy, illustrated essays regarding a broad range of topics relevant to science in the twentieth century. It covers everything from the use of statistics and scientific management principles in business to developments in the electronics and pharmaceutical industries, science in public policy, science fiction and science, cancer research, computer science, and atomic and molecular science. Also included is a section on science in various countries and regions of the world, such as the United Kingdom, India, and the United States. A general index is also provided.

McGraw-Hill Encyclopedia of Science & Technology. 10th ed. 20 vols. New York: McGraw-Hill, 2007.

Now in its tenth edition, this set of encyclopedias has long been considered the standard in basic reference tools for the sciences. It contains more than seven thousand articles on topics related to almost one hundred separate fields of science. Each signed article is written by an expert in the field, including twenty-five Nobel Prize winners. Owners of the tenth edition also have access to a companion website that provides updates and additions as well as a wide range of supplemental graphics and illustrations. The printed work also has extensive analytical and topical indexes and a range of study guides.

Indexes and Bibliographies

History of Science, Technology, and Medicine. History of Science Society. www.hssonline.org/teaching/teaching_database.html.

This electronic database provides access to citations for materials relevant to the development and influence of science from prehistory to the present. It combines four major tools for the study of the history of science: *Isis Current Bibliography of the History of Science*, *Current Bibliography in the History of Technology*, *Bibliografia Italiana di Storia della Scienza*, and citations from the *Wellcome Library for the History and Understanding of Medicine* (incorporating the former *Wellcome Bibliography for the History of Medicine*). Members of the History of Science Society have free access to this database; many libraries subscribe to it as well.

Web of Science. New York: Thomson Reuters. http://thomsonreuters.com/products_services/scientific/Web_of_Science.

The *Web of Science* is the interface for access to the three ISI Citation databases: *Arts & Humanities Citation Index*, *Social Science Citation Index*, and *Science Citation Index Expanded*. The *Science Citation Index Expanded* indexes more than 7,100 major journals in more than 150 disciplines. Date range coverage depends on your library's subscription.

Sources and History

Heilbron, J. L., ed. *Oxford Companion to the History of Modern Science*. Oxford: Oxford University Press, 2003.

The *Oxford Companion to the History of Modern Science* contains short, dictionary-like signed articles covering major topics in the history of science, including ethics and science, mind-body problems, the fossil record, and modernity/postmodernity. A thematic overview precedes the main entries, arranged alphabetically by topic. Each entry provides a few citations for suggested readings. There is a larger "Further Readings" section at the end of the book, along with a list of Nobel Prize winners in the sciences and a general index.

Hessenbruch, Arne, ed. *Reader's Guide to the History of Science*. Chicago: Fitzroy Dearborn, 2000.

This guide provides an overview of some of the most highly recommended readings related to various topics within the history of science. An alphabetical list of entries and a thematic list of entries are found at the beginning. The themes covered include "Alternative Science," "Chemical Sciences," "Engineering and Technology," "Individuals," "Medical and Health Sciences," and "Social Sciences." The bulk of the work is made up of entries arranged alphabetically by topic. Each entry begins with a bibliography of relevant readings related to the topic, followed by an essay giving a brief overview of the subject and then summarizing the main points and importance of each of the items cited in the bibliography. An index of all books and articles cited within the work is found at the back of the book, arranged alphabetically by author; there is also a general index.

Lindberg, David C., and Ronald L. Numbers, eds. *Cambridge History of Science*. Cambridge: Cambridge University Press, 2003–.

Volume 5 of this series, *The Modern Physical and Mathematical Sciences*, edited by Mary Jo Nye, and volume 6, *Modern Life and Earth Sciences*, edited by Peter J. Bowler and John V. Pickstone, both cover the history of various scientific disciplines from the nineteenth and twentieth centuries. Volume 5 includes essays relevant to physics, astronomy, chemistry, mathematics, geoscience, environmental sciences, computer science, and biomedical science. Volume 6 discusses such topics as botany, biology, zoology, embryology, pathology, geochemistry, paleontology, and physiology. In-depth scholarly essays written by experts in the field are provided for each topic. (See the "Social Sciences" category for another relevant volume in this series.)

Olby, R. C., ed. *Companion to the History of Modern Science*. New York: Routledge, 1990.

Compared with the *Oxford Companion to the History of Modern Science*, listed above, this volume contains longer, more in-depth scholarly essays on a variety of topics related to the development of modern science in the Western world from the Renaissance forward. Part 1 covers "The Study of the History of Science," including the history of the field and various analytical approaches, such as Marxism and feminism. Part 2 is "Selected Writings," which is broken into three sections devoted to "Turning Points," "Topics and Interpretations," and "Themes," such as science and religion, science and literature, science and imperialism, science and war, and more. Both a name index and a subject index are provided.

SOCIAL SCIENCES

Dictionaries and Encyclopedias

Calhoun, Craig, ed. *Dictionary of the Social Sciences*. Oxford: Oxford University Press, 2002.

Dictionary entries from fifty to five hundred words in length cover basic terms, concepts, theories, schools of thought, methodologies, techniques, topics, issues, and controversies within various social science disciplines. Almost three hundred biographies of major figures are also included.

Outhwaite, William, ed. *Blackwell Dictionary of Modern Social Thought.* 2nd ed. Malden, MA: Blackwell, 2003.

More than a dictionary of definitions, this work provides in-depth, signed scholarly articles on currents of thought in the social sciences and related disciplines. In addition to an entry for "Modernism and Postmodernism," the work covers topics such as "Eugenics," "Industrial Society," "Totalitarianism," and "Social Democracy." Brief lists of recommended readings accompany each essay, and there is an extensive bibliography at the back.

Smelser, Neil J., and Paul B. Baltes, eds. *International Encyclopedia of the Social and Behavioral Sciences.* 26 vols. Amsterdam: Elsevier, 2001.

This work is the current standard for a multivolume encyclopedia covering all of the social sciences. It is broad and inclusive and provides an international perspective on disciplines within the social sciences (anthropology, education, linguistics, psychology, and more), intersecting fields (neuroscience, religious studies, environmental studies, gender studies, etc.), and methodologies and applications. The encyclopedia is available in print and online editions and contains four thousand articles with ninety thousand bibliographic references. It also provides comprehensive name and subject indexes.

Stearns, Peter N., ed. *Oxford Encyclopedia of the Modern World: 1750 to the Present.* 8 vols. Oxford: Oxford University Press, 2008.

This comprehensive encyclopedia covers social, economic, cultural, and political topics from the mid-eighteenth century to the present time. Heavily illustrated with maps and pictures, it features scholarly articles focused on various countries, regions, and ethnicities, covering social history, demography, religion, technology, and culture broadly defined.

Indexes and Bibliographies

PsycINFO. American Psychological Association. www.apa.org/psycinfo/.

The *PsycINFO* database has more than two and a half million records covering journal literature, book chapters, dissertations, and other secondary materials related to psychology. Sources include *Psychological Abstracts* and *Psychological Index,* which may be found in some libraries in their print formats. Researchers in modern British literature may be particularly interested in the database's historic content, some of which goes back to the nineteenth century and most of which reaches to the early twentieth century.

Sociological Abstracts. ProQuest-CSA. www.csa.com/factsheets/socioabs-set-c.php.

The standard for sociological databases, this tool provides indexing and abstracting of the international literature in sociology and related disciplines, including psychology, economics, social work, and women's studies. Almost two thousand serial publications are indexed as well as books, book chapters, dissertations, and conference papers.

Web of Science. New York: Thomson Reuters. http://thomsonreuters.com/products_services/scientific/Web_of_Science.

The *Web of Science* is the interface for access to the three ISI Citation databases: *Arts & Humanities Citation Index*, *Social Science Citation Index*, and *Science Citation Index Expanded*. The *Social Science Citation Index* provides indexing for 2,100 journals in fifty social science disciplines as well as 3,500 of the world's leading scientific and technical journals. Date range coverage depends on your library's subscription.

Sources and History

Lindberg, David C., and Ronald L. Numbers, eds. *Cambridge History of Science*. Cambridge: Cambridge University Press, 2003–.

Volume 7 of this series, *The Modern Social Sciences*, edited by Theodore M. Porter and Dorothy Ross, provides scholarly essays relevant to the development of the social sciences from the eighteenth century forward. Topics include psychology, economics, sociology, anthropology, political science, geography, history, and statistics, and the involvement of the social sciences in government, business, education, culture, and social policy. Part III is particularly relevant for topics related specifically to the twentieth century. (See the "Science and Medicine" category for two other relevant volumes in this series.)

Bibliography

Beall, Jeffrey, and Karen Kafadar. "The Proportion of NUC Pre-56 Titles Represented in OCLC WorldCat." *College & Research Libraries* 66, no. 5 (September 2005): 431–435.

Bradbury, Malcolm. "Modernism and the Magazines." Pp. 187–313 in *Transcultural Encounters—Studies in English Literatures*, edited by Heinz Antor and Kevin L. Cope. Heidelberg: Winter, 1999.

Budd, John. "Characteristics of Written Scholarship in American Literature: A Citation Study." *Library and Information Science Research* 8, no. 2 (1986): 189–211.

DeZelar-Tiedman, Christine. "The Proportion of NUC Pre-56 Titles Represented in the RLIN and OCLC Databases Compared: A Follow-up to the Beall/Kafadar Study." *College & Research Libraries* 69, no. 5 (September 2008): 401–6.

Larkin, Phillip. "A Neglected Responsibility: Contemporary Literary Manuscripts." Pp. 98–108 in *Required Writing*. Ann Arbor: University of Michigan Press, 1999.

Library of Congress. "Collection Overview: Anglophone/Commonwealth Literature." 2008. www.loc.gov/acq/devpol/colloverviews/anglophone.pdf, p. 1 (21 May 2009).

Mahood, Aurelea. "Fashioning Readers: The Avant Garde and British *Vogue*, 1920–9." *Women: A Cultural Review* 13, no. 1 (Spring 2002), 37–47.

Openhym, Evelyn Tennyson, and Alan Littell, comp. *Bibliography of the Openhym Collection of Modern British Literature and Social History, Herrick Memorial Library, Alfred University*. Alfred, NY: Alfred University Press, 1980.

Schwarz, Daniel R. *Reading the Modern British and Irish Novel, 1890–1930*. Hoboken, NJ: Wiley-Blackwell, 2005.

Thompson, Jennifer Wolfe. "The Death of the Scholarly Monograph in the Humanities? Citation Patterns in Literary Scholarship." *Libri* 52 (2002): 121–36.

Washington State University, Manuscripts, Archives, and Special Collections. *The Library of Leonard and Virginia Woolf: A Short Title Catalog*. www.wsulibs.wsu.edu/Holland/masc/woolflibrary.htm (10 April 2009).

Watson-Boone, Rebecca. "The Information Needs and Habits of Humanities Scholars." *RQ* 34, no. 2 (1994): 203–16.

Woolf, Virginia. *A Room of One's Own*. New York: Harcourt, 2005.

———. *Three Guineas*. New York: Harcourt Brace Jovanovich, 1938.

Index

About the Author

Alison M. Lewis is assistant teaching professor in the library and information science program at Drexel University's College of Information Science and Technology in Philadelphia. She holds both an MLS degree and MA in English literature from Florida State University and a PhD in English literature from Temple University, with a specialization in modern British literature.

4648406R00132

Made in the USA
San Bernardino, CA
29 September 2013